ACADEMIC FREEDOM

A Guide to the Literature

Compiled by **Stephen H. Aby**
and **James C. Kuhn IV**

Bibliographies and Indexes in Education, Number 20

GREENWOOD PRESS
Westport, Connecticut • London

Library of Congress Cataloging-in-Publication Data

Academic freedom : a guide to the literature / compiled by Stephen H. Aby and James C.
  Kuhn, IV.
      p.   cm.—(Bibliographies and indexes in education, ISSN 0742–6917 ; no. 20)
    Includes bibliographical references and indexes.
    ISBN 0–313–30386–X (alk. paper)
      1. Academic freedom—United States.   2. Academic freedom—United States—History.   I.
  Aby, Stephen H., 1949–   II. Kuhn, James C., 1966–   III. Series.
  LC72.2.A29   2000
  378.1'21—dc21   99–059136

British Library Cataloguing in Publication Data is available.

Library of Congress Catalog Card Number: 99–059136
ISBN: 0–313–30386–X
ISSN: 0742–6917

First published in 2000

Greenwood Press, 88 Post Road West, Westport, CT 06881
An imprint of Greenwood Publishing Group, Inc.
www.greenwood.com

Printed in the United States of America

The paper used in this book complies with the
Permanent Paper Standard issued by the National
Information Standards Organization (Z39.48–1984).

10 9 8 7 6 5 4 3 2

ACADEMIC FREEDOM

Contents

Introduction

Overview of Academic Freedom

The freedom of academics to pursue knowledge and truth in their research, writing, and teaching is a fundamental principle of contemporary higher education in the United States. However, this freedom has been hard won and regularly abridged, reinterpreted, and violated. Academic freedom is not a static right, but an ever-changing relationship between faculty and their disciplines, students, university administrations, communities, and governmental bodies. Its development reflects the changing influences and interests of these elements.

The contemporary model of academic freedom is of fairly recent vintage. Early American colleges and universities were primarily training grounds for clerics, and faculty were the means by which various religious beliefs were transmitted. They were not free to teach what they liked or to challenge the predominant orthodoxies of their institutions. It was not until the onset of industrialization that the role of the university, and therefore its academics, began to change to a new model. Universities and their faculty were required to train the intellectuals and skilled employees of a burgeoning economy. With this new role came a growing freedom and responsibility to push back the boundaries of knowledge and to transmit this to students.

Despite this new role and a corresponding increase in support for academic freedom, violations of that freedom were common. The turn-of-the-century academic freedom cases of Edward Bemis, Edward Ross, Richard Ely, and Scott Nearing illustrate how vested political and economic interests, either in the community or on Boards of Trustees, exerted undue influence in firing faculty and limiting academic freedom. However, the founding of the American Association of University Professors (AAUP) in 1915 established an organization devoted to the increasing professionalization of faculty, the establishment of professional standards, and an active defense of academic autonomy. Academic freedom was one of the Association's earliest preoccupations, as reflected in the establishment of its Committee A on academic freedom. That committee, through its investigation and potential censure of institutions that violated academic freedom, was an early attempt to provide a model and safeguard for the free pursuit of knowledge.

The AAUP presented its own formal articulation of the principles of academic freedom in its *1940 Statement of Principles on Academic Freedom and Tenure*. Here, the organization attempted to establish professional standards for the treatment of faculty and the protection of their academic freedom. Though most colleges and universities subscribe to these principles, alleged and actual violations of academic freedom have continued. The McCarthy period, the political movements of the 1960s and 1970s, and the more recent "culture wars" have all given rise to notorious academic freedom cases. Clearly, the incorporation of principles of academic freedom into policy does not neutralize the various constituencies in higher education, nor does it diminish the role of politics and ideology in the operation of university administrations, departments, and disciplines. "The devil is in the details," as the saying goes, and exactly how academic freedom should be interpreted and applied as a codified principle in individual cases has never been a completely settled question.

Abiding questions remain: about the relationships and conflicts between academic freedom as an institutional right and as a right of individual faculty and students; about how the distinction is made between special rights accruing to faculty or students and civil liberties available to all citizens; about whether the right of academic freedom actually protects open debate and the free pursuit of truth, or (from a conservative critique that has recurred in recent years) merely protects an entrenched and ideologically biased status quo. New questions as well are cropping up: about whether restricting access to telecommunications equipment or networks (e.g. the Internet) violates principles of academic freedom; about the problem of hate speech and whether the parameters of academic freedom can be restricted in order to regulate the climate of debate or teaching on campus; about whether campuses, faculty, and students are constrained by a climate of political correctness that restricts the topics that can be addressed; about whether a conservative or liberal "canon" of acceptable literature limits the freedom of faculty to teach beyond the traditional bounds of their disciplines.

Such a broad range of issues has generated literature in a variety of disciplines. This selective, annotated guide will provide access to that literature and, hopefully, promote the further study of this most important topic.

Scope and Purpose

This guide provides descriptive annotations of 481 sources relevant to the topic of academic freedom. The focus is on post-secondary education in the United States, limited primarily to items published since the American Association of University Professors' *1940 Statement of Principles on Academic Freedom and Tenure*. However, some notable items published between 1915 (the AAUP's founding) and 1940 will be selectively included, as will some older works and historical treatments of academic freedom in earlier periods. Though a number of the chapters focus on topics that have generated a wide-ranging literature (e.g., the Cold War; political correctness), we have tried to limit our entries to those dealing significantly with academic freedom. Books, journal articles, book chapters, World Wide Web sites, organization reports, policy documents, published conference presentations, and reference works are included. Articles published in legal periodicals are generally not included for two reasons: first, a comprehensive (though unannotated) bibliography of legal journal articles has recently been published; and second, the authors have little or no expertise in legal research. Sources dealing primarily with intellectual freedom or censorship are also excluded since numerous bibliographies in library science provide access to this literature.

English-language materials drawn primarily from literature published in the United States are included, as are selective sources from other countries, including Canada, Great Britain and Australia. Publications dealing with academic freedom in various countries around the world are included in their own chapter. Complete bibliographic citations accompany annotations of 50 to 300 words. All sources have been examined and annotated by the compilers.

Organization

The guide is organized into eleven chapters dealing with various aspects of academic freedom: Philosophy; History (General); History (1915 to World War II); History (Cold War); History (1960 to 1979); Current Issues and General Trends; Academic Freedom and the Culture Wars; Academic Freedom and Religion; Tenure - Defense, Critiques and Alternatives; Other Countries; and World Wide Web sites. Within chapters, entries are arranged alphabetically by author or, lacking an author, by title. Some cross-references to other entries are included in the annotations.

The chapter on **Philosophy** examines academic freedom from the perspective of individual philosophers (e.g., John Dewey, Rene Descartes, Immanuel Kant), the philosophical and theoretical contributions of other cultures (e.g., Germany), and earlier historical periods (e.g., the Enlightenment). Many entries examine the relationship between professors' academic freedom and the ethical obligations of their profession. Other topics discussed include the philosophical basis for the freedom and autonomy of higher educational institutions, as well as the political philosophies that justify the central place in a democracy of publicly-funded higher education, with its autonomies of teaching, conducting research, and studying. Finally, a number of entries attempt to carefully define the concept of academic freedom and its conceptual relationship to other educational and social values.

Five chapters covering historical periods occupy a central place in this bibliography. **History (General)** provides abstracts of early accounts of academic freedom, from its roots in medieval European universities up through specific late 19th century and early 20th century cases. Overviews of the history of academic freedom in the United States are also provided, some giving broad coverage of the topic throughout this century and before, others providing more localized geographic, institutional, or profession-specific coverage. Also included here are broad historical overviews of the work of the American Association of University Professors (AAUP) and other such advocacy groups. **History (1915 to World War II)** covers a critical period in the development of academic freedom in the United States. The founding of the American Association of University Professors (AAUP) in 1915 marked the beginning of efforts to professionalize teaching and protect academic freedom. Many entries in this chapter discuss this development, as well as the academic freedom cases that helped foster it. These cases relate to professors' opposition to World War I, their critiques of monopolies and vested economic interests, and their involvement in controversies over science and religion, among others. A number of entries also deal with the firing of professors for radical political views, developments that foreshadowed the McCarthy period. **History (Cold War)** covers the period from about the end of the World War II up though the end of the 1950s. Though not a long period in American history, this was a period in higher education marked by tremendous upheaval. This was due in large part to anti-Communist efforts at the Federal, State and local levels, as well as to the massive influx of veterans (and Federal spending) into public higher education. Specific anti-Communist cases are covered here, as are arguments for and against the rooting out of Communist elements on campus and the close scrutiny of professors' political views, both characteristics of McCarthyism. The period covered by **History (1960-1979)** was marked by political activism and financial exigency on American campuses. Controversies and academic freedom cases revolved around such issues as civil rights, student activism, opposition to the war in Vietnam, gender equity and affirmative action, financial exigency and retrenchment, governmental interference in research, and loss of funding, among others. The chapter on **Current Issues and General Trends** focuses on the years since 1980, during which attacks continued on educational funding, tenure, and the freedoms to teach and research. There was also the growing perception among some interest groups that leftist or radical professors were taking over campuses, and that tenured professors were not accountable. The entries in this section address these and other issues, reflecting a growing diversity of challenges to academic freedom.

The works cited in **Academic Freedom and the Culture Wars** deal with contemporary debates over and academic freedom cases relating to political correctness and campus speech codes. Both topics are part of the broad ideological debate over what knowledge and ideas are most worth teaching, the context in which they should be presented, and the role of educational institutions in society.

In **Academic Freedom and Religion** the entries examine the sometimes troubled coexistence of religious education and academic freedom. A number of the entries deal with alleged infringements of academic freedom at religiously-affiliated institutions. However, other articles argue for the central place of pluralism and academic freedom in such institutions, and for the essential compatibility of religious truth and the freedom to research or teach controversial topics. Even the AAUP's stance on religion in higher education is critiqued as a violation of principles of academic freedom.

Tenure - Defense, Critiques and Alternatives addresses the role played by tenure in protecting academic freedom rights. Included here are books and articles both defending and criticizing the institution of tenure. Some of the critical entries present arguments in favor of replacing tenure with other systems, such as post-tenure review and the expanded use of non-tenure-track and part-time positions. Others propose, for example, to allow faculty to bargain away tenure for higher salaries. Defenders of tenure argue for its continued importance in protecting academic freedom. They also find fault with some of the market-oriented alternatives to tenure.

Though limited in the number of countries covered, the chapter on **Other Countries** includes entries on histories of academic freedom, on specific academic freedom cases, and on studies of the relationship between human rights and academic freedom. Some of the entries are historical, such as those covering Peron-era academic freedom in Argentina or Nazi-era restrictions on academics in Germany.

World Wide Web Sites provides Internet addresses and annotations of sites maintained by such groups as the American Association of University Professors and the National Association of Scholars, or of such seminal documents as the 1988 "Lima Declaration on Academic Freedom."

A name index and a subject index are included to provide thorough access to the entries. The name index includes authors and editors, as well as contributors to edited collections or symposia who are listed in abstracts. Individuals treated as subjects and named within abstracts are also included and are indicated by the phrase "references to" before the entry numbers. The subject index includes not only subjects, but also organizations, associations, and other proper names. Multiple access points are provided for each entry.

Acknowledgments

A number of individuals have helped us in the preparation of this work, which was begun while the authors were colleagues at Bierce Library of the University of Akron. The authors are grateful for the unqualified support and assistance of Bierce Library faculty and staff. In particular, we would also like to thank our editor, George Butler, for his assistance. Martha McNamara helped edit the work, for which we are most grateful. Ellen Brink did a superb job with the indexing. The professional staff at Greenwood Press have been extremely patient and helpful in assisting our efforts. Finally, we would like to thank Martha McNamara, Ruth Ilan and Katherine Anne Kuhn for their moral and intellectual support. This bibliography is better for the input and involvement of the individuals mentioned above. The remaining deficiencies, however, are the responsibilities of the compilers.

Chapter 1

Academic Freedom—
Philosophy

1. Ahmad, Iqbal. "Karl Jaspers' Idea of Academic Freedom." **Intellect** 101(2344): 95-96, November 1972.

Jaspers was excluded from administrative positions, removed from his professorship, and forbidden to publish his own writings under the Nazi regime not only because he was married to a Jewish woman but also because of his uncompromising position on academic freedom. A brief overview of his definition of academic freedom and some of the details of his own experience with academic freedom violations under Hitler are recounted.

2. American Association of University Professors. **Policy Documents & Reports.** Washington, D.C.: American Association of University Professors, 1995. 274p.

Known as the AAUP "Redbook," this volume includes "a wide range of policies as they have been formulated by standing and special committees" (1984 ed., p. ix) of the American Association of University Professors (AAUP). These policies are clustered together under ten major chapter headings: academic freedom, tenure, and due process; professional ethics; research and teaching; discrimination; college and university government; collective bargaining; students rights and freedoms; college and university accreditation; collateral benefits; and constitution (of the Association). A chapter may include anywhere from one to more than a dozen documents, each accompanied by the citation to the issue of *Academe* or the *AAUP Bulletin* in which the item originally appeared. The chapter on academic freedom, tenure, and due process is the largest and includes such documents as the *1940 Statement of Principles on Academic Freedom and Tenure*, "Procedural Standards in the Renewal or Nonrenewal of Faculty Appointments," and "On Freedom of Expression and Campus

Speech Codes." There is also a brief but useful introduction, as well as an appendix of court decisions that have referred to various AAUP policy documents.

3.   Boas, George and Sidney Hook. "Symposium: The Ethics of Academic Freedom." In Morton White, editor. **Academic Freedom, Logic and Religion.** Philadelphia: University of Pennsylvania Press, 1953. pp. 1-38. (American Philosophical Association Eastern Division, 1953, v. 2). LC 52-4984.

In two back-to-back papers, Boas and Hook address ethical issues of academic freedom. Boas argues that restraints on knowledge-seeking and discovery should be explicitly limited to issues of logic and methodology. All other limits threaten academic freedom and are in direct opposition to the interests of science and society. In contrast, Hook holds that advancement of knowledge is but one justification for academic freedom. Referring to his book *Heresy, Yes—Conspiracy, No*, Hook briefly addresses issues of Communism and its threat to academic freedom. Hook argues further that certain breaches of professional ethics should be considered evidence of incompetence, holding that refusals to answer Congressional inquiries might be ethical lapses even if found to be legal.

4.   Brown, William R. "Contemporary Cartesians: An Essay on the Academician's Organizing Principles." **Liberal Education** 70(3): 263-74, Fall 1984.

Brown argues that the autonomy of the modern academician is traceable back to a normative style of work best represented in Descartes' "Discourse on Method." The six principles governing Descartes' method of inquiry that still characterize the work of autonomous academics are: that intellectual activity should be pursued independently and individually; that inquiry should have no limits; that the amount of time spent should be dictated by assessments of need made by the scholar himself; that objectivity or detachment from the object of study is required; that rationality is universal; and that a secure and stable environment is essential for scholarship. Brown gives specific examples of how these principles govern the work, relationships, and personal autonomy of contemporary professors.

5.   Butts, Robert E. "Philosophers as Professional Relativists." **Canadian Journal of Philosophy** 20:617-624, December 1990.

This 1990 Presidential Address to the Canadian Philosophical Association calls on philosophers to adhere to a principle of "professional relativism," regardless of any personal or professional commitment they may have to positions of "epistemological absolutism." Calling this the "professional philosopher's schizoid split," Butts says that support for professional relativism would not only have the effect of institutionalizing intellectual and academic freedom within the philosophic community, but would also help the discipline flourish, given that philosophy thrives on disagreement.

6.　　Cahn, Steven M. **Saints and Scamps: Ethics in Academia.** Totowa, NJ: Rowman & Littlefield, 1986. 113p. ISBN 0-8476-7517-3.

Cahn discusses ethical aspects of academia, with chapters on the "professorial life," teaching, scholarship and service, personnel decisions, and graduate education. Issues of academic freedom are addressed in sections of these chapters, dealing with such topics as the role of the teacher and how to best evaluate teaching; departmental obligations to professors and their work; faculty appointment, dismissal, and tenure; and the responsibilities of graduate students to their intended profession and of professors to their graduate students.

7.　　Capen, Samuel P. "Reflections on Freedom in Education." **Philosophy and Phenomenological Research** 8(4): 494-507, June 1948.

Capen points out that some faculty and invited campus speakers have been persecuted in various ways for their "unorthodox views." He suggests that while many universities give rhetorical support to academic freedom in the abstract, they often fail to live up to this ideal in the concrete. Protecting academic freedom means protecting faculty's freedom to investigate, publish, disagree, and be controversial, among other things. Furthermore, keeping and advancing in a faculty position should be dependent only upon one's competence. If universities support this principle, then they should defend it even if it costs them financial or moral support. The protection of the free search for knowledge will ultimately lead to the truth and the discovery of knowledge. This also provides the appropriate model of valuing freedom for students preparing for professional careers and leadership positions. Capen points out that the AAUP has been the primary defender of academic freedom, and that presidents and trustees have been derelict, for the most part, in protecting freedom. With freedom comes responsibility, which is imposed on faculty by the scientific method, and on students by their conduct and work. Ultimately, the university can defend democracy by being an example of it, says Capen, and by defending the principles of free inquiry.

8.　　Chermside, Herbert B. "Some Ethical Conflicts Affecting University Patent Administration." **Journal of the Society of Research Administrators** 16(3): 23-34, Winter 1985; 16(4): 11-17, Spring 1985.

Chermside, in a two-part article, addresses the ethical dilemmas posed by the profit to be had by publicly-funded universities when they exercise proprietary rights over the intellectual property produced by researchers on campus. A utilitarian ethical imperative common to discussions of federal support for universities is addressed here. Specific reference is made to the 1980 federal Patent and Trademark

Amendments which allow universities to retain title to inventions made using federal funds, provided that public access to these patents is ensured in times of need. A number of potential conflicts of interest are addressed, including, among others: faculty involvement in and profit from research; equity participation; university licensing and revenue management; inappropriate commercial uses of a university's name.

9.   Cowley, W. H. "Professional Growth and Academic Freedom." **The Journal of Higher Education** 21(5): 225-236, May 1950.

Cowley argues that there are prerequisites to any freedom. These include the need to survive, to have social order, to manage competing conceptions of order, to strive for a better world, and to select a source of authority for managing the world. However, these needs pose questions or dilemmas. How does a society maintain democracy and social order at the same time? In an academic setting, how can free institutions and free faculty be maintained? Though state legislatures and boards of trustees have formal control over colleges and universities, faculty and alumni exert increasing influence in academic matters. This, says Cowley, is a positive and democratic development. However, faculty are also becoming increasingly obsessed with professional specialization and are not becoming better educated in freedom. To counter this development, and to promote and preserve academic freedom, the faculty, the public, and those students receiving general collegiate education need to be educated in the value and importance of general and academic freedom.

10.   Dewey, John. "Academic Freedom." **Educational Review** 23: 1-14, January 1902.

Writing at the beginning of the 20th Century, Dewey argues that the established, physical sciences have fewer problems with academic freedom than some of the newer, fledgling sciences (e.g., sociology, psychology). The former have methods and techniques that are considered advanced and unassailable, so their findings are more accepted. The findings of the social sciences, however, are given less credence, particularly when they conflict with cherished beliefs related to daily life. Yet because they often deal with matters of social importance, these sciences need to be granted much freedom. Dewey is optimistic that overt abridgements of freedom are declining. However, he does express concern over subtle infringements on the freedom to work, which is the backbone of the university. The need to raise money, for example, may gradually become an end in itself and make universities susceptible to self-censorship. Similarly, scholarly specialization may encourage academics to avoid the larger issues which would now fall outside of their narrow sphere. Also, the centralization of administration has the potential to diminish "initiative and responsibility." Ultimately, Dewey is optimistic that individual initiative, "the need of the community for guidance," and the growing community of inquirers will preserve academic freedom.

11. Dewey, John. "The Social Significance of Academic Freedom." **Education Digest** 50(1): 37-39, September 1984.

In this reprint of an April, 1936 article in the same journal, Dewey argues that academic freedom for teachers and students is essential for the creation of intelligent citizens and the support of democracy. The denial of freedom to some students, brought about by our restrictive industrial system and an acquiescent school system, has led some students to see violent social change as their only redress. As such students see it, social intelligence is not valued by the system as a means of influencing or affecting social and political reality. What is needed, says Dewey, is free inquiry by teachers and students, so that they can see the value of "intelligent action" in the development of society.

12. Dworkin, Ronald. "We Need a New Interpretation of Academic Freedom." **Academe** 82(3): 10-15, May-June 1996.

An excerpt from the author's 1996 book *Freedom's Law: The Moral Reading of the American Constitution*, this essay is one in the Academic Freedom and the Future of the University lecture series. Dworkin argues that the conventional defense of academic freedom as necessary for the pursuit of truth is not enough to help decide when or if it must yield in favor of other competing values. Arguing that higher education contributes to a "culture of independence" as opposed to a "culture of conformity," Dworkin argues further that academic freedom supports and nurtures an ideal of "ethical individualism" that is essential for such a culture to flourish. The two most important responsibilities in this ideal of ethical individualism are the responsibility not to profess what one believes to be false, and the duty to speak out for what one believes to be true. Arguing that academic freedom reinforces these values in students and scholars, Dworkin also acknowledges that academic freedom is but one value among many, and as such must sometimes be limited in favor of supporting competing values. As an example of a rationale for limiting academic freedom, the author cites the case of hate speech: deliberate insults or intentional infliction of emotional harm. Comparing the Stanford University and University of Michigan speech codes, Dworkin sees a key difference in that the Stanford code requires a proof of intent on the part of the speaker, whereas the Michigan code (found unconstitutional by the U.S. Supreme Court) did not. He outlines various possibilities of arguments for compromising academic freedom, concluding that a "culture of independence" will always and necessarily include elements that ridicule or insult. Academic freedom should be defended, Dworkin holds, as an important ethical element of the traditions and social institutions of higher education.

13. Fischer, Louis. "The Academic Freedom of John Dewey." **High School Journal** 60(8): 379-386, April 1977.

Fischer reviews some of the ideas of John Dewey regarding the role of freedom in education. Dewey felt that the purpose of schooling was to foster a "democracy of mind" that would preserve a democratic social order. To do this, both teachers and students had to be democratically involved in the pursuit of knowledge. Teachers should have meaningful involvement in "the selection of goals, curricula, books, techniques, and materials" (p. 380). Students need to become active and disciplined learners who can identify, study and solve problems. Academic freedom has also been expanded into the public schools, says Fischer, supported in part by the liberal arts background of teachers, the rise of national teacher organizations, and court decisions. For Dewey, the nurturing of the freedom of thought and the freedom of expression is critical in perpetuating democracy. How we educate must necessarily reflect these values.

14.   Gardner, David P.   "Faculty Responsibility for Professional Ethics." **Educational Record** 52(4): 343-347, Fall 1971.

Gardner believes that unless bodies of faculty begin to discipline breaches of professional conduct by professors, the authority to do so is unlikely to be expanded upon. Faculty self-governance in accordance with principles of academic freedom and standards consistent with the AAUP's 1940 Statement of Principles requires sanctioning abuses which infringe upon freedom to learn. The author does not argue that academe adopt a code of conduct, but rather that it accept responsibility for disciplining colleagues charged with abuse of professional standards so as not to risk losing its hard-fought authority and prerogatives.

15.   Gewirth, Alan. "Human Rights and Academic Freedom." In Steven M. Cahn, editor. **Morality, Responsibility and the University: Studies in Academic Ethics.** Philadelphia: Temple University Press, 1990. pp. 8-31. ISBN 0-8772-2646-6.

Gewirth addresses conflicts between higher education's moral values of academic freedom and the societal value placed in education. He examines those areas where freedom-based rights of professors may collide with the intellectual standards-based rights of students or the community at large. The relationship between human rights and academic freedom is addressed along with two interpretations of the right to academic freedom. The first is based on a generalized libertarian interpretation placing in a larger societal context the freedoms of academics. The second is a workplace libertarian interpretation which focuses on freedoms of specific professional academic activities, placing these within the broader context of employee rights. After addressing possible grounds for disputing the distinction between human and academic rights as well as possible grounds for justifying academic freedom on the basis of human rights principles, Gewirth then presents the obligations academics have by virtue of these rights. The specific case study of creation science is used to illustrate his indirect justification of academic freedom as a human right, one that implies limiting obligations. Gewirth concludes his test case by charging that known creationists should not be given tenure in the natural science departments of secular universities and that teaching of these ideas should not be required. But once tenured, creationists cannot be dismissed solely on those grounds.

16. Gutmann, Amy. "Is Freedom Indivisible?: The Relative Autonomy of Universities in a Liberal Democracy." In J. Roland Pennock and John W. Chapman, editors. **Liberal Democracy.** New York: New York University Press, 1983. pp. 257-286. (Nomos: The Yearbook of the American Society for Political and Legal Philosophy, 25). ISBN 0-8147-6584-X.

Gutmann presents two theoretical positions regarding university autonomy from government control: corporate pluralism and liberal democracy. In the former, the corporate rights of university ownership are asserted; in the latter, the necessity for democratic politics of free inquiry is asserted. Gutmann elaborates on both ideas, supporting the latter position over the former.

17. Held, Virginia. "The Independence of Intellectuals." **Journal of Philosophy** 80(10): 572-582, October 1983.

These papers by Held, Rorty and MacIntyre make up an American Philosophical Association "Symposium on the Social Responsibilities of Intellectuals." Held argues that the social role of intellectual carries with it a special social obligation to provide critique of societal norms and values, and that these obligations are above and beyond any that are associated with such roles as citizen, member of a certain profession, or even as human being. The activism required for intellectuals to appropriately fill this role is spelled out. Rorty argues in response to Held that her justification of activism requires an impossibility - that societal values and norms can be adequately determined (or even determined at all) independently of the community which holds them. An abstract of the response provided by MacIntyre looks at the difference between Held and Rorty as differing responses to the rejection by modern society of a social life rooted in the traditions of rationality.

18. Kerr, Clark. "Knowledge Ethics and the New Academic Culture." **Change** 26(1): 8-15, January/February 1994.

Kerr sees "disintegration" in ethics among academics and calls for acceptance of an academic code of conduct that should govern discovery and dissemination of knowledge. Kerr compares the current academic culture unfavorably with that of the past. In an academic culture that has more economics-driven elements and more off-campus political concerns than in the past, Kerr sees more necessity for formal codes of behavior as well as for independent judicial tribunals. A statement outlining obligatory actions for "the ethics of knowledge" is included. Problems with academic self-government are outlined. The historical autonomy of universities is seen as a direct result of their ethical conduct. Noteworthy because of its absence is any argument basing institutional autonomy on foundational principles of academic freedom.

19. Kirk, Russell. **Academic Freedom: An Essay in Definition.** Westport, Conn.: Greenwood Press, 1977, c1955. 210p. ISBN 0-8371-9566-7.

Kirk argues that, contrary to much scholarly opinion, religion and religious institutions have made a profound contribution to academic freedom. He provides philosophical and historical analysis in support of this argument and also points out some limitations of prominent secularist and doctrinaire liberal models of academic freedom (e.g., Henry Steele Commager, John Dewey, Sidney Hook, Robert Maynard Hutchins). Academic freedom is best served when its purpose is to seek the Truth, rather than just to serve the community's needs, to promote democracy, or to engage in social reconstruction. Kirk is also somewhat critical of William F. Buckley's conservative proposals for higher education (in Buckley's *God and Man at Yale*), which would impose an individualist and religious orthodoxy. This constrains academic freedom, as does Buckley's view of faculty as, in effect, servants of administrators and trustees. Finally, Kirk examines legislative investigations of faculty loyalty, loyalty oaths, and faculty members taking the 5th Amendment.

20. Leslie, David W. "Academic Freedom for Universities." **The Review of Higher Education** 9(2): 135-157, 1986.

Leslie attempts to explain the origins of the principle of institutional academic freedom or autonomy for universities. Through historical analysis and the review of some landmark court decisions, Leslie analyzes the extent of the autonomy and discretion that universities are allowed in conducting academic affairs. Though court decisions are somewhat contradictory, universities nonetheless seem to have some institutional latitude in protecting and providing for academic freedom and in making academic decisions (e.g., retention and tenure). The author also discusses cases and circumstances in which freedom of individual expression and institutional academic freedom conflict.

21. Machlup, Fritz. "On Some Misconceptions Concerning Academic Freedom." **American Association of University Professors Bulletin** 41(4): 753-784, Winter 1955.

Machlup begins by offering the following definition of academic freedom: "Academic freedom consists in the absence of, or protection from, such restraints or pressures – chiefly in the form of sanctions threatened by state or church authorities or by the authorities, faculties, or students of colleges and universities, but occasionally also by other power groups in society – as are designed to create in the minds of academic scholars (teachers, research workers, and students in colleges and universities) fears and anxieties that may inhibit them from freely studying and investigating whatever they are interested in, and from freely discussing, teaching, or publishing whatever opinions they have reached." Machlup goes on to clarify this definition by discounting thirteen critical statements on academic freedom. Debunked in turn are the following issues: whether academic freedom is merely an aspect of the constitutional guarantee of free speech; whether it is a privilege solely benefitting a special interest group (academia); whether it extends no further than the relationship between a professor and his university's board of trustees; whether it is limited to the issue of protection from dismissal and therefore is fairly synonymous with tenure; whether there are special or uniquely moral responsibilities that must be adhered to by those benefitting from academic freedom; whether academic freedom must really be extended to protect dissenters; whether academic freedom must protect those who "abuse" their freedom; whether the rights and protections of academic freedom are confined only to a specific scholar's area of competence; whether it includes the right to advocate subversive ideas; whether it should be granted only to those loyal to the government; whether academic freedom extends to cover those without "independence of thought;" whether it should be denied to all those who would "destroy" freedom; whether academic freedom is consistent with an oath prescribed by those in authority. In each of these thirteen areas, the author argues closely how such restrictions on the freedom to teach cannot be consistent with principles of academic freedom. Reprinted in Louis Joughin, editor, *Academic Freedom and Tenure* (Madison: University of Wisconsin Press, 1967).

22. MacIntyre, Alasdair. "Moral Arguments and Social Context." **Journal of Philosophy** 80(10): 590-591, October 1983.

See Held (entry #17).

23. Metzger, Walter P. "The German Contribution to the American Theory of Academic Freedom." **American Association of University Professors Bulletin** 41(2): 214-230, Summer 1955.

Metzger addresses the dependence on German concepts that were selected and transformed in the early development of the principle of academic freedom as it related to American colleges and universities. After outlining the institutional freedoms common to German universities of the 19th century, Metzger cites three basic concepts as playing key roles in the formation of the German concept of academic freedom. The first of these concepts is Wissenschaft, or a calling to search for ultimate meanings. Such a focus on disinterested, objective research was encouraged by two other important foundational concepts in German intellectual life: Lernfreiheit and Lehrfreiheit. The first of these, Lernfreiheit, means an absence of administrative control over the learning process—the student's freedom of inquiry, which was fairly significant in scope and reach. The second of these, Lehrfreiheit, embraced the freedom of professors' inquiry and teaching. Post Civil War and pre-World War I American intellectuals spoke in praiseworthy terms of the freedoms they saw inherent in the German universities where many of them had studied. In fact, eight of the thirteen signers of the 1915 AAUP Declaration of Principles had studied in Germany. One difference that evolved between American and German conceptions of academic freedom turned on the question of advocacy in the classroom. Whereas there was a German idea of "convincing" one's students, Americans tended to call for preserving neutrality of teaching on controversial issues and restraining professional speech on topics outside one's area of competence. That American universities included undergraduate colleges while their German counterparts did not helps in part to explain this difference, according to Metzger. For a reprint of this article, see entry #60.

24.   Metzger, Walter P. "Professional and Legal Limits to Academic Freedom." **Journal of College and University Law** 20(1): 1-14, Summer 1993.

Metzger attempts to refocus attention on what he, as well as the founders of the AAUP, considers to be appropriate limitations on academic freedom. These include the expectations that faculty reach conclusions in a scholarly manner, that they be "judicial" and "fair" with students, and that they be mindful of "the dignity of their calling and the good reputation of their institutions" (p. 2) in their extramural utterances. The "ethical injunctions" on faculty behavior were part of the definition of academic professionalism, says Metzger. The AAUP founders felt that a such professional restraint could be "content-neutral" and therefore not an infringement on academic freedom. More recently, however, the courts have supported more expansive views of academic freedom, at the expense of the original ethical injunctions. Furthermore, the AAUP, in at least one case, has gone along with this development, at the expense of its original views of academic responsibilities and obligations. Metzger discusses the case in question, Levin v. Harleston, and its implications for the exercise of appropriate restraints on academic freedom.

25.   Moodie, Graeme C. "On Justifying the Different Claims to Academic Freedom." **Minerva** 34(2): 129-150, Summer 1996.

Moodie is primarily concerned with justification of academic freedom as a special case of freedom beyond those civil liberties enjoyed by citizens. Moodie argues for a narrow definition of scholarly freedom, restricting the range of activities to which such protections are extended. He addresses three different claims to academic freedom: that of the scholar's right of unconstrained decision making (here called "scholarly freedom"), that of the institution's freedom from externally imposed restraints (here called "university autonomy"), and that of the decision-making rights of groups of academics (here called "academic rule"). Each depends for its validity on differing considerations, here spelled out.

26.   Pincoffs, Edmund L., editor. **The Concept of Academic Freedom.** Austin, Texas: University of Texas Press, 1975. 272p. ISBN 0-2927-1016-X.

This book presents the proceedings of the 1972 "Conference on the Concept of Academic Freedom" held at the University of Texas at Austin. Those who presented principle papers or participated in panel discussions were given the opportunity to revise or reply to respondents. A radical class-based analysis of the concept is presented by Milton Fisk in an essay called "Academic Freedom in a Class Society;" responded to in essays by Bertram H. Davis and Hardy E. Jones called (respectively) "Academic Freedom, Academic Neutrality and the Social System," and "Academic Freedom as a Moral Right." Fisk hopes to provide an alternative model of the working class intellectual as opposed to the intellectual working in service for a capitalist system, and he calls on academics to explicitly identify themselves with the working class. In so doing he questions what he calls the "myth" of academic neutrality as being impossible, given the evident coincidence of material interests between a professor and the capitalist society in which he labors. Davis' response is in part based on an affirmation that academic neutrality is no myth, but on the contrary an obligation that broadens academic freedoms. Jones reasserts a rights-based theory as a necessary underpinning of academic freedom, here criticizing a utilitarian justification of academic freedom. Jones holds that there is a moral obligation for scholars to seek the truth, an obligation to seek out the knowledge necessary to better determine "what we ought to do." In the second part of this book, William Van Alstyne and John Searle present conflicting views of the basis of academic freedom in essays called "The Specific Theory of Academic Freedom and the General Issue of Civil Liberty," and "Two Concepts of Academic Freedom." This essay of Searle's is a section from the chapter on academic freedom from his book *The Campus War*. Van Alstyne argues that academic freedom is a subset of basic constitutionally protected civil liberties and outlines the tensions between academic freedom as liberty from restraint versus a right that implies an enforceable claim against others. Searle writes of a "special theory" and a "general theory" of academic freedom which, when taken together, Searle claims will cover most of the cases of violation of academic freedom. The third section presents a panel discussion on the issue of tenure by Rolf Sartorius, Alexander Ritchie, Grahamn Hughes, and Amelie Oksenberg Rorty. The final two sections cover panel discussions on free speech issues and issues related to university regulation of research. Essays here are by Hugo Bedau, and Alan Pasch (free speech); and by T.M. Scanlon, and Judith Jarvis Thomson (research). A "Proposed Statement on Academic Freedom" was drawn up by Thomson and is reproduced at the end, along with a bibliography of suggested readings provided by Fritz Machlup.

27.   Rand, Richard, editor. **Logomachia: The Conflict of the Faculties.** Lincoln: University of Nebraska Press, 1992. 218 p. ISBN 0-8032-3884-3.

This compilation includes some of the papers read at a 1987 symposium called "Our Academic Contract: 'The Conflict of the Faculties' in America." The focal point is philosopher Immanuel Kant's long-neglected essay *Der Streit der Fakultaten*, in which he presents a model for the modern research university, for the societal role of the university, and for the protection of academic freedom. Jacques Derrida's 1980 essay "Mochlos; or, The Conflict of the Faculties" reintroduced Kant's work, and is provided here for the first time in English translation. Presenters at the conference were asked to read both Kant's and Derrida's essays and respond. Essays included here are by Jacques Derrida, Christie McDonald, Timothy Bahti, Peggy Kamuf, Robert Young, John Llewelyn, and Alan Bass. Also included is an interview with Derrida conducted by the editor. Topics discussed include not only deconstructive readings of Kant's work, but also: historical analyses of the French, British, and American origins of the modern university; psychoanalytic and literary perspectives on medicine and science in higher education; a Heideggerian reading of Kant and Derrida.

28.   Rendel, Margherita. "Human Rights and Academic Freedom." In Malcolm Tight, editor. **Academic Freedom and Responsibility.** Milton Keynes: Society for Research into Higher Education/Open University Press, 1988. pp. 74-87. ISBN 0-3350-9531-3.

Rendel discusses how provisions in various international and regional human rights documents relate to academic freedom. Provisions banning discrimination as well as those in support of rights of travel, freedom of expression and opinion, conscience and religion are all spelled out. Treaty obligations and enforcement through the UN Human Rights Committee and court decisions in the UK and Europe are all cited in reference to issues of academic freedom. After outlining how human rights principles can be applied to support academic freedom rights of individuals and institutions, the author calls for an International Charter drawn up by academics in preparation for a (proposed) treaty, the Convention on Academic Freedom. See entry #461 for a description of the full volume of essays.

29.   Rorty, Richard.   "Does Academic Freedom Have Philosophical Presuppositions?" **Academe** 80 (6): 52-63, November/December 1994.

The author holds that academic practices would be better served if academics stopped relying on their most common presupposition for academic freedom, that of depoliticizing a search for objective truth. According to Rorty, any number of beliefs about the nature of truth and rationality can be held to justify academic freedom. In arguing that it is more important to strengthen socio-political grounds for academic freedom than epistemological grounds, Rorty discusses both his philosophical debate with John Searle on the nature of truth and knowledge, and his own affinity with John Dewey and other American pragmatist philosophers.

30. Rorty, Richard. "Postmodern Bourgeois Liberalism." **Journal of Philosophy** 80(10): 583-589, October 1983.

See Held (entry #17).

31. Scott, Joan Wallach. "Academic Freedom as an Ethical Practice." **Academe** 81(4): 44-48, July-August 1995.

A lecture in the series "Academic Freedom and the Future of the University," this essay argues that the power of academic freedom lies in an ambiguity inherent in putting any universal principle at work in historically circumscribed relationships. Scott draws on John Dewey's 1902 essay "Academic Freedom," on Arthur Lovejoy's 1937 entry in the *Encyclopedia of Social Sciences*, and on Glenn Morrow's 1968 entry in the *International Encyclopedia of the Social Sciences* in examining the relationship between the academic freedom of individuals and the demands of their disciplines for establishing truth claims or submitting to standards of inquiry and knowledge-production. The ambiguity at work here is that the protection provided researchers by a discipline is one affording freedom of inquiry while simultaneously being confining and regulatory. Scott notes that more and more often, a choice is being forced between the traditional disciplines and critical inquiry, a rigid choice between a tradition-bound dogmatism on the one hand and a moralistic interdisciplinarity on the other. This polarization can best be seen, she says, by comparing the attacks on disciplinarity and on postmodernism, the former attacked as enforcing empty standards and the latter attacked as being mere political advocacy. At its best, academic freedom can mediate between discipline and criticism in a way that both judges and intervenes when a discipline is enforcing specific exclusions that interfere with an individual's ability to pursue his or her inquiry autonomously. Academic freedom must remain an ideal that is "blind to power in order to be able to see how power is abused in particular cases," Scott argues. Only then can the two functions of the academy, discipline and criticism, be integrated as an ethical as well as academic practice.

32. Shils, Edward. **The Order of Learning: Essays on the Contemporary University.** Philip G. Altbach, Editor. New Brunswick: Transaction Publishers, 1997. 376p. LC 96-47503. ISBN 1-5600-0298-0.

Part three of this edited collection of works by Shils includes three chapters on academic freedom. The first chapter provides an overview of academic freedom, including discussion of its rights and obligations, as well as sources of infringements. Shils' discussion includes both historical and cross-national analysis. The second chapter addresses tenure, with Shils exploring both its strengths and weaknesses. On balance, Shils supports the continuance of permanent tenure. He suggests that it provides a modest amount of protection to non-mainstream ideas, though he generally feels there is a "spirit of tolerance." However, he sees the political correctness movement as a threat to this tolerance, with the more tradition-minded academics potentially being most at risk. The third chapter focuses almost exclusively on restrictions on the freedom of research and teaching in the social sciences. Shils observes that certain topics and disciplines are most susceptible to controversy, thereby placing the professor's freedom at risk. Threats to one's freedom can come from inside and outside educational institutions, originating with doctrinaire colleagues, administrators, trustees, or external "patriotic" organizations. Furthermore, limitations can range from subtler forms of intimidation, such as a lack of cordiality, to overt and tangible punishments, such as denial of raises and promotions or, in the worst instance, dismissal.

33.   Shirley, Robert C. "Institutional Autonomy and Governmental Control." **Educational Forum** 48(2): 217-22, Winter 1984.

Shirley addresses the basic freedoms that should be accorded to public educational institutions in a "Bill of Rights" for institutions. Three basic freedoms often being denied in this area are: freedom to define the institutional mission, goals, and strategic plan independent from governmental influence; the freedom to manage fiscal issues constrained only by the total appropriated amount and a commitment not to transfer funds between operating and capital budgets; and the freedoms to define organizational structure, workloads, and selection or promotion of personnel.

34.   Simon, Robert L. "A Defense of the Neutral University." In Steven M. Cahn, editor. **Morality, Responsibility and the University: Studies in Academic Ethics.** Philadelphia: Temple University Press, 1990. pp. 56-75. ISBN 0-8772-2646-6.

Simon addresses the question of whether universities should act as political agents in support of social causes. The concept of institutional neutrality is fleshed out here. Arguing not only that institutional neutrality is possible, Simon argues also that what he calls a "critical neutrality" is desirable in order to protect individuals' rights of free critical inquiry. Critical neutrality, for Simon, does not require value neutrality, but requires adherence to rules of critical inquiry that are independent of any substantive positions that are taken one way or another. Simon addresses such "hard cases" as university regulation of student behavior through anti-drug and sexual activity policies. And Simon considers, as a counter-example, the case of divestment of financial holdings in apartheid South Africa as a possible case in which universities should not be neutral. The author emphasizes the necessity of a critical procedural neutrality, one that parallels state neutrality with regard to religion: respect for individual rights along with a prohibition from active institutional support for specific social causes.

35. Sjoberg, Gideon. "Democracy, Science, and Institutionalized Dissent: Toward a Social Justification for Academic Tenure." **Sociological Perspectives** 41(4): 697-722, Winter 1998.

In this broad, sociological defense of tenure, Sjoberg argues that tenure is critical for "sustaining intellectual dissent," which in turn sustains science and democracy. Freedom requires that individuals be able to challenge authority and propose alternative social arrangements. Tenure provides the "buffer" that allows this work to be carried out. It also provides a certain amount of freedom to focus on long-term problems, in contrast to the short-term focus of many corporations and governmental bodies. Much of Sjoberg's focus is on modern, large-scale organizations (particularly corporations) and their relationship to the democratic process. Sjoberg identifies some of the tensions and conflicts between the system-maintenance and profit goals of some organizations and the socially necessary protection of institutionalized dissent, which advances social and cultural freedom.

36. Stelzmann, Rainulf A. "Kant and Academic Freedom." **Thought** 43(169): 187-201, Summer 1968.

The author addresses Kant's definition and defense of academic freedom principles, while also dispelling what Stelzmann sees as common fallacies regarding Kant's concept of the State. In sections devoted in turn to the metaphysical problem of freedom, personal freedom, and academic freedom, Stelzmann discusses the freedom of the individual from the points of view of Kantian pure reason and practical reason. But he also addresses the Prussian educational system and Kant's personal experiences with restrictions on freedom of study (as a student) and on freedom of expression (as a professor). Stelzmann writes that indictment of authoritarian rules gradually became more and more part of Kant's own writings on religion; writings that earned him official rebukes from the government and later from the King. But after the death of Frederick Wilhelm II Kant took up the issue of academic freedom directly, in writings which called for the study of philosophy to be completely free from external regulations. Stezmann concludes by addressing how Kant's conception of academic freedom eventually formed the basis for German educational policies.

37. Strike, Kenneth A. "Liberality, Neutrality, and the Modern University." In Kenneth A. Strike and Kieran Egan, editors. **Ethics and Educational Policy.**

Boston: Routledge & Kegan Paul, 1978. pp. 22-35. ISBN 0-7100-8423-4. LC 77-30516.

Strike discusses attacks on the concept of institutional neutrality, particularly those that claim that value neutrality is "impossible" in higher education institutions. The author addresses the difference between logical and factual possibility, as well as the difference between neutrality of opinion and neutrality of consequence. A third sense of impartial neutrality is developed here, along with an outline of how universities have shifted from a liberal "marketplace of ideas" focus to a more social service-oriented focus. In the context of changing and often conflicting institutional values, the concept of institutional neutrality is in flux and not easy to generalize about. Strike calls for further inquiry into how changing institutional values impact traditional liberal values in higher education.

38.   Sutton, Robert B. "The Phrase *Libertas Philosophands.*" **Journal of the History of Ideas** 14(2): 310-316, April 1953.

The author discusses the European Enlightenment call for freedom in philosophizing as the source for today's call for academic freedom. A 1622 defense of Galileo by Tommaso Campanella may be the earliest use of the exact phrase "libertas philosophands" in support of scientific freedom. The conceptual origins are traced to writings of Giordano Bruno and Galileo from the late 16th century regarding the search for "philosophic freedom." Uses of the phrase by Descartes, Spinoza, Milton, Nathanael Carpenter, and others are here discussed, as is the conceptual difference between academic freedom as we now know it and philosophic freedom as it was understood in the 16th and 17th centuries.

39.   Tierney, William G. "Academic Freedom and the Parameters of Knowledge." **Harvard Educational Review** 63 (2): 143-160, Summer 1993.

Tierney presents a social constructivist critique of the conceptual relationships between academic freedom, academic community, and knowledge, taking issue with conservative critics of the academy. The first section of this essay identifies a common theme in varying definitions of academic freedom, that of being defined by what limits it. Tierney here examines the "cultural politics" behind a model of academia under which academic freedom is necessary to ensure the free search for an objective truth, that search being the common good of academic community (p. 147). The second section presents a case study of homophobia at a university involved in establishing a sexual orientation clause in its policy on nondiscrimination. Lesbian and gay individuals and communities were marginalized as deviant; similarly, gay studies were limited by being branded as not legitimate forms of knowledge. The author identifies epistemological issues related to the social construction of knowledge as underlying these problems of social justice, individual rights, and academic freedom. That what counts as knowledge is always a function of social forces points to the need for what the author calls "community founded on difference rather than similarity" in academe (p. 158).

40.   Tight, Malcolm. "Academic Freedom Re-examined." **Higher Education Review** 18(1): 7-23, Autumn 1985.

To fully explore the concept of academic freedom, Tight dismantles it into five constituent questions: academic freedom for whom; academic freedom for what; academic freedom from whom/what; academic freedom in return for what; and how is academic freedom to be ensured? Tight examines these questions in some detail, with occasional examples drawn from higher education in Great Britain. Some of the related issues he addresses concern distinctions between institutional autonomy and individual academic freedom, sources of threats to academic freedom (e.g., internal versus external), conflicts between accountability and academic freedom, the distinction between academic freedom and a civil right, and the role of tenure in ensuring academic freedom. Tight concludes that academic freedom "can only be maintained and protected by force of law" (p. 21).

41.   Wallerstein, Immanuel. "Academic Freedom and Collective Expressions of Opinion." **The Journal of Higher Education** 42(9): 713-720, December 1971.

In order for society to remain free and vital, major institutions and social groups must give collective expression to their opinions on key social issues. Wallerstein identifies the church and the university as two such important social institutions. If they do not engage in open debate on such matters, their silence gives tacit support to the status quo. Opponents of institutional involvement suggest that it endangers individual rights, diverts attention from the institution's real functions, and risks "social and economic retaliation." Wallerstein refutes these arguments by arguing that: 1) individuals can and do live with a certain amount of ambiguity in their social groups and institutions; 2) the true function of universities is to question the truth; and 3) "retaliation is always a function of political strength" (p. 718), which is more ably resisted by collective response. Faculty self-deception, timidity and elitism are the chief dangers to academic freedom, says Wallerstein. The creation of the critical university is academic freedom's best safeguard.

42.   Wright, Quincy. "The Citizen's Stake in Academic Freedom." **The Journal of Higher Education** 20(7): 339-345, October 1949.

Wright's argument is that the world is becoming increasingly interdependent and interconnected culturally, politically, and economically. At the same time, there are countervailing forces at work that celebrate nationalism and isolationism. However, interconnectedness and multiculturalism are the future, says Wright, and should be valued in a contemporary definition of citizenship. International cooperation will be required to address the two greatest threats to civilization, poverty and war. Given this context, academic freedom is necessary in universities to help create a microcosm of a diverse, tolerant and interconnected world. Academic freedom will foster the variety of opinions needed to solve the world's problems.

Chapter 2

Academic Freedom—History (General)

43. Appel, Stephen. "'Expediency Was Struggling With Principle and Expediency Won:' Kendrik P. Shedd's Dismissal from the University of Rochester." **Journal of Educational Administration and History** 25(1): 41-57, January 1993.

Appel explores the political and economic issues that played a role in the 1911 forced resignation of Shedd, an active Socialist in Rochester, Professor of German, and Head of the Department of Romance Languages. In this, Appel argues that the University of Rochester became the first American university to dismiss a professor due to his political beliefs and activities. The case provides an example of the extent to which capitalist business interests (in this case, George Eastman) can influence personnel decisions at American universities.

44. Beauregard, Erving E. "Academic Freedom: A Cause Célèbre Revisited." **Continuity: A Journal of History** 3:111-119, Fall 1981.

The author here examines the case of the 1897 firing of Professor James Allen Smith by Marietta College, concluding that Hofstadter and Metzger (see entries #53 and #59) were inaccurate in their conclusion that this was a violation of academic freedom. Examining archives of Marietta College, Beauregard finds evidence that financial exigency, rather than displeasure with Smith's left-leaning views played the larger role in his dismissal.

45. Beauregard, Erving E. **History of Academic Freedom in Ohio: Case Studies in Higher Education, 1808-1976.** New York: P. Lang, 1988. 300p. (American University Studies; 14). ISBN 0-8204-0666-X.

This book is divided into two parts, the first covering 19ᵗʰ-century Ohio academic disputes over religion, slavery, and other topics; the second covering 20ᵗʰ-century Ohio academic disputes over religion, war and independence movements, communism and politics, economic and social events, and institutional governance. Appendices include, among other things, an exhaustive list of academic freedom cases in Ohio, the Cedarville College Doctrinal Statement (a statement of Baptist faith that all faculty, staff, and trustees must sign annually); and the test of the Ohio State University Faculty "Oath of Allegiance" to the Constitution of the State of Ohio (in place at OSU until 1984). Especially noteworthy are an extensive bibliography, along with extensive quotations throughout the text from primary source material and contemporary commentary.

46.   Berquist, Harold E., Jr. "The Edward W. Bemis Controversy at the University of Chicago." **AAUP Bulletin** 58(4): 384-392, December 1972.

Berquist reviews the historical, documentary evidence relating to the landmark academic freedom case of Edward Bemis. Two competing explanations of Bemis' firing have been put forth. The first is that Bemis was fired because he was either incompetent in his field or was unable to cover his own salary from his extension course teaching. Berquist suggests that neither of these explanations is supported by the documentary evidence. Bemis was renown and well published in his field, which was why he was hired in the first place. Prior to his firing, his competence had never been questioned by the key administrators involved in his termination (except J. Laurence Laughlin). Furthermore, Bemis was never notified that his teaching enrollments had to cover his salary costs. In any event, he was on track to teach as many extension courses as some of the more prolific teachers. The alternative explanation for Bemis' firing, one which Berquist supports, is that Bemis' critical and anti-monopolistic views on economic and social policy questions alienated key trustees and corporate benefactors of the university. He was, therefore, fired for his political opinions.

47.   Courtenay, William J. "Inquiry and Inquisition: Academic Freedom in Medieval Universities." **Church History** 58(2): 168-181, June 1989.

This study examines ecclesiastical control over academic judicial proceedings in the thirteenth and fourteenth centuries. The medieval European university allowed for open debate on a number of issues, and there are numerous examples of people who went on to positions of importance in universities or cathedrals even after their ideas or propositions were officially censured by the Church. From about the beginning of the thirteenth through the early decades of the fifteenth centuries, an internal process of review by university or regent-masters of theology passed judgement on academic heresy. This right of autonomy was more durable than any external imposition of papal or ecclesiastical control, and freedom of thought or expression were more generally permitted among scholars at medieval universities than among the general population.

48. DeGeorge, Richard T. **Academic Freedom and Tenure: Ethical Issues.** Lanham, New York: Rowman & Littlefield, 1997. 231p. ISBN 0-8476-8331-1. LC 96-39513.

This volume is divided into two distinct but related parts. Part one is, in effect, a primer on academic freedom written by DeGeorge. He systematically discusses what he sees as the justifications for academic freedom and tenure, as well as the rights, responsibilities and ethical obligations that should accompany the status. Also included here is a discussion of the Michael Levin and Leonard Jeffries academic freedom cases at the City College of the City University of New York. Part two is a collection of important historical works in the development and consideration of academic freedom. These include some American Association of University Professors (AAUP) documents, such as the "1940 Statement of Principles on Academic Freedom and Tenure" and the more recent "On Freedom of Expression and Campus Speech Codes." Also included are analytical essays by Ralph Fuchs ("Academic Freedom - Its Basic Philosophy, Function, and History"), Robert McGee and Walter Block ("Academic Tenure: An Economic Critique"), Richard Rorty ("Does Academic Freedom Have Philosophical Presuppositions?" - see entry #29), and John Searle ("Rationality and Realism, What Is at Stake?").

49. DeVinney, Gemma. "Academic Librarians and Academic Freedom in the United States: A History and Analysis." **Libri** 36(1): 24-39, March 1986.

DeVinney traces the history of academic freedom as it relates specifically to academic librarians. Recounting a 1937 case of a dismissed librarian and the lack of response of the American Library Association, this essay also traces early moves by the ALA to present tenure as a right available to all in the library profession and as a necessary condition for guaranteeing the intellectual freedom of library users. The post World War II movement to achieve faculty status for academic librarians began by presenting tenure as a privilege of academic status rather than as a right, as compared with the AAUP model of academic freedom. Whether construed as necessary to protect the rights of library users or as a right associated with job security and due process, the concept of academic freedom for academic librarians differs from the concept of freedom of teaching and research. DeVinney concludes by calling on academic librarians to better define the professional freedoms associated with academic librarianship.

50. Eaton, Clement. "Professor James Woodrow and the Freedom of Teaching in the South." **Journal of Southern History** 28(1): 3-17, February 1962.

Given as the 1961 Presidential Address to the Southern Historical Association, this essay recounts the late 19th-century extended academic freedom battles of James Woodrow regarding his freedom to teach evolution in the Columbia Theological Seminary. In the case of his dismissal, unsuccessfully appealed to the highest court of the Southern Presbyterian Church, Woodrow argued that evolution was not in conflict with the Bible or the Church. He went on to become president of the University of South Carolina. Eaton concludes by calling directly on the Southern Historical Association to stand for what he calls "the meaning of academic freedom today;" that of overcoming racial discrimination and segregation in higher education and within the SHA itself.

51.   Hamilton, Neil. **Zealotry and Academic Freedom: A Legal and Historical Perspective.** New Brunswick, NJ: Transaction Publishers, 1995. 402p. ISBN 1-5600-0205-0.

In Part I Hamilton addresses threats to academic freedom that have arisen from seven waves of ideological zealotry since the late 19th century and throughout the 20th century: 19th century religious fundamentalism, late 19th century unfettered capitalism, World War I-era patriotism, pre-World War II anti-Communism, McCarthyism, 1960s student activism, and a current campus leftism. Hamilton compares "the current fundamentalism" of today's radical academic left with previous historical trends, finding many similarities, particularly with McCarthyism. In Part II the meaning and justification of and limits to the theory of professional academic freedom is addressed. The final part focuses on buttressing the defense of academic freedom. Emphasized here are correlative duties of academic freedom to defend students and faculty from zealotry, and to enforce professional and ethical standards of behavior. Throughout the work, Hamilton continually returns to the threat he sees posed by academic leftists to academic freedom and the professional autonomy of academics.

52.   Hansen, W. Lee, editor. **Academic Freedom on Trial: 100 Years of Sifting and Winnowing at the University of Wisconsin-Madison.** Madison: University of Wisconsin Press, 1998. 352p. ISBN 0-9658-8341-8.

This volume presents the proceedings of the 1994 100th anniversary celebration of academic freedom at the University of Wisconsin-Madison. A central theme here is the 1894 "sifting and winnowing" statement of the UW Board of Regents: "Whatever may be the limitations which trammel inquiry elsewhere, we believe that the great State University of Wisconsin should ever encourage that continual and fearless sifting and winnowing by which alone the truth can be found." The first part of this volume covers the emergence of an institutional commitment to academic freedom at the University, traceable to the 1894 "trial" of Richard T. Ely, an economist who was accused of union and socialist sympathies. Included here is an essay by A.W. Coats on "Economists, the Economic Profession and Academic

Freedom in the United States." The second part focuses on hate speech codes and presents a variety of perspectives on their constitutionality, effectiveness, and desirability. Included here is an essay by Nat Hentoff called "Academic Freedom: the Indivisibility of Due Process." Much of the rest of the volume is devoted to essays by UW-Madison students, professors, and administrators on rededicating a "sifting and winnowing" plaque, the current state of academic freedom at the University, and the future academic freedom challenges likely to be faced at UW-Madison. A photographic essay concludes the book.

53.   Hofstadter, Richard. **Academic Freedom in the Age of the College.** New Brunswick, N.J.: Transaction Publishers, 1996. 284p. ISBN 1-5600-0860-1.

This volume represents the first half of Hofstadter and Walter Metzger's *The Development of Academic Freedom in the United States*. The companion volume is Metzger's *Academic Freedom in the Age of the University* (see entry #59). Hofstadter traces the development of intellectual freedom in European institutions from the Middle Ages. Though such freedoms operated within the parameters of religious doctrine, Hofstadter nonetheless shows how intellectual boundaries were pushed and degrees of freedom were realized. The evolution of academic freedom in this country is analyzed from the beginnings of Harvard College through the first half of the 19th century, with particular focus on such institutions as Harvard, Yale, Princeton, and William and Mary.   Some of the key developments examined include the establishment of lay government in colleges, religious freedom for students, the secularization of learning, faculty involvement in decision-making, and efforts to avoid sectarianism.

54.   Imber, Jonathan B. "Arthur O. Lovejoy and 'The Revolt Against Dualism.'" **Society** 32(6): 73-83, September 1995.

Arthur Lovejoy was a notable early twentieth century philosopher and the first secretary of the American Association of University Professors (AAUP). This article provides an intellectual biography of Lovejoy, focusing in part on his involvement in academic freedom issues and their relation to his views on knowledge and the intellectual calling. In 1901, Lovejoy resigned from Stanford University in protest over the firing of Edward Ross and George Howard. Imber points out that Lovejoy became an advocate for due process in the treatment of faculty. In 1913, he was involved, on behalf of the American Philosophical Association and the American Psychological Association, in investigating the academic freedom case of John Moffatt Mecklin at Lafayette College. During the McCarthy period, Lovejoy argued that members of the Communist Party (as well as German and Italian fascist parties) should not be employed as teachers since their allegiance was to their parties and not to the truth. Imber concludes by attempting to relate Lovejoy's ideas to more recent developments in higher education.

55.   Joughin, Louis, ed. **Academic Freedom and Tenure: A Handbook of the American Association of University Professors.** Madison: The University of Wisconsin Press, 1967. 343p. LC 67-25947.

Since its founding in 1915, the American Association of University Professors (AAUP) has regularly issued guidelines, principles, and procedures relating to the academic profession in general and the protection of academic freedom and tenure in particular. This volume is a compilation of many of these key documents and statements. It is divided into four major parts. Part one includes a "Model Case Procedure" for dealing with an academic freedom complaint on campus. Part two includes the texts of a number of landmark AAUP statements issued on important topics. These include the classic "1940 Statement of Principles on Academic Freedom and Tenure," as well as statements on procedural standards for dismissals, extramural utterances, academic freedom of students, national security, professional ethics, conflict of interest in government-sponsored research, and more. Part three includes resolutions from annual meetings on such matters as censorship of textbooks, teachers' oaths, racial segregation, and speakers on campus, among others. There are also some advisory letters and lists, including a list of censured administrations. Finally, the original 1915 AAUP "Declaration of Principles," as well as some classic articles on academic freedom, are included in the appendices.

56.   Lewis, Lionel S. "Academic Freedom: A New Threat?" **The Journal of Higher Education** 44(7): 548-561, October 1973.

Lewis categorizes and analyzes the perceived causes of 217 contested academic dismissals from 1916 through 1970. Up until 1945, interpersonal behavior was the most frequently cited reason for termination, both by the faculty and the administration. After 1945, however, the faculty member's ideological position was the most frequently cited cause. This covers the McCarthy period, as well as 1960s faculty activism relating to racial integration, civil rights, nuclear disarmament, and the Vietnam War, among others. In the late 1960s, faculty challenges to university governance became the main cause of dismissals. Furthermore, there was a noticeable increase in the number of contested dismissals per year. As Lewis observed, "[w]hen radical ideology was combined with active defiance of the administration's claim to power, dismissals resulted" (p. 555). The evidence suggests, says Lewis, that academic freedom is being "eroded" in the current period, and that the primary "threat comes from within the university rather than from without" (p. 552).

57.   Ludlum, Robert P. "Academic Freedom and Tenure: A History." **Antioch Review** 10(1): 3-34, March 1950.

Ludlum traces early academic freedom cases, from the late 19th century until the founding of the AAUP and up through 1950. Early cases here discussed include anti-slavery movements at seminaries, public, and private institutions of higher education; early movements for independence of faculties and presidents from trustee control; the landmark 1900 case of Edward A. Ross, ousted from Stanford for his views on politics and economics; and the 1913 case of John M. Mecklin, who resigned under pressure from Lafayette College due to his teachings on evolution. The latter two cases marked the first time that professorial and scholarly organizations weighed in to publicly condemn such dismissals. The American Philosophical Association and American Psychological Association issues statements condemning Lafayette, and the American Economic Association issued a report concluding that Ross had not 'overstepped the limits of professional propriety.' Ludlum traces the early development of the AAUP and some of the early actions and reports of the Committees on Academic Freedom and Tenure. Examples are provided of cases referred to Committee A in the years between 1916 and 1950.

58. McGill, William J. "The University and the State." **Educational Record** 58(2): 132-45, Spring 1977.

The President of Columbia University provides an historical perspective on academic freedom, federal regulation, and governmental interference into academe. Suggestions are given for improving the writing and enforcing of federal regulations. Problems cited include: overlapping jurisdictions of federal agencies; conflicting guidelines among different agencies; bureaucracy as a threat to academic freedom; the fact that public and private institutions have become equally dependent on federal dollars; activist political philosophies that drive an interventionist (rather than incentive-based) approach to encouraging institutional changes. Complaining that compliance with federal regulation is often required in order to continue receiving funding, McGill calls instead for a nonadversarial perspective on the part of the state and for greater flexibility in enforcement of regulations.

59. Metzger, Walter P. **Academic Freedom in the Age of the University.** New York: Columbia University Press, 1955. 232p. LC 61-2328.

Covering the period from the mid-19th century to the founding of the American Association of University Professors, this volume is a companion to Richard Hofstadter's *Academic Freedom in the Age of the College* (entry #53). Both volumes were initially published as *The Development of Academic Freedom in the United States*. After reviewing the nature of higher education and academic freedom in the ante-bellum college, Metzger addresses the developments and ideas that led to a "revolution" in higher education, with implications for academic freedom. These major factors included the influence of Darwinism, the impact of the German college and university system on American academics, the growing role of big business in higher education, and the founding of the American Association of University Professors (AAUP) in 1915. Metzger also discusses World War I, the narrow interpretation of faculty loyalty, and the challenges this presented to the preservation of academic freedom. In addition, he discusses the principles of due process, tenure, professional competence, and free inquiry that comprised the AAUP's formulation of academic freedom.

60.   Metzger, Walter P, ed. **The American Concept of Academic Freedom in Formation: A Collection of Essays and Reports.** New York: Arno Press, 1977. various paging. LC 76-55209. ISBN 0-405-10037-X.

Spanning the late 19th and 20th centuries, these essays and documents address a range of issues and concerns in the historical development of academic freedom. Many of the essayists are well-known scholars and academics, including Albion Small, Charles W. Eliot, Nicholas Murray Butler, Arthur O. Lovejoy, John Dewey, and Walter Metzger, among others. Some of the essays (e.g., Andrew West, William Hyde, John Dewey, Ralph Fuchs) are general or philosophical in nature, exploring the definition and parameters of the evolving concept of academic freedom. Other essays deal with more specific issues: the Germanic roots of the concept of academic freedom (Walter Metzger; see also entry #23); the nature of freedom during the Cold War (Harry Gideonse); the influence of trusts and powerful economic interests on academic freedom (Thomas Elmer Will, Albion Small). The rest of this collection consists of reports and policy documents issued by the American Association of University Professors (AAUP). Included here are reports on academic freedom in wartime (1918) and academic freedom and the quest for national security (1956). There is also the initial (1915) AAUP report on academic freedom and tenure, as well as the 1940 "Statement of Principles" and subsequent procedural standards for dismissal (1958) and renewal/nonrenewal (1971).

61.   Metzger, Walter P. "Some Perspectives on the History of Academic Freedom." **Antioch Review** 13(3): 275-287, September 1953.

Metzger addresses three issues. First, he questions the tendency to assess the state of academic freedom by examining cases of its repression, comparing this oversimplification to a history of the labor movement examining only strikes. The second question here addressed is a comparison of the differences between American and British approaches to academic freedom. Finally, Metzger compares contemporary anti-Communist efforts with the first "Red Scare" crisis in academia which began in 1917. Metzger recounts ways that the current troubles are worse and ways in which they are better than previous problems.

62.   Morrison, Joseph L. "Josephus Daniels and the Bassett Academic Freedom Case." **Journalism Quarterly** 39(2): 187-195, Spring 1962.

In 1903 John Spencer Bassett, a professor of history at Trinity College (now Duke) was defended and not dismissed by the college trustees despite strong public calls for his dismissal for calling Booker T. Washington "the greatest man save General Lee born in the South in a hundred years." Some of the strongest criticism of Bassett came from the editor of the Raleigh North Carolina News and Observer, Josephus Daniels. This article recounts the political and racial background for the positions taken by Bassett and Daniels, who was an otherwise staunch supporter of academic freedom and progressive politics in North Carolina.

63. Poch, Robert K. **Academic Freedom in American Higher Education: Rights, Responsibilities, and Limitations.** Washington, D.C.: The George Washington University, 1993. (ASHE-ERIC Higher Education Report No. 4, 1993). 92p. ISBN 1-8783-8025-9. LC 93-61674.

After reviewing the history of the development of academic freedom, Poch devotes chapters to 1) the Supreme Court's interpretation of and support for AAUP principles on academic freedom and tenure, and 2) contemporary issues of academic freedom. As Poch indicates in his review of key Supreme Court decisions, academic freedom seems to have been accorded near Constitutional protection as an extension of free speech or one's civil rights and as a necessary requirement for the advancement of knowledge. The court also tends to defer on academic matters to the professional judgement of academics, though not at the expense of due process. Poch also discusses the freedom to research and the limits on the confidentiality of one's work. Similarly, there is a review of the Court's view of the rights and limitations of classroom communication and extramural utterances. The contemporary issues that Poch discusses include artistic expression, political correctness, academic freedom in church-related colleges, and subpoenaed information and protected sources. Throughout, Poch interweaves discussion of AAUP policy statements, taken from the 1940 *Statement of Principles on Academic Freedom and Tenure*, the AAUP's *Policy Documents and Reports* (1984), and court decisions.

64. Porter, Earl W. "The Bassett Affair: Something to Remember." **South Atlantic Quarterly** 72(4): 451-460, Autumn 1973.

John Spencer Bassett was the founder and editor of *South Atlantic Quarterly*, and in fall 1903 published an essay he had written about the equality of the races, praising Booker T. Washington as the greatest Southerner after General Lee in the past 100 years. Press attacks on Trinity College (now Duke -- where Bassett was a faculty member), the journal and Bassett were statewide throughout North Carolina and sustained. The role of Trinity College President John Carlisle Kilgo is here detailed, along with the plan for all faculty members (including Kilgo) to submit their resignations if the Board voted to accept Bassett's resignation. The Board voted it down, and issued a strong statement in support of "academic liberty" that was reprinted in a 1904 issue of the journal.

65.   Shryock, Richard H.   "The Academic Profession in the United States." **American Association of University Professors Bulletin** 38(1): 32-70, Spring 1952.

This address of the retiring President of the AAUP gives an historical overview of higher education in the United States. Tracing historical trends in American higher education back to German universities, Shryock details delays (until mid- to late 19th century) in founding research universities in the United States. Also addressed are such issues as the changing professional status of intellectuals and academics, the expansion of roles of universities, and the changing dynamics of boards of trustees, presidents, and faculty.   Early (pre-1900) academic freedom cases and other developments leading up to the organization in 1915 of the AAUP are detailed. The final sections deal with some of the issues faced by Committees A and T between 1915 and 1950. Shryock ends by discussing recent loyalty oath cases.

66.   Slaughter, Sheila. "The Danger Zone: Academic Freedom and Civil Liberties." **The Annals of the American Academy of Political and Social Science** 448: 46-61, March 1980.

The author argues that in order to obtain limited job security for the profession as a whole, and through the process of seeking uniform acceptance of tenure, the AAUP sacrificed the civil liberties of individual academics. Slaughter uses an historical overview of AAUP statements on academic freedom to highlight the organization's ongoing lack of support for reinstatement or restitution in cases of dismissal. Justifications of academic freedom that are grounded in society's need for specialized knowledge and that stress the role of the objectivist researcher in increasing the well-being of society effectively deny the revolutionary potential of knowledge. Slaughter cites early examples of the AAUP's failure to protect the rights of unfairly dismissed professors from World-War I-era dismissals of professors opposing the war to 1920s and 1930s-era violations of the academic freedom of politically active professors. In contrast with the 1915 Declaration of Principles and the 1925 Conference Statement (which made explicit a professorial code of conduct), the 1940 Statement of Principles outlined a tangible job security that professors should expect. But in so doing, Slaughter claims, the AAUP exchanged full civil liberties for tenure. The AAUP narrowly prescribed the "extra-mural utterances" of professors but at the same time backed away from any obligation it might have to defend professors who engage in unpopular political activity. Slaughter here cites the lack of action on the part of the AAUP in defense of the dismissed City College professors who were called before the New York Rapp-Coudert Committee investigating communist activities in the schools in the early 1940s. Going on to cite the 1956 AAUP position paper on national security and the 1970 interpretive comments on tenure, Slaughter recounts numerous examples of Cold War-era cases where tenure did not protect the academic freedom of professors engaged in overt political actions. Slaughter concludes with a call for the profession and AAUP to work harder to safeguard the rights that it claims for its members.

67. Stein, Harold. "Note for the Good of the Order: Safeguards for Academic Freedom at Princeton." **American Political Science Review** 54(4): 981-983, December 1960.

Stein recounts the history of academic freedom policies at Princeton, tracing them back to 1918 faculty resolutions in support of tenure rights. Changes to these rules over the years have expanded the job protections and external appeals to all members of academic staff and faculty, not just those employed in tenure track positions.

68. Trinity College Board of Trustees. "Trinity College and Academic Liberty." **South Atlantic Quarterly** 3(1): 62-72, January 1904.

The Board of Trustees of Trinity College (later Duke) issued this strong statement in support of academic freedom at its December 1, 1903 meeting after strong public calls for the resignation of Professor John Spencer Bassett due to his publishing an essay in *South Atlantic Quarterly* called "Stirring Up the Fires of Race Antipathy." Also reprinted here are a message from the Faculty to the Board and a supporting editorial from the Trinity College student newspaper. While vowing that they disagree with Bassett's view, the Board refused to accept his resignation and emphasized their position in favor of tolerance, for permitting professors the same freedoms enjoyed by other Americans, and against persecution of those with unpopular views. The faculty statement also issued on December 1, 1903 put the controversy in a broader context which finds academic freedom as a necessary condition for seeking truth and for promoting the welfare of the college.

69. Van Alstyne, William W., editor. **Freedom and Tenure in the Academy.** Durham, N.C.: Duke University Press, 1993. 429 p. ISBN 0-8223-1333-2.

This compilation was previously published as vol. 53, no. 3 of *Law and Contemporary Problems Journal* (Summer 1990). Republished with new material, it includes reprints of the 1915, 1940 and 1967 AAUP statements on academic freedom, as well as an unannotated bibliography of articles published in legal journals from 1940 to the present. Essays are by Walter Metzger, William Van Alstyne, Judith Thomson, Robert O'Neil, Rodney Smolla, David Rabban, Michael McConnell, Ralph Brown and Jordan Kurland, Matthew Finkin, and Janet Sinder. Topics discussed include: analysis of the 1940 statement, an historical overview of Supreme Court rulings, ideological aspects of faculty reappointment and tenure, artistic freedom as it relates to academic freedom, hate speech, 'individual' vs. 'institutional' perspectives on academic freedom, academic freedom at religious colleges, the relation of tenure to academic freedom, and tenure's relation to the legal aspects of employment practices.

Chapter 3

Academic Freedom—History (1915 to World War II)

70. American Civil Liberties Union. **The Story of the Bertrand Russell Case.**
     New York: ACLU, 1941. 16p. LC 41-2246.

     This pamphlet recounts the controversy surrounding the 1940 appointment of
     philosopher Bertrand Russell to a professorship at City College in New York that was
     struck down by the courts. Reviewed here are the efforts by the city's Board of
     Higher Education to appeal court interference with their appointments, efforts by
     Russell to appeal the decision, and press comments on the controversy. Signed by
     many local prominent members of the ACLU, this pamphlet also lists serious threats
     to civil and academic liberties presented by the case.

71. American Civil Liberties Union. **What Freedom for American Students? A
     Survey of the Practices Affecting Student Activities and Expressions.** New
     York: ACLU, 1941. 48p. LC 41-11487.

     Covering the academic freedom rights of college students, this study begins by
     outlining a student "Bill of Rights." A survey was conducted in 1940 of 111 colleges
     and universities querying the academic rights of students. Conclusions of the survey
     are outlined in such areas (among others) as: peace, military training, outside
     speakers, college press, free speech, and student democracy.

72. American Civil Liberties Union. Committee on Academic Freedom. **The Gag
     on Teaching: The Story of the New Restrictions by Law on Teaching in
     Schools, and by Public Opinion and Donors on Colleges.** 3rd ed. New York:
     ACLU, 1940. 63p. LC 43-49773.

This report covers such issues of the day as: legislative restrictions on teaching in public schools, loyalty oaths, tenure laws, teacher unionizing, and college restrictions on faculty and students. Outlined in separate chapters are: the freedom of teaching, principles of academic freedom, and the relationship between academic freedom and tenure. Previous editions were published in 1936 and 1937.

73.   American Civil Liberties Union. Committee on Academic Freedom. **Special Oaths of Loyalty for School Teachers: Memorandum of Fact and Arguments Against Such Laws, With Particular Reference to New York State.** New York: ACLU, 1934. 16p. LC unk836899.

This pamphlet describes the passage and defeat in many states after World War I of a Daughters of the American Revolution-sponsored legislative bill requiring special loyalty oaths from teachers and college professors, oaths not required of other public servants. In Spring of 1934 such a bill was introduced in the New York state legislature; this essay argues specifically against that bill. Arguments both for and against loyalty oaths are here presented with quotes from educational leaders in public schooling and higher education, from Governor Alfred Smith's 1920 veto of a teacher's loyalty bill, as well as from newspaper editorials of the day.

74.   "Conference on Academic Freedom." **School and Society** 21(526):   101, January 24, 1925.

Nine national college and university associations sent representatives to a 1924 meeting in Washington where they adopted statements on academic freedom and academic tenure. The organizations in question were: The Association of American Universities, The Association of American Colleges, The American Association of University Professors, the American Association of University Women, the Association of Land Grant Colleges, the Association of Urban Universities, the National Association of State Universities, the American Association of Teachers Colleges, and the Association of Governing Boards. The full texts are provided of these statements in support of the rights of academic freedom and tenure.

75.   Dewey, John. "The Democratic Faith and Education." **Antioch Review** 4(2): 274-283, Summer 1944.

Written toward the end of World War II, Dewey discusses the imbalance he sees between the extensive scientific knowledge accumulated by humanity, and comparatively meager acquisitions of social and moral knowledge. The imbalance is due, Dewey asserts, to a failure to use scientific methods in seeking "social or humane knowledge and human engineering." Dewey discusses attacks against the scientific method of free and open inquiry by those who blame science for the persistence of World Wars, hunger and other social ills. Dewey argues that democratic ideals must inform pursuits in both hard science and social science. Collective and cooperative human efforts must be based on educational systems that rely on the openness and objectivity of the scientific method. Only then can efforts to "humanize science" prevail, bringing humanity's social knowledge into harmony with its physical knowledge.

76. Dewey, John, and Horace M. Kallen, eds. **The Bertrand Russell Case.** New York: Da Capo Press, 1972. 227p. LC 78-37289. ISBN 0-306-70426-9.

A reprint of a book published in 1941, this edited collection criticizes the firing of Bertrand Russell from the City College of New York. Hired to teach courses in the philosophy of mathematics and science, Russell was deprived of the position even before he began it. A lawsuit was brought against the Board of Higher Education by a Mrs. Jean Kay, who charged that Russell should not be allowed to assume the teaching position because 1) he was an alien and 2) his writing and teaching promoted sexual immorality. The justice in the case, John E. McGeehan, decided in favor of Mrs. Kay. McGeehan passed negative judgement on the quality of Russell's scholarship, ignoring the favorable professional opinions of hundreds of academics and numerous professional associations. Russell was, in fact, a distinguished philosopher. In handing down his decision, the judge afforded Russell no opportunity to answer any of the charges. As the contributors to this collection point out, Russell's scholarship on issues relating to sex and morality was thoughtful and well within the bounds of academic freedom and the pursuit of truth. According to the contributors, those who attacked Russell, including the judge, seemed willfully to misread his work and to make patently false accusations against him. Justice McGeehan's decision is appended, as is a statement of the Committee on Cultural Freedom.

77. Dugger, Ronnie. "Nobel Prize Winner Purged at the University of Texas." **Southern Exposure** 2(1): 67-70, Spring/Summer 1974.

In 1946, biologist Hermann J. Muller was awarded the Nobel Prize for genetics work he had done in 1926 at the University of Texas. This essay recounts the events leading up to his being fired in 1936 for suspected Marxist views, and for his visits to Russian genetics labs in the early 1930s. He was fired by President H.Y. Benedict, who professed to believe that teachers should live by the same personal standards as preachers.

78. Gatewood, Willard B., Jr. "Embattled Scholar: Howard W. Odum and the Fundamentalists, 1925-1927." **Journal of Southern History** 31(4): 375-392, November 1965.

Gatewood recounts the controversy over a University of North Carolina publication called the *Journal of Social Forces*, edited by Odum. Anti-Darwinian evangelicals as well as more mainstream Protestant church leaders vehemently and publicly condemned Odum for publishing articles on religion and genetics by L.L. Bernard of Cornell and Harry Elmer Barnes of Smith College. The actions of individual theologians, of Baptist associations, of ministerial associations and of legislators are all here recounted. In the end, Odum's critics were unsuccessful in imposing restrictions on the journal or on the University of North Carolina. This success provided an early boost to efforts to defend academic freedom in the south.

79. "General Report of The Committee on Academic Freedom and Academic Tenure." **The American Political Science Review** 10(2, part 2): 1-29, May 1916.

The 15 members comprising this AAUP committee were drawn predominantly from the American Economic Association, the American Political Science Association, and the American Sociological Society, all of which had participated in the creation of an earlier joint report on academic freedom and tenure. This landmark report focuses on the fundamental principles that should form the foundation of academic freedom (i.e., freedom of inquiry, freedom of teaching, and freedom of extramural utterance), and the broader institutional and professional considerations that affect them. Academic authority resides in the Boards of Trustees, and it is incumbent upon them to safeguard the public trust. To do so, they must not bind the "reason or the conscience of any professor" (p. 9). Nor should faculty be seen as employees, as in a business setting. Rather, they should be granted the "dignity" and "independence" to pursue their scholarly inquiries. Only then can faculty earn the public's confidence and support. Finally, the ability of faculty to effectively advance knowledge and train students is dependent upon its integrity, which requires academic freedom.

80. Greenberg, Michael, and Seymour Zenchelsky. "The Confrontation with Nazism at Rutgers: Academic Bureaucracy and Moral Failure." **History of Education Quarterly** 30(3): 325-349, Fall 1990.

Greenberg and Zenchelsky review the historical evidence surrounding the firing in 1935 of Lienhard Bergel, a faculty member in the German department at the New Jersey College for Women (Rutgers). Bergel was the lone anti-Nazi in a department chaired by an avowed pro-Nazi, Professor Friedrich Hauptmann. Hauptmann terminated Bergel in 1933 for incompetency, and that decision was upheld by the Dean, the university President, and the Board of Trustees. However, in reviewing the evidence, Greenberg and Zenchelsky document the political motivation for Bergel's firing, its coverup and minimization by university officials, and the violation of Bergel's academic freedom. Even a mid-1980s official reassessment of the case by

Rutgers University historians failed to acknowledge all of the evidence and the infringement on academic freedom. Greenberg and Zenchelsky argue that, over and above the injustice to Bergel, the case indicates the ease with which administrators can still conceal the political motivations of academic dismissals.

81.   Gruber, Carol Signer. "Academic Freedom at Columbia University, 1917-1918: The Case of James McKeen Cattell." **AAUP Bulletin** 58(3): 297-305, September 1972.

James McKeen Cattell was a world famous psychologist at Columbia University who, despite his stature in the field, was fired from the university in 1917. As Gruber documents, a combination of circumstances led to his difficulties. Cattell was a constant and unwavering critic of administrative and trustee interference in academic affairs. Not surprisingly, the university trustees had been trying since 1910 to retire him. However, key faculty members continued to support Cattell, arguing that he should not be fired for his "eccentricities" nor for his criticisms of the university President and trustees. Ultimately, the event that precipitated Cattell's firing was his support of conscientious objectors during World War I, which was part of his overall opposition to the war. In a predominantly nationalistic environment, Cattell's position was considered unpatriotic and served to alienate him further from many faculty and administrators. It also violated university president Nicholas Murray Butler's "wartime moratorium on academic freedom." Ultimately, the trustees fired both Cattell and Henry Dana for promoting disloyalty. Gruber discusses the subsequent faculty discontent, the resignation of Charles Beard and others, and the role that faculty ambivalence and "internal tensions" played in these events.

82.   Gutfeld, Arnon. "The Levine Affair: A Case Study in Academic Freedom." **Pacific Historical Review** 39(1): 19-37, February 1970.

Gutfeld explores the 1919 case of Professor Louis Levine's dismissal from the State University of Montana. Author of a book critical of Montana's tax structure, Levine's outspokenness led to investigations of him by the state legislature and State Board of Education which led to political pressure being exerted on Chancellor Edward C. Elliott to suspend Levine. One of the earliest investigations by the AAUP ensued, and the board reinstated Levine with back pay in April of 1919. No explanations from the Chancellor or Board of Education were ever provided as to why Levine was dismissed or reinstated. Gutfeld here details the controversial tax issues as well as the campus proceedings of Levine's case.

83.   Howlet, Charles F. "Academic Freedom Versus Loyalty at Columbia University During World War I: A Case Study." **War & Society** 2(1): 43-53, May 1984.

The question of the effects of war on academic freedom is examined through this case study of an overzealous board of trustees which set up a "Committee of Nine" (five deans, four faculty) to look into the extent of teaching of subversive or disloyal doctrine at Columbia. The angry reponse of professors, along with quotes from contemporary issues of the *Nation* and the hard line approach taken against perceived sedition by Columbia President Nicholas Murray Butler are given as background to the case of leading psychology professor James McKeen Cattell. An arrogant and outspoken man, he was dismissed over the issue of loyalty after he sent a petition in 1917 on university letterhead to three Congressmen urging them not to approve a pending bill which would have allowed sending American draftees into battle in Europe. The resignations (including that of Charles Beard) and dismissals of other faculty that followed prompted a request from John Dewey for formal investigation submitted to A. A. Young, the chair of the AAUP's Committee on Academic Freedom and Tenure. No investigation ever came about, largely through the AAUP's indecisiveness about the paper's relationship between war and academic freedom. Also recounted here are Harvard President Abbott Lawrence Lowell's condemnations of Columbia, as well as the World War I era loyalty fights at other U.S. universities.

84. Hunt, Erling M. "Pressure Groups and Academic Freedom." **Harvard Educational Review** 9(3): 316-329, May 1939.

Should the activities of pressure groups, and in particular the propaganda disseminated to further their causes be permitted in a democracy? If so, what obligations do those in academia have in pro- or anti-propaganda activities, and in what ways have propagandists limited freedom of teaching? These questions are addressed here in the context of a bibliographic essay on publications of the 1920s and 1930s on various aspects of freedom of teaching and the influence of public opinion on higher education.

85. Irvine, A.D. "Bertrand Russell and Academic Freedom." **Russell** New series 16(1): 5-36, Summer 1996.

Irvine addresses Russell's life and philosophy in terms of how each relates to his uncompromising defense of academic freedom. Born to freethinkers and educated at Trinity College Cambridge, Russell became an active pacifist during World War I, serving jail time and suffering dismissal from a teaching position at Trinity for publishing essays against the war effort. He faced legal battles in the United States as well. In addressing the opposition he faced from government and courts, Irvine compares Russell's lot with that of Socrates. Irvine discusses Russellian arguments in favor of free and open debate as being essentially utilitarian: the advancement of knowledge requires the individual scholar's and all educational institutions' autonomy. It is to the wide benefit of society (not just academia) that opinions be tested openly in an atmosphere of free speech for the individual and academic freedom of the higher education institution. Irvine cites John Stuart Mill as the source for Russell's views on these points. The author concludes with a section discussing the tension between freedom and utility. Rather than arguing from political first principles, Russell's justification of freedom of inquiry and debate depends on the assumption of a fundamental societal benefit in advancing knowledge. Faced with the nuclear arms race, Russell's 1950 Nobel lecture touched on the dangers inherent in too much technical knowledge. That such advancement may not prove ultimately beneficial to society undercuts his defense of freedom.

86. John Dewey Society. Yearbook Committee. "Survey of Attitudes of Propaganda Organizations Towards Academic Freedom." In Harold B. Alberty, Boyd H. Bode, editors. **Educational Freedom and Democracy: Second Yearbook of the John Dewey Society.** New York: D. Appleton-Century Co., 1938. pp. 261-282. LC 43-16927.

A survey of 143 special interest and public policy groups and civic organizations was conducted in 1937. Statements were requested from each group in favor of freedom in schools and universities. Only four antagonistic replies were received, but most replies to the survey were neutral. The text of some responses are here provided, with identification of the individuals who wrote them and the organizations they represent. A full list of organizations receiving the survey is also provided.

87. Lowell, Abbott Lawrence. "Academic Freedom." In Abbott Lawrence Lowell. **What a University President Has Learned.** Freeport, NY: Books for Libraries Press, 1969. pp. 117-133. (Essay Index Reprint Series). ISBN 0-8369-1303-5.

Originally published in 1938, this essay by the then-President Emeritus of Harvard covers the principles behind limitations on a professor's "liberty of speech." Four issues are addressed in turn, having to do with issues that fall inside or outside of a professor's expertise, and differences between speech within a classroom and outside of it. Professors should be entirely free from interference in classroom teaching and extra-mural activities within a professor's field of study. But rights of professors to speak or act on their own views inside the classroom may violate the university's obligation to students. Professors do, however have the same rights as all citizens to engage in extra-mural activities and speech. Lowell argues that restraining professors' rights as citizens would do more harm than they ever could in exercising these freedoms.

88. Marsh, Daniel L. "Teachers' Oaths and Academic Freedom." **Schools and Society** 42(1089): 651-653, November 9, 1935.

The President of Boston University, in his annual report to the Trustees (here excerpted) recommends that all instructors comply with the new Massachusetts law requiring oaths of loyalty to the U.S. and Massachusetts constitutions, and to consider them as oaths to uphold the Bill of Rights and the Massachusetts Constitutional Preamble's statement that "the people have a right to alter the government." As one of a number of Massachusetts college and university presidents who put themselves on record as opposing anything that could stifle academic freedom, March worries that corrosion of these rights could put U.S. institutions of higher education in the position of many European universities suffering under political repression in Russia, Italy and Germany.

89. Matsen, William E. "Professor William A. Schaper, War Hysteria and the Price of Academic Freedom." **Minnesota History** 51(4): 130-152, Fall/Winter 1988.

In 1917, the Chair of the University of Minnesota Department of Political Science was dismissed on suspicion of having anti-American sentiments. After manufacturing washboards for a time, Schaper ran for Governor on the Farmer-Labor ticket. After his loss he became a professor of finance at the University of Oklahoma. His fight against the nomination of Pierce Butler to the U.S. Supreme Court is here recounted. Butler was his chief accuser on the university Board of Regents. In 1938, the board approved a resolution reinstating Schaper as professor emeritus and paid him his salary for the 1917-1918 academic year. The resolution included language resolving that the University of Minnesota should not in any way limit the freedom of teaching. This language later (in 1945) became part of the University of Minnesota's code for tenure.

90. Meiklejohn, Alexander. "Teachers and Controversial Questions." In Erich A. Walter, editor. **1939 Essay Annual.** Chicago: Scott, Foresman, 1939. 112-125.

Reprinted from the June 1938 *Harper's Magazine*, this essay argues that the conflict between Capitalism and Communism must be taught, that teachers must take sides on the issue in classroom discussion, and that school boards and university trustees must make sure that Communists are appointed to teaching positions. While education must remain engaged with societal controversies, and professors must engage students in questioning their beliefs, teachers/professors should not engage in propagandizing. Meiklejohn spells out a distinction between "teacher-advocacy" (here supported) and propaganda.

91. Meiklejohn, Alexander. "To Whom Are We Responsible?" In Alexander Meiklejohn. **Freedom and the College.** Freeport, N.Y.: Books for Libraries Press, 1970. pp. 3-26. (Essay Index Reprint Series). ISBN 0-8369-1990-4.

Originally published in the September 1923 issue of *Century Magazine*, this essay addressed the responsibilities of college faculties and college presidents. In turn, Meiklejohn concludes that colleges are not responsible to students, their parents, the public, donors, the church, alumni, trustees, the state, oneself, or one's academic peers. Instead, they are primarily responsible to the pursuit of truth and knowledge.

92. Metzger, Walter P. **Professors on Guard: The First AAUP Investigations.** New York: Arno Press, 1977. various paging. LC 76-55213. ISBN 0-405-10040-X.

Included here are reprints of American Association of University Professors committee reports on five academic freedom cases dating from the earliest years of the organization (i.e., 1915-1917). The reports deal with cases at the University of Utah, the University of Colorado, Wesleyan University, the University of Pennsylvania, and the University of Montana. These early committee reports not only illustrate the AAUP's methods for investigating such cases, but also highlight many of the fundamental principles that the AAUP valued and wanted to protect, such as academic freedom, the sanctity of terms of appointment, and due process in the review of faculty. Many of these cases demonstrate the excessive level of external interference in faculty evaluations and firings during this historical period. The case of Scott Nearing at the University of Pennsylvania is one of the more historically noteworthy cases, though all five reports are instructive.

93. Mulcahy, Richard P. "The Dark Side of the Cathedral of Learning: The Turner Case." **Western Pennsylvania Historical Magazine** 69(1): 37-53, January 1986.

The author makes use of the files of Chancellor John G. Bowman in describing the events leading up to and aftermath of the 1934 University of Pittsburgh dismissal of Professor of History and social activist Ralph Turner. A push to finish the campus Cathedral of Learning led Bowman to suppress academic freedom in order to help ensure that wealthy trustees were not offended.

94. Oshinsky, David M., Richard P. McCormick, Daniel Horn. **The Case of the Nazi Professor.** New Brunswick, N.J.: Rutgers University Press, 1989. 157p. ISBN 0-8135-1363-4.

Written by a committee of historians authorized in 1985 by the President of Rutgers, this book reexamines the case of dismissal in 1935 of a New Jersey College for Women (Rutgers) instructor of German with strong anti-Nazi views. Lienhard Bergel was dismissed, he claimed, because Friedrich J. Hauptmann, the Chair of the German Department, was a Nazi official who required that his professors distribute

Nazi literature in class. Bergel claimed that his refusal to do so was the only reason for his being labeled incompetent and fired. A committee of trustees (convened in 1935 after protests by students, alumni and local citizens) ruled in favor of the dismissal and cleared Hauptmann of the charge by Bergel. Fifty years later, in the face of mounting pressure for a University apology and exoneration of Bergel, this committee of Rutgers historians reexamined the case, concluding among other things that there were legitimate grounds for Bergel's dismissal, and that while Hauptmann was indeed a Nazi, his propaganda activities were minimal and no evidence was found to support the charge that he was a spy.

95.   Pollitt, Daniel H., and Jordan E. Kurland. "Entering the Academic Freedom Arena Running: The AAUP's First Year." **Academe** 84(4): 45-52, July-August 1998.

    Pollitt and Kurland recount the founding of the American Association of University Professors (AAUP) in 1915 and its immediate undertaking of five major academic freedom investigations at the University of Utah, the University of Colorado, Wesleyan University, the University of Pennsylvania, and the University of Montana. The broad details of these five cases are reviewed, including that of Scott Nearing at University of Pennsylvania. As a result of the experiences gained in these investigations, the AAUP issued both some general principles of academic freedom and practical proposals to protect it. The principles argued that faculty need academic freedom in their research, teaching and extramural utterances in order to best serve the university, society and their profession. The practical proposals addressed the need for due process, fairness, and proper faculty involvement in appointments, tenure and non-reappointments.

96.   Slaten, A. Wakefield. "Academic Freedom, Fundamentalism and the Dotted Line." **Educational Review** 65(2): 74-77, February 1923.

    This author addresses the requirement at some religious institutions of higher education that faculty sign a statement of faith. Activities of fundamentalist Christians to extend promulgation of their doctrines to private and sometimes public schools are addressed, with quotations from the policies of Baylor University in Texas as well as resolutions presented at State Baptist Conventions in Texas and Colorado. Slaten argues that requirements for signing statements of faith threaten the academic freedom of professors at denominational colleges.

97.   Smith, Andrew C. "May Academic Freedom Become an Instrument of Subversive Propaganda?" **The Southern Association Quarterly** 4(3): 449-452, August 1940.

The text of an April 11, 1940 radio broadcast at Atlanta station WSB, this essay takes the position that academic freedom is beneficial to society, a right of teachers that furthers their function in society. Quoting from the 1940 academic freedom statement of the Association of American Colleges, a 1935 Walter Lippmann column, and the 1925 Supreme Court Gitlow Case decision, Smith concludes that academic freedom is best served, and propaganda best fought, when we agree that certain truths are fixed and have preferential rights of expression over falsehood and error.

98. Springarn, J. E. **A Question of Academic Freedom: Being the Official Correspondence Between Nicholas Murray Butler, President of Columbia University and J.E. Springarn, Professor of Comparative Literature and Chair of the Division of Modern Languages and Linguistics in Columbia University During the Academic Year 1910-1911, With Other Documents.** New York: Printed for Distribution Among the Alumni, 1911. 53p. LC 12-2475.

Springarn was dismissed from Columbia in March of 1911 after introducing a faculty resolution in support of a recently dismissed Professor Henry Peck who was then suing President Butler for libel. The correspondence between Springarn and Butler are here reprinted, along with a chronology of events, and appendices reprinting letters of support for Springarn from students, alumni, and scholars.

99. Tap, Bruce. "Suppression of Dissent: Academic Freedom at the University of Illinois during the World War I Era." **Illinois Historical Journal** 85(1): 2-22, Spring 1992.

The superpatriotic environment that existed in the United States during World War I made it difficult for faculty members to express opposition to or reservations about the war. This environment was evident at the University of Illinois, where such beliefs as pacifism, opposition to conscription, opposition to the sale of Liberty bonds, and sympathy with anything German got a number of faculty in trouble. Tap reviews the historical events, transcripts and documentary evidence surrounding the investigations of the suspect faculty. While none of the faculty were immediately fired, all but one were forced out of the university within a few years. Furthermore, the university President's acquiescence to public opinion and the patriotic cause compromised academic freedom for years and set a precedent for the use of "sociopolitical orthodoxy" in the hiring and firing of faculty.

100. Thurstone, L. L. "Academic Freedom." **The Journal of Higher Education** 1(3): 136-140, March 1930.

Thurstone suggests that in order to protect academic freedom, the AAUP and other professional associations need to implement two policies or procedures. First, the AAUP needs to keep a list of accredited colleges, with accreditation being based on following guidelines and standards for the protection of free inquiry. Those college and universities that fail to meet this criterion will be removed from the list. Unaccredited institutions will then be deemed unacceptable places for academics to accept teaching positions. Second, the various academic professional associations should agree to revoke the membership of those academics who accept positions at unaccredited institutions. These two steps could prove a serious deterrent to institutions that infringe on free inquiry. As Thurstone put it, if "the college wants to enjoy the advantages of a competent teaching staff and...a good reputation in the academic world, it must voluntarily pay the price of academic freedom" (p. 137). These procedures would more effectively defend academic freedom, while avoiding "militant aggression" on the part of faculty.

101. Wilcox, Clifford. "World War I and the Attack on Professors of German at the University of Michigan." **History of Education Quarterly** 33(1): 59-84, Spring 1993.

This essay recounts the 1917-1918 purge of the University of Michigan German Department in which six professors were permanently discharged on suspicions of disloyalty. Provided here is background to the case, and the possible alternatives to dismissal that could have been followed. Wilcox argues that the AAUP's narrowly constructed definition of academic freedom meant it could pose no opposition to a case of dismissal of professors due to who they were rather than what they said, wrote, or taught.

102. Witmer, Lightner. **The Nearing Case: The Limitations of Academic Freedom at the University of Pennsylvania by Act of the Board of Trustees, June 14, 1915: A Brief of Facts and Opinions.** New York: Da Capo Press, 1974. 123p. (Civil Liberties in American History). ISBN 0-3067-1978-9.

A reprint of the 1915 edition, with a new forward by Stephen Whitfield, this volume addresses the 1915 dismissal of Wharton School Assistant Professor of Economics Scott Nearing by the Trustees of the University of Pennsylvania. Nearing was outspoken on matters related to child labor and poverty. His dismissal was investigated by the AAUP's Committee A which found that he was indeed fired (without a fair judicial hearing) for his opinions and teaching and for reasons with which Nearing's peers on the faculty did not approve or agree. About the same time that the AAUP took on the case, Witmer's book was published; the new foreword puts the contents in historical perspective. Chair of the U. of Pennsylvania's psychology department, the author collected sympathetic articles from Philadelphia newspapers, added documents from both sides of the dispute and presented his own reflections on what had happened to his colleague. The involvement of corporate and political donors to the University, the secret deliberations of the board of trustees, and its relationship to the alumni and the faculty are all here addressed.

Chapter 4

Academic Freedom—History (Cold War)

103. Association of American Universities. **The Rights and Responsibilities of Universities and Their Faculties: A Statement by the Association of American Universities, Adopted Tuesday March 24, 1953.** Princeton, N.J.: Distributed by the Princeton University Dept. of Public Relations, [1953]. 12p. LC 54-7633.

The AAU begins by addressing the role of the university in American life, goes on to define the university in terms of academic freedom as the "surest safeguard of truth" and then addresses the duties which qualify and limit the freedoms of faculty members. This statement ends by addressing "The Present Danger" of members of the Communist Party holding academic positions. The AAU affirms that such membership should disqualify a person from any position at an American university. But the AAU concludes here by asserting that condemning Communism should not be interpreted as a willingness to limit research or impose conformity of belief on faculty.

104. Bloom, Samuel W. "The Intellectual in a Time of Crisis: The Case of Bernhard J. Stern, 1894-1956." **Journal of the History of the Behavioral Sciences** 26(1): 17-37, January 1990.

Drawing on a previously unpublished archival collection of Stern's papers deposited at the Meiklejohn Civil Liberties Institute, Bloom recounts the case of Marxist sociologist Stern's targeting by congressional committees from 1938 through 1953, and his 1953 dismissal from Columbia University.

105. Buckley, William F. **God and Man at Yale: The Superstitions of "Academic Freedom."** Introduction by John Chamberlain, with a new Introduction by the author. Chicago: Regnery Books, c1986. 240p. ISBN 0-8952-6697-0.

Buckley's memoir about his post-World War II years at Yale sparked controversy when it was first published in 1951. In this reissued edition, a new introduction by Buckley addresses and rebuts many of the reviews and criticism the book initially received. Throughout, Buckley's focus is on how Yale abandoned its conservative moral (and financial) roots in Christian individualism to expound a curriculum marked by socialism and atheism. Masquerading as non-political, impartial and value-neutral, Yale educators nevertheless exhibited a bias in favor of values and interests not held by the university trustees or alumni, who in large part subscribed to Christian, anti-Communist, and pro-free-market values. Buckley goes on to argue that value-neutrality, even if it were possible, should not be practiced in teaching. He calls for a return at Yale to a higher education rooted in Christian individualist traditions. Focusing first on religion on campus and then on the study of economics, Buckley examines what he sees as a duplicitous relationship between the institution and its alumni in which large sums of money were raised from alums who were denied any active role in governance, curriculum-writing, and the shaping of campus life. In a chapter called "The Superstitions of Academic Freedom," Buckley examines and rebuts arguments against "value orthodoxy" made by supporters of academic freedom, and examines specific cases on the Yale campus in which a professed impartiality in the search for truth disguises the promulgation of secular or socialist values. Appendices focus on specific curricula from Yale courses in the late 1940s, documenting a disdain for religious truth and a bias towards atheism and collectivism.

106. Buder, Leonard. "'Refuse to Testify' Einstein Advises Intellectuals Called in by Congress." **New York Times** June 12, 1953, pp. A1, A9.

Responding to the case of a high school teacher being called before the Senate Internal Security Subcommittee, Albert Einstein wrote an open letter in which he said that "Every intellectual who is called before one of the committees ought to refuse to testify..." The text of the letter is reproduced here.

107. Bundy, McGeorge. "Were Those the Days?" **Daedalus** 99(3): 531-67, Summer 1970.

Bundy poses the question of whether characteristics of universities during the relatively quiet 1950s can provide insights for universities during the (then) future decade of the 1970s. The author was a professor and later a Dean at Harvard during the 1950s. He disputes some recently-made charges against universities during the 1950s. Among the claims he objects to here are that universities were run by boards of trustees purely for the political and monetary interest of the ruling classes; that the university was the instrument of political powers in Washington and/or of the military industrial complex, CIA, or foreign policy establishment. Some of the failures on the part of the universities of the 1950s addressed here include overly expensive support for intercollegiate athletics and the neglect of governance issues and how they impact on faculty roles and responsibilities. Lessons for the future include an admonishment for universities to leave the role of running the government to the politicians, and for students and professors who move between the worlds of politics and academia to accept that "they cannot be in both places at once." Bundy concludes by calling on universities to reestablish a commitment to academic community and respect for "the dignity and humanity of all its members."

108. Carleton, Don E. "'McCarthyism Was More Than McCarthy:' Documenting the Red Scare at the State and Local Level." **Midwestern Archivist** 12(1): 13-20, 1987.

Carleton recounts his experience in researching McCarthyism in Houston, Texas as a case study in how to locate and research local archival collections. Resources examined include the personal papers of victims, accusers, and prominent observers (e.g., reporters), as well as institutional records such as those of the Daughters of the American Revolution. Clipping files of local papers and universities, official records of conservative pressure groups and community organizations, the records of local and state governmental agencies or elected officials can all usefully document local anti-Communist activities of the 1950s.

109. Chomsky, Noam, et al. **The Cold War & the University: Toward an Intellectual History of the Postwar Years.** New York: The New Press, 1997. 260p. LC 96-25426. ISBN 1-56584-005-4.

The articles comprising this collection concentrate on the intersection between personal experiences of and structural limitations on academic freedom during the Cold War. Rather than focusing just on specific academic freedom cases, these articles also address such issues as 1) when, how, and what kinds of academic research were funded, 2) the gradual influence of geopolitical concerns on such research, and 3) the growing role of the federal government in funding and directing research. The common thread running through many of the articles is the way in which research agendas and paradigms within academic fields were constrained by the Cold War, thus limiting the topics that could be safely addressed and the perspectives from which they could be examined. Some of the essays are somewhat autobiographical in nature, written from the perspective of individual scholars and their experience of the Cold War in academia. Specific articles discuss some effects of the Cold War in the fields of history (Howard Zinn), English (Richard Ohman), Anthropology (Laura Nader), Earth Science (Ray Siever), Area Studies (Immanuel

Wallerstein), and Political Science (Ira Katznelson). More general articles on the university during the Cold War were contributed by R. C. Lewontin, Noam Chomsky, and David Montgomery.

110. Coker, Francis W. "Academic Freedom and the Congressional Investigations: Free Speech and the Silent Professor." **Journal of Politics** 16(3): 491-508, August 1954.

Coker addresses two questions here. One is what a teacher should do in response to investigative inquiries he feels are improper; the other is what a college should do when one of its teachers refuses to answer questions raised by an investigative committee or answers in ways which call into question his professional competency or integrity. Coker feels that the cause of free speech is better served by speech than by silence. He also holds that membership in the Communist Party is itself an abdication of academic freedom that should automatically disqualify the party member from any teaching duties. Coker holds that universities have the right to reconsider the employment of faculty who refuse to testify or who have been shown to be Communist Party members.

111. Columbia University. Faculty of Political Science. "Statement on Academic Freedom in Relation to Legislative Investigations of Colleges and Universities, Adopted by the Faculty of Political Science of Columbia University, May 21, 1953." **School and Society** 78(2011): 11, July 11, 1953.

Asserting that investigations are unnecessary and unwise, that refusal to testify is not grounds for dismissal, and that fitness to teach must be determined with reference only to conduct, this statement goes on to request that the university administration put in place procedures for termination that permit involvement and review by faculty committees whenever the terminated scholar believes that an issue of academic freedom is involved in his dismissal.

112. Committee for the Reinstatement of Professor Burgum. **Academic Freedom & New York University: The Case of Professor Edwin Berry Burgum.** New York: The Committee, February 1954. 80p. LC 54-43375.

Dr. Burgum invoked his 1st and 5th Amendment rights under questioning about his membership in the Communist Party by the Senate Sub-Committee on Internal Security (the McCarran Committee) in 1952. The day of his testimony he was suspended from his position as a Professor of English at NYU. A chronology of events is presented, as well as quotations from denunciations of the legislative investigative committees (including AAUP policy statements and quotes from Albert Einstein and Harry S. Truman). The appropriateness of exercising 5th Amendment rights in such situations is defended, and a section spells out how the principles of academic freedom bear on this case and all other cases of red baiting. Appendices reprint Burgum's testimony before the Faculty Committee of the University Senate as well as the supporting testimony of other faculty members (including Alexander Meiklejohn).

113. **Communism and Academic Freedom: The Record of the Tenure Cases at the University of Washington Including the Findings of the Committee on Tenure and Academic Freedom and the President's Recommendations.** Seattle: University of Washington Press, 1949. 125 p.

Issued by the University of Washington Board of Regents, this volume deals with the issues surrounding six 1949 tenure cases in which three professors were dismissed for being Communists and three retained on condition of their signing affidavits that they are not now members of the Communist Party. The full text of the faculty Committee on Tenure and Academic Freedom is presented, along with President Raymond Allen's analysis of that report and his recommendations to the Board of Regents. An appendix lists the charges against each faculty member leveled by the Canwell Committee (a Washington State Legislative Committee on Un-American Activities). Source documents are presented without further analysis other than a cover "Letter of transmittal to the people of the State of Washington" from the Board of Regents.

114. Davis, Horace B. "Reply to President McGrath." **School and Society** 79(2035): 188-189, June 12, 1954.

Excerpts are given from the August 4, 1953 statement of Horace Davis before the Board of Trustees and President Earl J. McGrath of the University of Kansas City, Missouri. The Board was convened to question Davis' fitness for teaching after he was called before the Senate Internal Security Subcommittee (the Jenner Committee). Davis asserts that the Jenner Committee is anti-intellectual more than anti-Communist and that a university should not impose political qualifications on staff selections. Davis was dismissed from his position not for refusing to answer political affiliation questions before the Congressional Committee, but for refusing to answer the same questions when posed by the University's Board of Trustees.

115. Diamond, Sigmund. **Compromised Campus: The Collaboration of Universities with the Intelligence Community, 1945-1955.** New York: Oxford University Press, 1992. 371p. LC 91-15668. ISBN 0-19-505382-6.

Focusing primarily on Harvard and Yale, Diamond traces the extent to which both institutions cooperated with the intelligence community and sacrificed their intellectual and institutional independence to support the surveillance of students and faculty. As Diamond documents, the universities' public pronouncements indicated a commitment to academic freedom.   However, behind the scenes, selective administrators, trustees, faculty, and students collaborated to spy on members of the university community, to affect hiring and firing, and to make the university secure from alleged Communists or sympathizers. Diamond relies upon archival research and information gained from Freedom of Information Act documents to demonstrate the degree of cooperation and collusion between university personnel and organizations such as the FBI. Throughout its surveillance of students, faculty, and campus organizations, the FBI attempted to maintain secrecy about the information it supplied to and received from campus authorities.

116. Dollard, Charles. "The Freedom of American Scholarship." **The American Journal of Economics and Sociology** 14(1): 37-38, October 1954.

The President of the Carnegie Corporation, in an excerpt from his July 12, 1954 testimony to the Reece Committee of the U.S. House of Representatives, writes that the freedoms of scholars are no different than those freedoms enjoyed by all American citizens. He addresses the question of the obligations of private foundations in light of principles of freedom of thought. Dollard testifies that the Carnegie Corporation should not tell grant recipients what conclusions to draw in research, how or what to teach students, or what to write in their books.

117. Duryea, E. D., Jr. "Academic Freedom: A Long View." **The Journal of Higher Education** 24(7): 345-348+, October 1953.

According to Duryea, the intolerance of different or "subversive" viewpoints during the Cold War poses an educational challenge for defenders of intellectual freedom. They need to "sell" a potentially supportive public on the virtues and social benefits of free inquiry and the search for truth. Duryea recommends making three key points in defense of academic freedom.   First, universities provide both "perspective on the present" and new ideas (p. 348). Second, an unpredictable future requires us to develop the best variety of potentially useful ideas. A "hardening of the nation's intellectual arteries" (p. 348), fostered by the hysteria against subversion or dissent, is counterproductive to this goal. Third, Duryea favorably recommends Karl Mannheim's argument to the effect that tolerance of intellectual difference goes hand-in-hand with the democratic method.

118. Eckelberry, R. H. "Academic Freedom at Ohio State University." **Journal of Higher Education** 22(9): 493-498, December 1951.

The Governor of Ohio requested that the Board of Trustees investigate the controversial invitation of Harold O. Rugg to speak at a conference sponsored by the OSU Department of Education. Rugg was criticized as a socialist and subversive in the Columbus, Ohio press. In response to the situation, the Board passed a policy requiring that all proposed invitations to outside speakers be cleared first with the President's Office. The aftermath of this Board decision is outlined, including: resolutions adopted by the local chapter of the AAUP and by the OSU Graduate Council condemning the decision; a straw poll of OSU students in which 2,986 to 637 voted against the speaker-screening; the refusals due to the gag rule of a number of invited campus speakers.

119. **The Efficiency of Freedom: Report of the Committee on Government and Higher Education.** Baltimore: Johns Hopkins Press, 1959. 44 p. LC 59-11781.

Organized and funded by the Ford Foundation's Fund for the Advancement of Education to study the relationship between state governments and public institutions of higher education, this committee sought to define and suggest limits on the scope of state control over higher education. Chaired by Milton S. Eisenhower (the then-President of Johns Hopkins University), the committee surveyed higher education administrators, state attorneys-general and governors in 39 states on questions related to institutional autonomy. Proposals are outlined for improving relations between state governments and public higher education in the areas of budgeting, personnel, legal autonomy, and building. More complete research findings are outlined in a companion volume, *The Campus and the State* (by Malcolm Moos and Francis E. Rourke).

120. Emery, Sarah Watson. **Blood on the Old Well.** Dallas, Texas: Prospect House, 1963. 240 p. LC 90-148729.

Emery decries a spiritual and intellectual decline she perceives at the University of North Carolina in the late 1950s and early 1960s. This is due, she claims, to the increasing influence of communists and atheists among faculty and staff, particularly in the Philosophy Department. Throughout, the author cites the principle of academic freedom as being a smoke screen for helping to justify anti-American and anti-Christian activities. The author recounts (and in many cases reprints) lectures by Philosophy Professor Maurice Natanson, a phenomenologist who wrote and lectured against Christianity. Emery also details campus events sponsored by the Philosophy Club at which existentialist and atheist sentiments were expressed. A former Communist, Professor David Hawkes, was hired as a visiting Professor of Philosophy in 1960. Emery reprints his testimony before the House Committee on Un-American Activities and those portions of the testimony of J. Robert Oppenheimer (before the US Atomic Energy Commission) where Hawkes is mentioned. Other issues addressed include suspicious deaths on campus and administrative efforts in 1957 to remove personnel form questions related to Communist Party affiliation of future faculty members. Appendices reprint HCUAC and AEC testimonies, Philosophy Club documents, American Legion resolutions against UNC student organizations, and other documents related to Communist activity at UNC.

121. Gardner, David P. "By Oath and Association: The California Folly." **The Journal of Higher Education** 40(2): 122-134, February 1969.

In 1950, 36 faculty members at the University of California were dismissed from their jobs for refusing to sign the California loyalty oath. Gardner reviews the chain of events that led to the dismissals. Designed as a means of placating the public and keeping Communists and subversives out of teaching posts, the oath was opposed by many California faculty. They felt that party membership, in and of itself, was not sufficient for termination; adherence to Communist Party discipline, and not to the search for truth, was the only indicator of unfitness. Faculty negotiated with the Regents of the university system in order to reach a compromise that would protect academic freedom, tenure, and self-governance. When that failed, many faculty refused to sign the oath as a matter of principle. Those faculty were fired, despite the fact that there was nothing in their professional behavior to warrant it. Gardner points out that oaths such as this have subsequently been found by the courts to violate academic freedom and civil liberties. Membership in a subversive organization is not sufficient grounds for termination.

122. Garrigues, George L. "The Great Conspiracy Against the UCLA Daily Bruin." **Southern California Quarterly** 59(2): 217-230, Summer 1977.

Conservative administrators at UCLA in the 1950s bowed to pressure from McCarthyism at the state and federal levels and took over the UCLA student newspaper, limiting publication of opinion pieces, and appointing a conservative editor-in-chief who amended the governance rules to call for popular election of editors by student votes. Garrigues argues that while very few Communists were actually involved with the paper, the level of anti-Communist rhetoric and actions taken against the Daily Bruin by the UCLA administration were extreme. Focusing largely on the early 1950s, Garrigues puts these events in a larger context. UCLA administrators attempted to focus public attention on the threat of campus Communism, a threat that Garrigues finds to be consistently overblown.

123. Gideonse, Harry D. "Changing Issues in Academic Freedom in the United States Today." **Proceedings of the American Philosophical Society** 94(2): 91-104, April 21, 1950.

This paper was read at a November 1949 Symposium on Academic Freedom at the Autumn General Meeting of the American Philosophical Association. The author, President of Brooklyn College, argues that academic freedom is undergoing many changes and new developments related to rising totalitarianism, three of which are discussed here. The first is the threat to academic freedom posed by Communists concealing their Party membership and hiding behind academic freedom principles while working to undermine liberty. The second is the undue limits placed on scientific research by (in some cases secret) federal security regulations. The third is the increasing financial support provided by foundations and the federal government which brings with it undue influence on academic priorities.

124. Goldblatt, Harold. "Academic Mobility and Cross Pressures on College Teachers During the McCarthy Era." **Sociology of Education** 40(2): 132-144, Spring 1967.

This research is an extension of Paul Lazarsfeld's and Wagner Thielens' *The Academic Mind* (see entry #135), a study of the behavior and attitudes of academics during the McCarthy period. Goldblatt traces the pressures created by downward or upward mobility from one's graduate program to one's teaching college, and the resulting effect on the academic's sense of apprehension regarding academic freedom. His data analysis suggests that the quality of an academic's graduate school did have an "independent influence on certain attitudes and values" (p. 144), such as feelings of apprehension. This finding complements and extends Lazarsfeld and Thielens' findings that the quality of one's teaching college had a significant effect on apprehensiveness.

125. Holmes, David R. **Stalking the Academic Communist: Intellectual Freedom and the Firing of Alex Novikoff.** Hanover, New Hampshire: University Press of New England, 1989. 288p. ISBN 0-8745-1466-5.

Holmes recounts the political, professional, and personal problems faced by Alex Novikoff because of his affiliation with the Communist Party. Novikoff was fired in 1953 from his teaching position at the University of Vermont and denied many other teaching and research positions due to his former political affiliation and his unwillingness to inform on political acquaintances. As Holmes points out, Novikoff was never a security risk, even in the peak of his political activities; his party membership and related activities were perfectly legal and, in fact, his right. Yet long after he left the party, he was still being persecuted for that previous membership. Though a case study, this work illustrates the degree of paranoia that existed about communists in society and, more specifically, in academia. It also demonstrates how readily academic freedom was sacrificed by politicians as well as university administrators and faculty members.

126. Hook, Sidney. "Communists, McCarthy and American Universities." **Minerva** 25(3): 331-348, Autumn 1987.

Hook takes exception to the arguments put forward in Ellen Schrecker's *No Ivory Tower*, a history of academic freedom in the McCarthy period. He argues that Schrecker is wrong when she suggests that Communist Party-affiliated faculty in the United States were still independent of mind and not slavish followers of the Party line. According to Hook, Schrecker presents no evidence for this contention. Hook argues, to the contrary, that faculty who are members of the Communist Party are not committed to an objective search for truth and therefore do not deserve the trust inherent in their teaching positions. They are incapable, he suggests, of independent or critical thought that runs counter to Party dictates. After chronicling a number of controversial Party positions or changes of position, he points out that Schrecker provided not one instance of a Party faculty member criticizing such positions. In fact, he argues, Schrecker displays poor scholarship by not even asking her interviewees such questions. He concludes by suggesting that the current New Left on campuses, while not beholden to a Party line, has made campus climates less free and more intolerant than ever.

127. Hook, Sidney. **Heresy, Yes, Conspiracy, No.** New York: John Day Company, 1953. 283p. LC 53-6587.

According to Hook, academic freedom is undermined by two different groups, the "cultural vigilantes" and the "ritualistic liberals." The cultural vigilantes see all heretical thought that diverges from their extremist anti-communism as dangerous and, therefore, not deserving of protection. At the other extreme, says Hook, are the ritualistic liberals who see no threat whatsoever from academics who are members of the Communist Party in the United States. Ritualistic liberals see Party membership as just another form of heresy, not as a political conspiracy. For Hook, academic freedom must protect heretical ideas arrived at freely in the search for truth. However, Hook argues strongly that members of the Communist Party in the United States hold allegiance to and take directives from a foreign power. Furthermore, they operate in a conspiratorial and secretive manner. As a result, they do not pursue truth freely and, therefore, are not deserving of academic freedom. Other chapters elaborate Hook's view of academic freedom, as well as his analyses of "guilt-by-association," the role of the teacher, authoritarian attitudes in education, and the Smith Act, among others.

128. Horn, Michiel. "Academic Freedom and the Dismissal of George Hunter." **Dalhousie Review** 69(3): 415-438, Fall 1989.

In 1949 the Board of Governors of the University of Alberta dismissed the tenured Head of the Department of Biochemistry for engaging in left-wing political advocacy in his classroom. Background of this case, and details regarding the Communist Party of Canada (which Hunter probably was not a member of), as well as details regarding Hunter's strained relations with the University administration are all provided. Not part of any anti-Communist push, Hunter's dismissal faded into obscurity. Reasons for this are speculated on. One issue this case has bearing on is whether it is appropriate to dismiss professors engaging in classroom advocacy of their own personal beliefs.

129. Hutchins, Robert M. "The Freedom of the University." **Ethics** 61(2): 95-104, January 1951.

The author defines the university as a center for independent thought and asserts that the only limitations which should be imposed on faculty members are the laws of logic and the laws of the country. Hutchins holds that the laws of the country should never seek to control thought. He argues not only that Communism should be studied and thought about at universities, but also that faculty appointments should be made without regard to a professor's political beliefs or association. Forcing conformity upon academics can never achieve the results sought by those patriots who seek to root out subversive activities on campus. Independent thought is better served by open inquiry and open criticism, rather than regulation.

130. Hutchins, Robert M. "The Meaning and Significance of Academic Freedom." **Annals of the American Academy of Political and Social Science** 300: 72-78, July 1955.

Hutchins claims that the country has been asking the wrong questions about education. The right question about a teacher is about his competence; the wrong questions are more about the questioner's fear of ideas than about the standards of competence in education. Hutchins relates principles of academic freedom to the activities of the U.S. House Reece Committee appointed to investigate subversives in tax-exempt foundations, and to the activities of the California Senate Committee on Un-American Activities.

131. Innis, Nancy K. "Lessons from the Controversy Over the Loyalty Oath at the University of California." **Minerva** 30(3): 337-365, Autumn 1992.

Innis recounts the University of California Board of Regents closed door vote in March of 1949 to require of all faculty an oath denying membership or support of any organization hostile to the United States. Text of the oath (here reprinted) was made public in June; no consultation with the faculty regarding this took place before then. Here covered are details of the ensuing controversy, such as the ultimatum requiring all faculty to sign by April 30, 1950 or be terminated. In compromise, the oath was abandoned in favor of a statement denying Communist Party membership inserted in the annual letter of appointment. Non-signers, calling themselves the "Group for Academic Freedom" were officially dismissed. A court case was brought on behalf of 20 of these. In October of 1952 the California Supreme Court decided that they must be reinstated. Members of the Group for Academic Freedom are given short biographies here. In a final section, Innis compares the external threats to academic freedom posed by the Regents with contemporary internal threats to academic freedom posed by liberal and politically correct professors.

132. Kerr, Willard. "The Measurement of Academic Freedom." **Journal of Applied Psychology** 38(2): 134, April 1954.

This short report details a 1953 survey devised by the Chicago Division of the American Civil Liberties Union Academic Freedom Committee to measure the academic freedom of the fifty higher education institutions in Illinois. Seventy-three replies were received from about 200 surveys sent to administrators, professors, and student leaders. The most and least secure aspects of academic freedom are noted for faculty; the least secure freedoms are noted for students. Faculty freedoms included: freedom from oaths, of association through faculty organizations, of research, of citizenship activities. Less secure freedoms included: self-government, tenure, criticism of curricula or administration. Insecure student freedoms included: hearing outside speakers, criticizing faculty or administration, organizing associations, of press and petition, and participating in off-campus activities.

133. Kirkland, Edward C. "Do Antisubversive Efforts Threaten Academic Freedom?" In Robert K. Carr, editor. **Civil Rights in America.** Philadelphia: AAPSS, 1951. pp132-139. (Annals of the American Academy of Political and Social Science, v. 275, May 1951). LC 51-4188.

Although concepts and procedures of academic freedom are widely endorsed and have been put into practice since 1915, the values of academic freedom clash with patriotic nationalist values expressed by anti-Communists. Responses to and support for antisubversive efforts differ from campus to campus, despite the AAUP stance that teachers should not be dismissed for joining a lawful party or group. The clash between on the one hand public pressures and legislative efforts to enforce loyalty on campus, and on the other hand the self-determination of faculties to decide on qualifications and choice of faculty members is addressed here. Examples are detailed, including the 1949 University of Washington dismissals of Communist faculty members and the University of California loyalty oath. The author concludes that the "negligible" numbers of Communists found in academia did not justify the "disastrous" effect on morale, productivity, and civil liberties of a campus-by-campus search for alleged subversives.

134. Larabee, Lottie B. **Administrators Who Subvert Learning: Their Residence & Education.** Garden City, NY: Education Press, 1957. 324p. LC 57-04526.

Based on AAUP-documented cases of denial of academic freedom or tenure between 1925 and 1950, this study gave corroboration for the author's thesis that college administrators participating in such cases had common backgrounds very similar to those of other administrators yet significantly different from other college staff members. Fifty eight administrators were compared with a randomly selected group of 150 educational administrators, staff members cited in *Who's Who in American Education*, and AAUP officers and councilors.

135. Lazarsfeld, Paul F., and Wagner Thielens, Jr. **The Academic Mind: Social Scientists in a Time of Crisis.** Glencoe, Ill.: Free Press, 1958. 460p. LC 58-6486.

   Lazarsfeld and Thielens analyzed the findings of a post-World War II survey of the attitudes and behaviors of over 2,400 social science faculty at 165 institutions of higher education. The purpose was to determine the impact of national security concerns and an anti-Communist climate on the academic freedom of those faculty most likely to deal with controversial topics. Through data analysis, the authors attempted not only to categorize the threats to faculty, but also to explore the subtle and not-so-subtle ways faculty responded to perceived and potential threats. A number of chapters deal with the degree to which faculty worried about their beliefs and professional behavior in a politically charged climate. Other chapters tried to gauge the incidence of cautious behavior that might have resulted from such worry. Summarizing these findings, the authors addressed the level of apprehension faculty felt about their reputations and job security. Measures of permissiveness toward controversial ideas or affiliations are also related to measures of apprehension. Additional chapters address patterns of caution among apprehensive faculty, as well as the social context of their apprehension.

136. Lerner, Max. "The Mandarins and the Pariahs." **American Scholar** 18(3): 337-341, Summer 1949.

   Part of a "Forum on Communism and Academic Freedom," Lerner's article decries the dismissal of three tenured faculty from the University of Washington. Lerner is not disturbed by the charge that they were members of the Communist Party, but rather by what he sees as the lack of evidence. Lerner holds that Communist Party membership should disqualify a professor from his office, but holds that "we shall match the intense dogmatism of the Communists with an almost parallel dogmatism of our own." He expressed further concern that this sort of reaction to the threat of Communism may be a more corrupting influence on students than the presence of Communists on faculty.

137. Lewis, Lionel S. **The Cold War and Academic Governance: The Lattimore Case at Johns Hopkins.** Albany: State University of New York Press, 1993. 318p. ISBN 0-7914-1493-0. LC 92-24053.

Owen Lattimore was a sinologist at Johns Hopkins University who, beginning in 1950, was investigated by Senate and House committees for possibly being a Soviet agent. His analysis of events in China, the Chiang Kai-shek nationalist government, and American foreign policy in the region were supposedly consistent with the Soviet "line" and contrary to American interests. This fact, along with some of his other activities and affiliations, brought him under the scrutiny of Congressional anti-communist committees. Lewis recounts in detail the investigation of Lattimore and, importantly, the university's response. There was much pressure brought to bear upon Johns Hopkins to fire Lattimore for being either a Soviet agent or a sympathizer. This pressure came from the public, alumni, politicians, and others. However, Lattimore was not fired. Though he was placed on leave with pay while he fought Congressional perjury charges, he was reinstated after the charges were dropped. Lewis analyzes documents from the university President, the Board of Trustees, faculty, administrators, alumni, and others to explain the source of Lattimore's support. Though administrative support may often have been reluctant, it nonetheless won out over the threats of what Lewis refers to as the "moral entrepreneurs." In the end, the university's concern for its academic reputation, the reactions of its faculty, and academic freedom were key factors. Lewis concludes with an analysis of the nature of university governance and the potential conflict between the bureaucratic nature of higher educational institutions and the professional norms of the faculty. He suggests that other universities, which generally did not support similarly accused faculty, could have done otherwise.

138. Lewis, Lionel S. **Cold War on Campus: A Study of the Politics of Organizational Control.** New Brunswick, N.J.: Transaction Books, 1988. 358p. ISBN 0-8873-8178-2.

Lewis examines the degree to which factors other than politics affected the course and outcome of the Cold War on college and university campuses in the United States. Specifically, he studied the records of over 100 cases of alleged infringement of academic freedom for political reasons. Lewis found that while the politics of the Cold War may have precipitated the campus cases, other factors, many of them non-political, played a crucial role in determining their outcome. These included such factors as whether the institution was public or private, whether the faculty member was tenured or not, the faculty member's cooperativeness with campus and off-campus investigating committees, and other variables. These factors often made a difference as to whether a faculty member was fired or not. Overall, however, Lewis indicts presidents and other academic administrators for their ready sacrifice of academic freedom to protect both the institution's image and their organizational control.

139. Lipset, S. M. "Opinion Formation in a Crisis Situation." **Public Opinion Quarterly** 17(1): 20-46, Spring 1953.

An interview was conducted in 1950 with a representative sample of the students attending the University of California at Berkeley regarding their opinions on the UC loyalty oath and policy of only hiring non-Communists. Previous experiences and attitudes, along with group affiliations helped determine student reaction. Attitudes towards academic freedom were found to be related to the same variables affecting other attitude formations. Among other findings were that, in comparison with those who did not support the oath, those who did support the oath believed that there were many more Communists among the student body.

140. Lovejoy, Arthur O. "Communism versus Academic Freedom." **American Scholar** 18(3): 332-336, Summer 1949.

Part of a "Forum on Communism and Academic Freedom," Lovejoy's article argues that while present Communist party membership could be legitimate grounds for dismissal without violating principles of academic freedom, dismissal on the basis of past membership is a violation. The specific case in question involves the 1949 dismissal of three tenured faculty members from the University of Washington (Joseph Butterworth, Ralph H. Gundlach, and Herbert J. Phillips) on the basis of membership or refusal to answer suspicions of membership in the Communist Party.

141. Lynd, Helen M. "Truth at the University of Washington." **American Scholar** 18(3): 346-353, Summer 1949.

The author believe that purging Communists is not in the interests of freedom of teaching or of democracy; in fact, it poses a threat to independent thought. Driving Communism underground and casting suspicion on anyone supporting liberal or progressive causes are the main results of purges like that which took place at the University of Washington. Lynd questions the integrity of specific witnesses called before the Board of Regents and speculates to the reasons behind exclusion of testimony by outside scholars.

142. Maccoby, Herbert. "Controversy, Neutrality, and Higher Education." **American Sociological Review** 25(6): 884-893, December 1960.

The author gathered data indicating that support for certain practices of academic freedom is stronger among academics engaged in such practices, and who have strong professional ties to the academic community and weak professional ties to the community. The practices in question are: social science instructor's discussion of controversial social issues, and instructors of any discipline expressing personal convictions when questioning traditional values in classroom topics. A mail survey in 1957-1958 was sent to all full-time academic personnel at 74 two-year colleges in fifteen states. Among the findings are that ideas and actions in academic freedom areas are largely determined by the position a person holds in the academic system and by the structure of the system.

143. MacIver, Robert M. **Academic Freedom in Our Time.** New York: Columbia University Press, 1955. 329p. LC 55-9094.

MacIver addresses the causes and consequences of attacks on academic freedom during the McCarthy period. He also systematically examines the rationale and necessary conditions for the protection of academic freedom and the scholarly search for truth. The book is divided into five parts. Part one identifies the "climate of opinion" in the United States during this period and the various types of groups and organizations that challenged academic freedom in the name of some orthodoxy. Part two contains chapters outlining the proper roles of various constituent groups in academic governance and the protection of academic freedom. These groups include university presidents, governing boards, faculty, alumni, and the public. Part three provides a fairly detailed overview of the various "lines of attack" on academic freedom, including those motivated for economic, religious, and political reasons (including anti-communism). Part four discusses a somewhat neglected aspect of academic freedom, the freedom of the student. Part five provides a broader social context for the mission of the university and the value of academic freedom and tenure. Throughout, MacIver reiterates the social contribution of academic freedom and necessity for an unfettered search for knowledge and truth.

144. "The McCarthy Era." **Academe** 75 (3): 27-30, May-June 1989.

The responses of the American Association of University Professors (AAUP) and its members to McCarthyism were varied. For years, the organization did not officially respond to alleged infringements of academic freedom that were based on one's alleged Communist political affiliations or beliefs. At the same time, many of the organization's members were opposed to McCarthyism; this was reflected in *AAUP Bulletin* articles, annual conference resolutions, and committee reports. This article captures the variety of those responses and opinions by presenting excerpts of those articles, resolutions, and reports on McCarthyism.

145. McCormick, Charles H. **This Nest of Vipers: McCarthyism and Higher Education in the Mundel Affair, 1951-1952.** Urbana, Ill.: University of Illinois Press, 1989. 229p. ISBN 0-252-01614-9. LC 88-30129.

McCormick recounts the facts surrounding the firing of Luella Mundel from the faculty of Fairmont State College in West Virginia. An art teacher, Mundel was fired allegedly for her political and religious beliefs, which were supposedly too "liberal" and agnostic for influential members of the community, university, and the West Virginia State Board of Education. Ultimately, college President George Hand was fired as well, in part for his support of Mundel, his impolitic handling of the matter, and his efforts at reforming the college. Mundel sued a member of the Board for libel, and the subsequent trials and news coverage involved any number of interest groups, including the local American Legion Post, the American Civil Liberties Union, and the American Association of University Professors. After an initial mistrial, Mundel lost a retrial of her case. McCormick's case study, however, does much to illuminate the climate of McCarthyism in general and the attitudes and beliefs of that particular West Virginia community.

146. McGrath, Earl J. "Academic Freedom and Academic Responsibilities." **School and Society** 79(2028): 65-67, March 6, 1954.

The President of the University of Kansas City Missouri explains the reasons behind the 1953 unanimous decision of the Board of Trustees to dismiss Horace B. Davis from his faculty position due to his refusal to answer whether he was ever a member of or in sympathy with the program of the Communist Party. Faculty of the University of Kansas City do not have the right to refuse to answer such questions when posed to them by "other members of this academic community."

147. Meiklejohn, Alexander. "The Teaching of Intellectual Freedom." **American Association of University Professors Bulletin** 38(1): 10-25, Spring 1952.

The author, a retired professor living in Berkeley at the time, sketches out a theory of constitutional justification for free thinking. He calls on the AAUP to oppose the University of California Board of Regents loyalty oath requirements, arguing on the basis of the main components of his theory: freedom of assembly, self-governance of faculties independent of "non-delegated powers," and electoral freedom from oath-taking. An institution ceases to meet the definition of a university when it limits intellectual freedom. Such freedom is a duty, not just a right, of all faculty members.

148. Metzger, Walter P. "Ralph F. Fuchs and Ralph E. Himstead: A Note on the AAUP in the McCarthy Period." **Academe** 72 (6): 29-35, November-December 1986.

During the McCarthy period, some faculty were fired for their alleged Communist political affiliations, their refusals to take loyalty oaths, and related causes. In fact, the American Association of University Professors (AAUP) had been asked to investigate two of the earliest and most famous cases of the period, at the University of Washington and the University of California. Yet the AAUP issued no formal reports on these or other alleged infringements of academic freedom. According to Metzger, the principal reason was the inaction of then general secretary Ralph E. Himstead. Himstead's increasing control over all aspects of the association's operations, his fear of criticism, his defensiveness, and his desire to protect his power combined to immobilize both him and the AAUP. Unable to keep up with all of the work, Himstead let much of the association's business fall behind. Fearing criticism of the reports on controversial academic freedom cases, Himstead never released them. It was only after Himstead's untimely death, and Ralph F. Fuch's assumption of the general secretary's position, that the organization resumed its role in the protection of academic freedom.

149. Moos, Malcolm and Francis E. Rourke, with the assistance of Glenn Brooks and Leo Redfern. **The Campus and the State.** Baltimore: Johns Hopkins Press, 1959. 414p. LC 59-10768.

This volume presents the detailed research findings of a two year Ford Foundation-funded study by the Committee on Government and Higher Education. A shorter companion volume called *The Efficiency of Freedom* was issued by this Committee. Questionnaires sent to state attorneys-general, governors, and university presidents and administrators form a large basis for the information here presented about growing centralization of state control over such formerly-autonomous public higher education functions as budgeting, purchasing and auditing, publishing, personnel, and building. A central question posed is whether the essential freedom of higher education from outside control is consistent with the legitimate governmental goal of ensuring efficient performance in public institutions. The argument is made that intense governmental control over day-to-day and long-range planning issues in higher education can prove detrimental to these institutions.

150. Murphy, Arthur E. "Concerning Academic Freedom." In William H. Hay, Marcus G. Singer and Arthur E. Murphy, editors. **Reason and the Common Good: Selected Essays of Arthur E. Murphy.** Englewood Cliffs, N.J.: Prentice-Hall, 1963. pp. 358-361. (Prentice-Hall Philosophy Series). LC 63-8665.

Originally presented at a symposium on Communism and Academic Freedom held in 1949 or 1950 at Yale Law School, this talk was not previously published. Murphy discusses his anti-Communism and his support for freedoms, including academic freedom. Murphy claims that removal of an individual professor does not violate academic freedom if the removal was due to the interference of partisanship in fulfillment of duties. But Murphy also claims that deplorable extra-curricular beliefs or political activity should not in and of itself be grounds for dismissal. Any firing based on political beliefs rather than competence not only injures the individual but also the scholarly community he is expelled from. Murphy does not agree that acceptance of Communist doctrine or party membership are sufficient evidence of incompetence in academia. Due process and a fair test of academic competence are required if freedom is to be protected, as most anti-Communists would hope.

151. Perry, Ralph Barton. "Academic Freedom." **Harvard Educational Review** 23(1): 71-76, Spring 1953.

Perry questions whether Congressional investigations into subversive activities should target higher education, whether academics should refuse to testify, and whether those who so refuse should be dismissed. Answering 'no' to all three questions, he also provides specific advice to academics called before such committees.

152. Riesman, David. "Interviewers, Elites, and Academic Freedom." **Social Problems** 6(2): 115-126, Fall 1958.

The author recounts the reactions of academic social scientists towards being interviewed about issues of academic freedom. A "Teacher Apprehension Survey" of 2,500 interviews at 165 colleges took place in 1955, commissioned by the Fund for the Republic and conducted by Paul F. Lazarsfeld. The sensitive nature of the questions combined with the national and often local pressures of McCarthyism meant that many interviewees were unwilling participants in this study of their experiences with and attitudes toward academic freedom. One quarter of the 212 interviewers were interviewed by Riesman; interviews were read and respondents also talked with; and a follow up questionnaire went to 750 respondents asking them to describe their interviewers. Concerns were expressed about the survey instrument, about the interviewers, and about the sponsoring agency. Regional, rural-urban, and educational quality differences between campuses were noted.

153. Robinson, James. "Academic Freedom and the Occupation of Germany and Japan." **Bulletin of Concerned Asian Scholars** 6(4): 49-58, November-December 1974.

The author addresses the relationship between academic anti-Communism and the democratization/Americanization efforts of post-World War II occupation forces in Germany and Japan which opposed and undermined left-wing political activity in the occupied areas. Of particular focus here is New York University and the activities through the CIA-sponsored American Congress for Cultural Freedom (founded in Berlin in 1952) of such liberal anti-Communists as Sidney Hook and James Burnham. Anti-Communist purges at NYU from 1948 through 1954 corresponded to some degree with the movement of former civil and military occupation personnel into NYU positions, from the level of the Board of Trustees down to Deans and development officers. The influence of, and government support for Sidney Hook's accusations against Professor Edwin Berry Burgum are detailed. Robinson concludes with a call for research into direct or indirect connections at other universities with post-war democratization programs, and the connections between government agents in overseas occupation posts and academics on U.S. campuses.

154. Rogow, Arnold A. "The Loyalty Oath Issue in Iowa, 1951." **The American Political Science Review** 55(4): 861-869, December 1961.

At a time when many states either had passed or were passing loyalty oaths for public employees (including teachers), Iowa was the only state that declined to pass such legislation. Introduced in 1951 by Senator Alden L. Doud, the Iowa bill would have denied state employment to subversives, required agencies to identify them, required employees to take a loyalty oath, and fined or imprisoned those "teaching or conspiring to teach the overthrow of the government" (p. 862). Rogow believes that Doud may have been encouraged to introduce the legislation by a government agency. Its secondary purposes were to identify opponents of the legislation, to provide a basis for prosecuting perjurers, and to neutralize and ensure the loyalty of teachers and professors. Ultimately, however, Doud's bill failed because of strong opposition by the education community, its questionable constitutionality, and its perceived irrelevance and ineffectiveness.

155. Sanders, Jane A. "Clio Confronts Conformity: The University of Washington History Department During The Cold War." **Pacific Northwest Quarterly** 88(4): 185-194, Fall 1997.

During the Cold War in the late 1940s and 1950s, the University of Washington was a focus of anti-communist legislative investigations by the state's Canwell committee. The committee was interested in identifying Communist faculty, who it felt were not deserving of academic freedom. Two faculty members in the history department came under investigation, and 11 faculty overall were required to testify before the committee. In a subsequent hearing on six of these faculty members, the Faculty Senate Committee on Tenure and Academic Freedom recommended that only one of these six be fired. However, the President of the university, Raymond Allen, recommended and the Board of Regents concurred that three tenured faculty be fired. Two members of the History department, W. Stull Holt (the department chair) and Max Savelle, were on the faculty committee and disagreed strongly with any firings. Holt unsuccessfully attempted to get the faculty Senate to pass a resolution opposing the Regents' interference. Passing judgement of the "competence" and "qualifications" of one's peers was a faculty responsibility, he argued. Other faculty opposed guilt-by-association and its probable effect on academic freedom and university morale. History department members were prominent in subsequent opposition to the banning of a speech by J. Robert Oppenheimer, to loyalty oaths, and to the prohibition against faculty membership in subversive organizations. Sanders demonstrates that for many years and in various crises, history faculty were staunch defenders of academic freedom.

156. Sanders, Jane. **Cold War on the Campus: Academic Freedom at the University of Washington, 1946-64.** Seattle: University of Washington Press, 1979. 243p. LC 78-21755. ISBN 0-295-95652-6.

Sanders provides a descriptive history of the effects of the Cold War on academic freedom at the University of Washington during an 18-year period. A number of notable developments occurred there that were illustrative of trends in higher education nationwide: professors Joseph Butterworth, Ralph Gundlach, and Herbert Phillips were fired for their alleged current or past Communist Party affiliations and their lack of candor and cooperation with university and State investigating bodies; professors E. Harold Eby, Garland Ethel, and Melville Jacobs were placed on probation for their affiliations; renown guest lecturers, such as J. Robert Oppenheimer and Kenneth Burke, were denied prestigious Walker-Ames Lectureships because of their political affiliations; faculty and staff were required to take loyalty oaths. While some faculty, administrators, and sympathetic civic organizations resisted infringements on academic freedom, many others agreed with or acquiesced to the pressures from "superpatriot" civic groups, state legislative bodies (such as the Canwell Committee), and federal Congressional committees (such as the McCarran Committee or the House UnAmerican Activities Committee).

157. Sanders, Jane A. "The University of Washington and the Controversy over J. Robert Oppenheimer." **Pacific Northwest Quarterly** 70(1): 8-19, January 1979.

Sanders details events at the University of Washington surrounding President Henry Schmitz's 1955 veto of a proposed Professorship for J. Robert Oppenheimer. Dubbed "the father of the atomic bomb," Oppenheimer had his federal security clearance revoked in 1953 after he testified before the House Un-American Activities Committee on suspicions of Communist ties. Schmitz's reasons for this veto, and the subsequent discord in faculty-administrative relations are outlined in this article, Among other things, the author relied on papers in the UW archives, on personal interviews, and on articles from the UW Daily and Seattle newspapers.

158. Sargent, S. Stansfeld, and Benjamin Harris. "Academic Freedom, Civil Liberties, and SPSSI." **Journal of Social Issues** 42(1): 43-67, Spring 1986.

Sargent and Harris examine the role of the Society for the Psychological Study of Social Issues (SPSSI) in defending academic freedom and civil liberties from 1936 to 1970. Drawing upon published and unpublished documents and correspondence, the authors review not only academic freedom violations against SPSSI officers and members, but also the University of California loyalty oath controversy of the early 1950s and the Department of Health, Education and Welfare security clearance system of the 1960s. Throughout, the nature and extent of the SPSSI response to these violations is discussed. Though often forthright in its defense of academic freedom, the SPSSI's success rate was, according to the authors, low. Furthermore, with many individuals and organizations involved in protesting these academic freedom violations, it is difficult to assess the specific impact of the SPSSI. Still, small and large victories were won and these, as well as the organization's failures, are reviewed by the authors. Sargent and Harris also explore the differences of opinion within the organization concerning the strength of its statement on academic freedom, its academic freedom fund, and the taking of the Fifth Amendment during testimony. A final listing covers the negative and positive experiences of this professional organization's 30 years of watchdog and whistle blowing roles.

159. Scanlan, John A. "Why the McCarran-Walter Act Must Be Amended." **Academe** 73 (5): 5-13, September-October 1987.

According to Scanlan, there is an historical chain of U. S. legislation, culminating in the McCarran-Walter Act of 1952, that allows the federal government to prohibit politically undesirable aliens from entering the country. These laws have been used to exclude or, in some cases, deport anarchists, Communists, and other "subversives" because of their opinions, speech, or writings. In many cases, the excluded aliens have been scholars and politicians who were coming here for academic and scholarly purposes, such as giving lectures or attending conferences. Scanlan argues that these laws violate principles of academic freedom and the marketplace-of-ideas and need to be overturned.

160. Schappes, Morris U. "Forty Years Later But Not Too Late." **Jewish Currents** 36(4): 12-25, April 1982.

As a prominent campus Marxist, tenured on the English faculty of Municipal College (now the City University of New York), Schappes was one of over 40 tenured and non-tenured teachers and staff members forced out of their positions by the New York State Legislature's Rapp-Coudert Committee in 1941. Officially known as the Joint Legislative Committee to Investigate State Monies for Public School Purposes and Subversive Activities, the Rapp-Coudert was established to root out public employees on the basis of their political beliefs and associations. Schappes recounts his involvement with a 1981 effort at CUNY by the Faculty Senate and Board of Trustees to officially apologize and pledge future protection of the rights of faculty, staff, and students.

161. Schrecker, Ellen. "Academic Freedom and the Cold War." **Antioch Review** 38(3): 313-327, Summer 1980.

Schrecker gives an overview of how academic freedoms were redefined in the Cold War era to exclude admitted communists from faculty bodies. Citing specific cases at the University of Washington (1948), Cornell (1951), Rutgers (1952) and Harvard (1952), Schrecker also covers the activities of various governmental investigatory bodies (such as the Senate Internal Security Subcommittee and the House Un-American Activities Committee) and the anti-Communist activities of professional organizations (such as the National Education Association and the Association of American Universities). Schrecker charges that the AAUP censuring of those institutions which fired tenured professors was ineffectual since it came too late (years after the firings in question), and because the AAUP did not seek to rectify the injustices they identified.

162. Schrecker, Ellen W. "Archival Sources for the Study of McCarthyism." **Journal of American History** 75(1): 197-208, June 1988.

Schrecker details the "basic structure of McCarthyism" and then lays out an overview of important archival collections that deal specifically with McCarthyism. Governmental repositories at the Federal and State level, as well as the personal papers of individuals important in the anti-Communist right wing of the 1950s are all listed. Schrecker also gives information on records relating to the victims of anti-Communism (including academics) as well as those institutions which opposed McCarthyism. The impact of McCarthyism on labor unions and the professions (including academia), Blacks, and the media can all be studied through some of the repositories described here. Schrecker concludes by calling for interviews, especially since many of those involved left no paper trail or written records.

163. Schrecker, Ellen W. **No Ivory Tower: McCarthyism and The Universities.** New York: Oxford University Press, 1986. 437p. ISBN 0-195-03557-7. LC 86-8417.

Schrecker provides an historical analysis of the origins, methods, and consequences of the academic anti-communism of the McCarthy period. She begins by reviewing the development of academic freedom from the late 19th century, discussing some of the more notorious cases (e.g. Richard Ely, Scott Nearing) and noting how readily academic freedom was sacrificed for the university's reputation and "corporate protection." After describing the nature and extent of communist and progressive activity on campus in the 1930s and 1940s, Schrecker tracks the academic anti-communist attacks from the 1930s onward. Of course, academics were at risk from external, state and federal congressional investigating committees, many of which considered communist party membership as disqualifying one from a teaching position. However, as she shows, many university administrations and faculty members shared this perspective and were active in purging their own ranks. Being a former party member, being unwilling to name other party members, taking the fifth amendment before an investigating committee, or simply being sympathetic with the wrong political groups and activities could also get one fired.

164. Smith, Philip M. "Teacher Loyalty and Academic Freedom." **Journal of Educational Sociology** 23(5): 251-257, January 1950.

Smith characterizes many post-war legislative efforts at uncovering teacher disloyalty as witch hunts, driven by a "misguided zeal." These legislative investigations have commonly resorted to such methods as misrepresentation and guilt-by-association in their anti-Communist fervor. They have created a climate in which it is more difficult for teachers to raise controversial issues or engage in critical examinations of American institutions or problems (e.g., the economic system; inequality). Those who criticize the status quo may be considered unpatriotic. The risk to freedom and the pursuit of truth is that teachers may be "coerced into voicing political views of only the dominant economic groups" (p. 253). However, one cannot compel loyalty; it is better given willingly. Furthermore, loyalty oaths would be ineffective since those intent on overthrowing our government would readily take a loyalty oath. In any event, Smith suggests that Communists are not taking over our education system. Teachers are predominantly conventional in opinion and middle class in background. If students fall prey to totalitarian ideas, there may be a problem with their education or training.

165. Smith, Stanley H. "Academic Freedom in Higher Education in the Deep South." **Journal of Educational Sociology** 32(6): 297-308, February 1958.

Smith argues that academic freedom in the Deep South is at risk, particularly when the issue of desegregation is being discussed. The social structure of the South is largely authoritarian, with power elites in some states rooted in a plantation economy. These elites work to maintain the status quo, which entails an opposition to desegregation. Higher educational institutions can be threatened with cuts in funding if they appear to support desegregation. This threat is aggravated by the close working relationship between institutional administrators and state legislators. Even private black colleges are at risk of sanctions, given that they are dependent upon the state for some services (e.g., teacher certification). Smith reviews particular policies and practices by state legislatures, trustees and college administrators in Alabama, Mississippi, Georgia, and South Carolina. Overall, academic firings and threats of funding cuts made academic freedom in those states precarious in the 1950s. This had the effect of scaring off good faculty and retarding the quality of these states' higher educational institutions.

166. Smith, T. V. "Academic Expediency as Democratic Justice in re Communists." **American Scholar** 18(3): 342-346, Summer 1949.

Part of a "Forum on Communism and Academic Freedom," Smith's essay argues that there is a tendency among academics to fight for the right of their peers to undermine the academy they all work in. Communists have no right to faculty privilege since they would subvert the mission of the university in which they serve. Also, faculty have no responsibility to themselves or to any principle of democracy or academia to tolerate Communists in higher education. Defending their rights as citizens is one thing; defending their right to the professional privileges of academia is another. Smith explains his agreement with the dismissals (on suspicion of Communist affiliations) of three tenured professors at the University of Washington.

167. Stember, Herbert. "Student Opinion on Issues of Academic Freedom." **Journal of Social Issues** 9(3): 43-47, 1953.

Stember recounts the findings of a 1953 survey of Columbia University student attitudes towards Congressional investigation of college faculty. These findings are compared with two similar surveys held at UCLA (1949) and Berkeley (1950) on the issue of student attitudes toward the loyalty oath. The Columbia survey occurred at a time when several Congressional committees were investigating the faculty members of a number of different universities (though not yet at Columbia). While one-half of the surveyed students felt it was worth investigating whether there were Communists on faculties, about three-quarters disapproved of the current investigations and of the principle of Congressional committee investigations of the political views of faculty members. In the California surveys, as well as in this one only a minority of students opposed employing Communists on faculties.

168. Summers, Robert E. **Freedom and Loyalty in Our Colleges.** New York: H.W. Wilson Co., 1954. 214p. (Reference Shelf, 26(2)). LC 54-7533.

This compilation reprints excerpts from journal and newspaper articles, federal and state committee reports, and position statements from professional organizations on the topic of college teachers accused of being Communists. A variety of perspectives are provided on such topics as national security, academic freedom, the Fifth Amendment, loyalty oaths, federal and state investigations. An extensive bibliography is also provided.

169. Tauber, Kurt P. "The Free University in an Open Society." **Harvard Education Review** 23(1): 3-16, Winter 1953.

Tauber examines the consequences of restricting academic freedom in the name of national security or in the name of asserting "acceptable value orthodoxies." Such arguments from fear in favor of restricting academic freedom violate democratic principles of pluralism since democracies are founded less on specific values than on methodological principles such as freedom of inquiry, expression, and association. Throughout this essay, Tauber argues against numerous points raised by Buckley in *God and Man at Yale* (see entry #105). He compares the role of the scholar in an open society that emphasizes tolerance and the rights of the individual with the role of the scholar in a closed society resting on orthodoxy and authoritarianism. Tauber, a former Harvard teaching fellow and official with the Massachusetts Civil Defense Agency, expresses concern that attacks on liberal education could put an end to the United States as an open society.

170. Taylor, Harold. "The Dismissal of Fifth Amendment Professors." **Annals of the American Academy of Political and Social Science** 300: 79-86, July 1955.

Taylor argues that the refusal to answer political questions in public is no reason for revoking tenure, since the criteria by which tenure is awarded have to do with scholarship and teaching ability. Political opinions or affiliations are not in and of themselves relevant to the question of fitness for teaching. Also, dismissal of professors who exercise their rights of citizenship betrays the responsibility of the university to society. Taylor discusses the 1948 University of Washington dismissal of tenured Communist and suspected Communist professors as an antecedent to the McCarthy and Jenner Committees. He discusses a number of specific Fifth Amendment dismissals, including those at Rutgers, the University of Vermont, and Harvard.

171. Wieder, Alan. "The *Brown* Decision, Academic Freedom, and White Resistance: Dean Chester Travelstead and the University of South Carolina." **Equity and Excellence in Education** 28(3): 45-49, December 1995.

Wieder reviews the academic freedom case of Chester Travelstead at the University of South Carolina. Travelstead was Dean of the School of Education from 1953 until 1956, when he was fired for publicly supporting integration. At the time, segregation was widely supported by both the state legislature and Governor George Timmerman. In response to a pro-segregation speech by the Governor, Travelstead wrote a letter to the Governor challenging some of the statements in that speech. He received no response to this letter. Later, in a speech to students and faculty in the School of Education, Travelstead "bemoaned the silence of educators and professional organizations in South Carolina that might support integration..." (P. 47). Because of these public statements favoring integration, the university's Board of Trustees fired Travelstead. While his firing was supported by many members of the public, others suggested that Travelstead's firing was a violation of his academic freedom and a clear indication that university officials would not tolerate contrary opinions regarding segregation.

172. Wright, Quincy. "The Citizen's Stake in Academic Freedom." **Journal of Higher Education** 20(7): 339-345, October 1949.

Wright begins by explaining a broader conception of world rather than national citizenship. Problems of war and poverty require such a broad understanding of citizenship and also require universities to be bound by principles of academic freedom if solutions are to be found. These universities are microcosms of the world, places where truth is an always evolving process that develops through the interaction of different ideas and free discussion of a variety of opinions. Wright concludes by discussing the too-narrow concept of Americanism and the too-narrow conception of the university which motivate proposed Illinois legislation designed to keep Communists out of teaching posts.

Chapter 5

Academic Freedom—History (1960-1979)

173. American Association of University Women. "AAUW Board Resolution on Academic Freedom." **AAUW Journal** 60(1): 2, October 1966.

The full text of this 1966 Resolution is presented in support of the principles of academic freedom. Branches and state divisions are encouraged "to make known this supporting position at appropriate times and in appropriate circumstances."

174. American Civil Liberties Union. **Academic Freedom and Civil Liberties of Students in Colleges and Universities.** New York: American Civil Liberties Union, 1970. 45p.

The ACLU argues that students are deserving of the same academic freedom rights as teachers. These guidelines cover such topics as: the student as a member of the academic community, freedoms of extra-curricular activity, political and personal freedoms, regulatory/disciplinary procedures and due process, students and the military, and the confidentiality of student records. An appendix covers recent court decisions on student rights.

175. Baldridge, J. Victor, David V. Curtis, George P. Ecker and, Gary L. Riley. "The Impact of Institutional Size and Complexity on Faculty Autonomy." **Journal of Higher Education** 44(7): 532-548, Oct. 1973.

This essay recounts a survey conducted by the Stanford Center for Research and Development in Teaching, called the Stanford Project on Academic Governance. Data were gathered from a random sample of 249 representative U.S. colleges, universities, and community colleges on the question of whether institutional size and complexity affects academic autonomy. Impact was measured using such issues as:

peer evaluation, departmental autonomy, freedom from administrative work regulations and overall decision decentralization. Among the findings is the assertion of a positive relationship between institution size and many aspects of professional autonomy. The authors describe a "professional autonomy index combined measure" of 54% advantage for large institutions, 41% for medium, and 33% for small.

176. Bowen, Howard R.   "Philanthropy and Academic Freedom."   **Liberal Education** 60(2): 168-174, May 1974.

Bowen argues that philanthropy is a "bulwark" of intellectual and academic freedom. It allows private schools to maintain their independence and thus serve as models of academic excellence and academic freedom.   This benefits public institutions as well, since it helps to maintain high standards of freedom and academic excellence. This is especially valuable in the current period, when the academic freedom and independence of public colleges and universities is compromised by a growing maze of regulations and accountability measures. Bowen suggests that philanthropy is needed to "resuscitate" the freedom and diversity in higher education. To accomplish this, new tax laws are needed that will provide tax concessions and thereby increase philanthropy. This promotes diversity and independence in higher education, which serves the public good..

177. Brewster, Kingman, Jr. "Academic Freedom and Federal Largesse." **Journal of Teacher Education** 26(2): 155-159, 1975.

Brewster calls "liberty" America's "distinctive genius." Though affluence and efficiency loom large in contemporary society, we must continue to put liberty and "having a choice" first. In higher education, this means we need to protect diversity, self-determination, personal choice and academic freedom. However, Brewster points to three threats that could endanger these freedoms: demographics (i.e., fewer students); inflation; and technology that displaces publications and classroom teaching. In tight economic times, universities may seek more support from the government. But such support may come with strings attached in the form of short-term funding, efficiency measures, and regulated uniformity. These could stifle innovation on campus, which is exactly why the government should not be the main influence in the acquisition and transmission of knowledge, says Brewster. Instead, we need strong state support for education that allows for self-determination, variety and choice.

178. Bronfenbrenner, Martin. "Notes on Marxian Economics in the United States." **American Economic Review** 54(6): 1019-1025, December 1964.

The author describes a perceived decline in diversity of economics theories presented at U.S. colleges and in particular a decline since World War II in the teaching of Marxian economics. Bronfenbrenner does not see violations of academic freedom in this decline, which is due less to outright discrimination or the invalidity of Marxist economic ideas than to the fact that few students at U.S. institutions are required to study Marxian theory, and to the fact that there are very few universities that go out of their way to employ Marxists in their economics faculties.

179. Brown, Michael E. "Academic Freedom in the State's University: The Ollman Case as a Problem for Theory and Practice." **New Political Science** 1(1): 30-46, Spring 1979.

The author sketches out the dilemma he sees in attempting to defend, by calling on the principles of academic freedom rather than the strategies of trade unionism, Marxist teachers in American state universities. Brown holds that universities such as the University of Maryland that are incorporated into the state are no longer places to which traditional arguments about academic freedom apply. Abstract principles of academic freedom and freedom of expression do not apply in state universities, where selection of teachers and curricula are handled by administrators more frequently. As an example, Brown cites the 1978 case of Bertell Ollman's lawsuit against the University of Maryland for overturning the Department of Government and Politics search committee's choice of Ollman for departmental chairperson. The author concludes by outlining a radical Marxist strategy for dealing with cases like Ollman's. In this strategy, the university is treated as a part of the state and the burden of proof in cases of denial of tenure or failure to rehire falls entirely on the university rather than on the professor in question.

180. Bunting, Mary I., Patricia A. Graham and Elga R. Wasserman. "Academic Freedom and Incentives for Women." **Educational Record** 51(4): 386-391, Fall 1970.

There have been historical trends of bias in academic freedom wherein women have been discouraged or prevented from entering the academic mainstream. However, progress is being made in opening up opportunities and in providing for more equality of status among women and men in academia. Focusing largely on women, especially those married to academics or to students, these authors note advances in such areas as increasing flexibility of part-time appointments, opportunities for research leave for part-time instructors, provision of institutional support for unaffiliated scholars married to faculty or staff, and such advances at the undergraduate level as co-residential housing and an increasing proportion of women in undergraduate classes. Programs for part-time instruction at Princeton and for research leave at the Radcliffe Institute are noted as promising examples of academic incentives and freedoms provided for women.

181. Bunzel, John H. "Costs of the Politicized College." **Educational Record** 50(2): 131-137, Spring 1969.

Concerned about political activities and protest on college campuses, the Chair of the Department of Political Science at San Francisco State College gave this testimony before the House Committee on Education and Labor Special Subcommittee on Education. Cited as threats to the freedoms to teach and learn are: a bomb found (and defused) outside his office door; a recent teacher's strike; and a student strike called as a result of the Black Students Union and Third World Liberation Front protests. The author claims that radicals were forcing the college to call police and "forcing the police to use clubs and violence." Bunzel describes the suspensions of students who consistently interrupted his lectures with Maoist shouts and verbal abuse and contends that the "inviolability of the classroom" is at the heart of academic freedom. The point is made here that contemporary assaults on academic freedom frequently come from individuals or groups from outside the academy with whom most faculty members are sympathetic. Faculty members often therefore feel value conflicts in these situations.

182. Burbank, Gavin. "Reagan and Academic Freedom at Berkeley, 1966-1970." **Canadian Review of American Studies** 20(1): 17-30, Summer 1989.

Burbank begins by recounting Reagan's first campaign for public office (in 1966) when he campaigned for Governor on a pledge that if elected he would "clean up the mess" at Berkeley. This essay recounts the concern felt by many Berkeley professors that Reagan would attack academic freedom, and the awkward position they were caught in regarding police action against violent student protest. An overview of the history leading up to Berkeley's becoming what this author calls the "first international capital of student protest," and a discussion of the backlash of public opinion are tied in here with an analysis of the effect on Berkeley's academic freedom through the responses of Governor Reagan and the California Board of Regents. The controversy surrounding Black Panther Eldridge Cleaver's book *Soul on Ice*, his 1968 visiting professorship, and the 1969 violent attacks on white students and faculty by the Third World Liberation Front are recounted as situations that spurred an increasingly popular Reagan to clamp down on student disturbances.

183. Chamberlain, Philip C. "Legalism on Campus: A New Challenge to Academic Freedom?" **JGE: The Journal of General Education** 29(4): 311-319, Winter 1978.

Historically, generalized constraints on academic freedom have been uncommon. Rather, most violations have been localized or campus-based. According to Chamberlain, however, the new legal environment may change that. "Legalism" refers to various federal laws (e.g., affirmative action; Title IX) or campus governance structures (e.g., collective bargaining) that can impose across-the-board constraints on the academy and academic freedom. These more legalistic or rule-governed structures undermine the "decentralized control and shared responsibility" that traditionally led to institutional autonomy and faculty involvement in governance. Collegial forms of governance are less codified and more dictated by tradition and shared values or principles. However, increasingly large, complex and multi-campus universities have spawned more centralized and rational decision-making. Centralized control can lead to top-down management, which may gradually limit the knowledge, involvement and freedom of faculty. Rational and regulated decision-making may become more premoral, quantified and codified. Collective bargaining particularly contributes to this kind of environment, says Chamberlain.

184. Daniloff, Nicholas. "The Marxist vs. Maryland." **Washington Post Magazine** November 12, 1978, pp. 23-29.

This article recounts the case of Bertell Ollman, an Oxford-educated NYU professor and Marxist who was offered the Chairmanship of the University of Maryland Government and Politics Department. He sued after University President John Toll said he wouldn't approve the appointment. Chronicling his early anti-Stalinist years as a University of Wisconsin student in the 1950s, and his turn towards Marxism, this essay also addresses the dynamics of the search committee which chose Ollman, interviewing members of the committee, the department, and the Maryland Board of Regents.

185. Ericson, Edward E., Jr. "What the Radicals Did for Academic Freedom." **JGE: Journal of General Education** 29(4): 289-298, Winter 1978.

Discussing the New Left impact on discussion in the late 1960s on academic freedom, Ericson calls the most important impact of the movement on the academy an epistemological, not political or social impact. The questioning of truth and methods of searching for it affirmed the personal and artistic as valid sources and methods of seeking truth. The author calls the New Left's attack on the methodology of objectivity right but for the wrong reasons. Examples are provided of political and religious situations where an objectivist framework of academic freedom would not help. These examples include a Shakespeare professor critiquing the Vietnam War through his readings of the plays or a religious scholar injecting spiritual readings into courses of secular literature. Ericson calls for rewriting the standard definition of academic freedom to take into account the idea that knowledge is not value-free; that personal and artistic elements have a role in any search for truth; and that an objectivist methodology is not the only legitimate one.

186. Franklin, H. Bruce. "The Real Issues in My Case." **Change** 4(5): 31-39, June 1972.

Franklin addresses specific charges leveled against him by the Stanford Administration and an Advisory Board of seven full professors in their decision to revoke his tenure. Franklin claims that his tenure was revoked primarily on the basis of his political activity with a local Marxist group called Venceremos, which had as members other campus employees who were also fired. Franklin claims that the anti-Communist political views of the faculty members serving on the Advisory Board influenced both their eventual recommendation to revoke tenure and the prejudicial manner in which initial charges were brought only weeks after Franklin's dismissal. He attests that these changes were thus heard in a highly politicized atmosphere. Franklin was fired from a tenured position for inciting students to violence, although no criminal charges were ever brought against him.

187. Glazer, Nathan. "Why a Faculty Cannot Afford a Franklin." **Change** 4(5): 40-44, June 1972.

Glazer argues that tenured Marxist Associate Professor H. Bruce Franklin was dismissed not for political advocacy (a legally protected form of free speech), but for incitement to lawless acts (not legally protected under the First Amendment). Two critical issues in the case are: whether Franklin had been punished solely for his views (this author says no); and whether there should be more to consider than just freedom of speech in deciding if a professor should be censured, disciplined or fired for political activity on campus (this author says yes). Glazer argues that not disciplining Franklin (who was fired for allegedly inciting students to violence and vandalism against Stanford, though no criminal charges were ever brought) "would have represented truly the ultimate degradation of academic life in the United States."

188. Hechinger, Fred M. "Academic Freedom in America." **Change** 2(6): 32-36, November/December 1970.

A member of the New York Times Editorial Board, this author outlines many threats to academic freedom, making the claim that it was under attack in 1970 as much as it ever was at any previous time in the U.S. Mention is made of the overt influence and prejudice against student protesters and radical professors by such politicians as then-Vice President Agnew, and then-Governor of California Ronald Reagan, but also of "left-totalitarianism" exercised by radical elements on college campuses who drown out speakers with whose views they disagree, shut down classes, and vandalize campus buildings. Hechinger compares this state of affairs, with attacks to academic freedom coming from various quarters, with the McCarthy period when, as he puts it, "the enemy was so easy to identify."

189. Herring, Mark Youngblood. **Ethics and the Professor: An Annotated Bibliography, 1970-1985.** New York: Garland, 1988. 605p. (Garland Reference Library of the Humanities, v. 742). ISBN 0-8240-8491-8.

Academic freedom issues, and academic rank and tenure issues are addressed in subsections of a chapter on professional ethics. Annotations are provided for articles from professional journals and monographs, as well as from news weeklies like the *Chronicle of Higher Education* and the *Times Higher Education Supplement.* Other chapters cover such topics as (among others): religious education, justice, and ethical issues of scientific research.

190. Holbrook, Sandra L. and James C. Hearn. "Origins of Academic Freedom Litigation." **Review of Higher Education** 10(1): 47-61, Fall 1986.

Addressing the question of which parts of post-secondary educational systems are most likely to produce academic-freedom-related litigation, the author proposes three hypotheses: that such litigation is more likely in the public than private sectors; that, within the public sector, such litigation is more likely to occur in complex "multiversities" than in smaller or more narrowly focused institutions; that such litigated disputes are more likely to occur in the human and social sciences than in other disciplines. To investigate these hypotheses, court decisions made between 1957 and 1982 were examined relating to academic freedom issues. Findings include corroboration of all three hypotheses. Theoretical and practical implications are discussed in the conclusion, especially those related to politicization of higher education, conflict resolution, and the sort of administrative responsiveness which helps to decrease the likelihood of academic freedom litigations.

191. Hook, Sidney. **Academic Freedom and Academic Anarchy.** New York: Cowles, 1969. 269p. LC 79-90060. ISBN 402-12211-9.

Hook argues that the radical student movement of the 1960s, in the name of fighting for various causes, abridged academic freedom on campus. He is equally critical of some administrators and faculty who acquiesced to and supported these students either out of fear or out of a misguided liberalism. Hook focuses particular attention on the Columbia University student protests, the Berkeley Free Speech Movement, and Students for a Democratic Society (SDS). He argues forcefully that when students resort to violence and intimidation to achieve their goals, it constitutes a "war against the democratic process." Hook is also critical of the view that says the scholar's role is to help liberate humanity. Herbert Marcuse is singled out for particular criticism in this regard. What happens when competing social "goods" collide, Hook asks, or when what is good collides with what is true? Resolving such issues should fall within the realm of politics, not scholarship. Appended are three articles or reprints on Berkeley, Columbia, and the University of Colorado.

192. Hook, Sidney, ed. **In Defense of Academic Freedom.** New York: Pegasus, 1971. 266p. LC 78-154562.

With a few exceptions, most of the articles in this edited collection represent critiques of the radical student movement of the late 1960s and 1970s and its effect on academic freedom. The dominant theme throughout is that this student movement was a genuine threat to academic freedom. According to the authors, radical students were attempting to politicize the university and force it to accommodate and support their political positions of radical social reform and opposition to the Vietnam War. This effort compromised the universities' openness to all points of view and its underlying goal of the objective pursuit of truth. Furthermore, in their zealous pursuit of their political goals, this minority of radical students infringed on the academic freedom of other students and faculty. This was reflected in such actions as campus sit-ins and the disruption of classes, according to some of the authors. Faculty were also criticized by some of the contributors for not staunchly defending academic freedom and for acquiescing to student demands and behavior. Contributors to this volume include Sidney Hook, Bruno Bettelheim, Henry Steele Commager, Jacques Barzun, Kenneth Clarke, Paul Kurtz, and John Searle, among others.

193. Hook, Sidney.   "The Principles and Problems of Academic Freedom." **Contemporary Education** 58(1): 6-12, Fall 1986.

According to Hook, academic freedom is a special right bestowed upon qualified teachers who are seeking the truth in their research and teaching. Academic freedom protects them in this search, even if their work appears to be wrong or unpopular. As Hook puts it, the scholar has "the right to heresy" in his or her field of expertise. The corresponding obligation is to be free of any ideology, whether religious or political, that might preclude the honest and open search for truth. Furthermore, faculty must be willing to take the unpopular stance of pointing out and disciplining violations of academic freedom within their own ranks.   This will prevent the unwelcome interference into academic affairs by outsiders, such as legislative oversight committees or watchdog groups like Accuracy in Academia. The activities of both kinds of groups are a threat to academic freedom, says Hook.

194. Hook, Sidney. "Who is Responsible for Campus Violence?" **Saturday Review** 52(16): 22-25, 54-55, April 19, 1969.

Hook points out that disruptions of campus speakers and classes by student protesters are widespread. He reviews some of the circumstances surrounding protests at Berkeley and Columbia and finds fault with faculty and administrators who do not protest this student violence. Why haven't campus rules and laws been invoked to punish these disruptions of academic freedom? Hook blames ritualistic liberals who seem unwilling to defend the underlying processes that support intellectual freedom on campus. Due process in the academic community requires the protection of reason and freedom in the pursuit of truth. By failing to respond to transgressions, university officials make matters worse. They must be willing to use police, if necessary, to preserve campus freedom and to prevent the coercion imposed by student protesters. Hook blames apathetic faculty for not upholding academic freedom and the "integrity of the educational process." However, campuses should also be open to hearing student grievances and proposals.

195. Katz, David A. "Faculty Salaries, Promotions and Productivity at a Large University." **American Economic Review** 63(3): 469-477, June 1973.

The author, a professor of economics, presents his findings in a quantitative study of the evaluation and rewarding of university professors. Interviews were conducted with department heads of a large university on their criteria for salary and promotion decisions; research ability, publication record, and national reputation were found to be the most important factors. Katz gathered data from university records and measured how these factors impacted some 596 professors at assistant or higher grades in eleven humanities, social science, hard science, and engineering departments. A regressive analysis was done to examine the effect of nineteen independent variables on salary and rank. Among Katz's conclusions are: that tenure does not seem to negatively impact lifelong productivity (as measured by publication record); that women are paid less than men; and that there are very uneven distributions of rewards across departments, with little written policy on the weighting of various criteria. Also found lacking are clear methods for ranking teaching performance. One expressed goal of the author is that quantitative analysis such as this could help administrators institute more equitable systems of evaluating and rewarding faculty members.

196. Kilgore, William J. "Academic Freedom in Texas." **Academe** 65(3): 177-185, April 1979.

This article recounts fifty years of Texan academic freedom issues. With seven AAUP-censured institutions, Texas in 1979 was the state with the largest number of censured institutions in the history of the AAUP. While Kilgore does not systematically recount all Texas cases, he does review some of the better known ones, including violations of academic freedom at the University of Texas, Texas Tech, Sam Houston State, Texas A & M, Odessa Jr. College, and community colleges generally. Academic freedom practices and policies vary widely among Texas colleges; these differences are here discussed.

197. Kilgore, William J. and Barbara Sullivan. "Academic Values and the Jensen-Shockley Controversy." **JGE: Journal of General Education** 27(3): 177-187, Fall 1975.

The authors address the academic freedom issues related to scientific claims made by William Shockley and Arthur Jensen for a racially-associated genetic basis for intelligence. Attacks on the freedom to express views linking intelligence and race came from some in academia who held that racism should not be given legitimacy by debating these theories on scientific grounds. Academic freedom, according to Kilgore and Sullivan, is not just a fundamental educational value but could also be of utilitarian value in this controversy by helping to weed out the substantive scientific claims and methodologies from the emotional and derogatory labeling engaged in by some critics. In the second section of this essay the authors question the internal validity of some of Jensen's findings as well as the generalizability of some of his claims. The authors conclude that further research into the possible genetic basis of IQ is justified, as conclusive evidence has not yet been found.

198. Kirk, Russell. "Central Political Power and Academic Freedom." **JGE: Journal of General Education** 29(4): 255-264, Winter 1978.

Kirk addresses the threat to academic freedom of federal government influence and interference in the work of universities. Various fund granting institutions, OSHA regulations, affirmative action, and Title IX are examples of the federalizing of higher education that has taken place between World War II and the early 1970s. University governance is more and more dictated by governmental bureaucracies and regulations.

199. Kohn, Hans. "Academic Freedom." In Hans Kohn. **Not by Arms Alone: Essays On Our Time.** Freeport, NY: Books for Libraries, 1971. pp. 33-39. (Essay Index Reprint Series). ISBN 0-8369-2461-4.

Kohn argues that academic freedom is a duty of the teacher as well as a right. Free scholarship and open questioning are only possible within a liberal political system. Enemies of academic freedom, of free speech, and of self-determination may not use academic freedom in their fight against it. Those who care about academic freedom should fight for freedom generally, not just in the university but also outside the college and outside the community.

200. Ladd, Everett Carll Jr. and Seymour Martin Lipset. **The Divided Academy: Professors and Politics.** New York: McGraw Hill, sponsored by the Carnegie Commission on Higher Education, 1975. 407p. ISBN 0-0701-0112-4.

The authors conducted a 1972 survey of 523 academics regarding their political views, structural and political sources of division between professors and disciplines, and some specific case studies, including 1960s era protests, the 1972 presidential election, and unionization. A remarkable consistency in ideas across a wide range of issues was found, with ideological thinking commonly found to be the source of polarization and controversy. This 1972 survey was based in large part on a 1969 Carnegie Commission Survey of Student and Faculty Opinion. Texts of both questionnaires, and some statistical information, are provided in appendices.

201. Lewis, Lionel S. "Faculty Support of Academic Freedom and Self-Government." **Social Problems** 13(4): 450-461, Spring 1966.

A 1964 survey of all 915 full time faculty at a northeastern U.S. state university examined two hypotheses: 1) that faculty in different schools or colleges within the same institution will have differing views on academic freedom and self-government; and 2) that faculty of different disciplines within the same institution will have differing views on academic freedom. Questions were posed regarding three aspects of academic freedom: adherence to academic freedom principles; belief about the wisdom of practicing academic freedom; and under what conditions it should be defended. Little unqualified commitment to academic freedom was found; in those areas in which over one half of faculty approve of academic freedom it is a belief in its principles rather than its practice that was approved. Reasons behind the opinions of those who believed that academic freedom should be restricted include the following (among others): mistrust of the survey and project; the potential jeopardy of defending academic freedom; the idea that it should be subordinate to the institutional interests. Some of the differences noted between faculties of schools or disciplines are explained by noting that those who feel most threatened are those most in favor of academic freedom and faculty self-governance.

202. Magsino, Romulo F. "Student Academic Freedom and the Changing Student/University Relationship." In Kenneth A. Strike and Kieran Egan, editors. **Ethics and Educational Policy.** Boston: Routledge & Kegan Paul, 1978. pp. 36-57. ISBN 0-7100-8423-4. LC 77-30516.

The author addresses various legal and academic justifications offered for student academic freedom, offers a definition of student academic freedom and concludes by elaborating on specific freedoms that student academic freedom encompasses. Included are primarily academic freedoms, or those freedoms which will further a student's search for and understanding of knowledge and truth.

203. Mainzer, Lewis C. "Scientific Freedom in Government-Sponsored Research." **Journal of Politics** 23(2): 212-230, May 1961.

The author examines the limits that political and bureaucratic pressures impose on federally-funded scientific freedoms, asking whether the freedoms necessary for scientific research are too much abridged by such pressures. Various means by which freedom of research is curtailed include: the pre-set goals of program planning by federal agencies, the differing allotments of funds from one Congress to the next, the undue influence of politicians and interest groups on project selection, research process or publication. The author concludes that neither productivity nor scientific integrity are unduly compromised by federal support. Though the pressures that come with federal funding are considerable, Mainzer concludes that the necessary scientific freedoms remain largely unabridged.

204. Matveev, V.M. "American Students for the Democratization of Education in Opposition to the Reactionary Direction of U.S. Foreign Policy." **Soviet Education** 13(1): 37-57, November 1970.

Matveev recounts the strengthening ties between American higher education, corporations, and the Nixon government as background for a discussion of progressive, radical, and anti-war student-led organizations and the resistance they posed to attempts to inculcate university students with anti-Communist and pro-capitalist ideals. Among the student organizations discussed are Black Panthers, Students for a Democratic Society, Association of Students of Mexican Origin.

205. Metzger, Walter P., et al. **Dimensions of Academic Freedom.** Urbana, Ill.: University of Illinois Press, 1969. 121p. LC 68-24623.

Included here are the texts of four lectures presented at a University of Illinois series on "Dimensions of Academic Freedom." Walter Metzger's essay suggests that colleges and universities have become delocalized institutions, thus increasing the influence of outside interests and processes that create new constraints on academic freedom. Some of these outside forces include the growth and economic impact of higher education, its centralized governance by states, the student movement, and the influence of political and research funding agencies. These influences were unanticipated at the AAUP's founding in 1915, and they suggest the need to reconceptualize the conditions needed to protect academic freedom. Sanford Kadish's essay argues that professorial strikes, whether for economic, academic, or political reasons, are unprofessional. However, he does discuss exceptional circumstances under which strikes may be acceptable. Arthur DeBarteleben's essay examines various external constituencies of the university and the threats some have posed to academic freedom. These constituencies may be political or, if they relate to university funding and research support, economic. He argues that academic freedom must be defended aggressively by faculty, administrators, and trustees in the face of any incursions by external constituencies. Finally, Edward Bloustein's essay argues that the hierarchical and paternalistic college system of the past has been undermined by a number of developments: 1) the growth, specialization, and social utility of knowledge; 2) the perception of college as a national resource; 3) the more active role of students in the learning process; and 4) the alienation, skepticism, and independent mindedness of contemporary students. All of these are factors explaining the student activism of the 1960s and the accompanying demise of academic authority.

206. Monro, John U. "The Black College Dilemma." **Educational Record** 53(2): 132-37, Spring 1972.

In a society still marked by racism, the black college is one of the few examples of institutional strength within the black community. Monro outlines some of the history, and some of the dilemmas, choices and conflicts of principle faced by these unique institutions. One dilemma is over the role of the black college in fostering community self-awareness and the necessary skills to fight an oppressive white power structure vs. fostering skills necessary to achieve personal success by blacks who end up participating in the institutions of general society. Monro calls for both activities, but has no clear answers to other dilemmas, such as whether to encourage the best and brightest freshman students to transfer to bigger and more prestigious state universities; or how black colleges should reach out to high school dropouts and other undereducated youth. Monro recommends strong teacher recruiting, soliciting assistance from business and cooperative faculty-exchange programs with predominantly white universities.

207. **Neutrality or Partisanship: A Dilemma of Academic Institutions.** New York: Carnegie Foundation for the Advancement of Teaching, 1971. 82p. (Bulletin, no. 34). LC 72-177054.

This volume reprints addresses made at the 1970 annual meeting of the Carnegie Foundation by Fritz Machlup, Walter P. Metzger, and Richard H. Sullivan. All three address the issue of social action and university neutrality. Machlup, in an essay entitled "European Universities as Partisans" addresses the history of the university and the slow development in Europe of the ideal of a non-partisan, secular institution of higher education. A brief bibliography on the subject is presented here as well. Also reprinted here for the first time is the text of a statement distributed by Machlup at Princeton in October of 1969 called "The Faculty: A Body Without Mind or Voice" in which he urges the impropriety of any faculty-sponsored "official" pronouncements on political, social or other issues of the day. Metzger, in "Institutional Neutrality, An Appraisal" addresses the issue of when and how institutions (rather than individuals) should take stands on public issues. He recounts how current pressures might modify Arthur Lovejoy's 1915 call for unflinching neutrality in institutions of higher education. Sullivan's essay "The Socially Involved University" addresses then-current attacks on academic freedom, tenure, and institutional neutrality and provides some recommendations about when a university should deliberately engage in social or political action.

208. Nixon, Richard M. "Academic Freedom: A Force in Human History." **Vital Speeches of the Day** 32(18): 550-552, July 1, 1966.

The 1966 Commencement Address at the University of Rochester, this speech addresses the limits that should be placed during wartime on "the four academic freedoms": freedom of the student to study and to engage openly in political activity; freedom of teaching and research; "freedom of the student from tyranny of the faculty, and conversely, freedom of the faculty from student tyranny." Nixon holds that those who openly advocate minority viewpoints such as Marxism should be protected by academic freedom, as should those who demonstrate their protest against the war effort. Yet he holds that a line must be drawn between those who exercise the rights that freedom protects and "those who would welcome victory for the enemy." To protect academic freedom, we must "defend it from its own excesses."

209. Pierce, Martin. "The Challenge to Academic Freedom: Part I and Part II." **Liberation** 11(7): 26-30, October 1966; 11(8): 34-37, November 1966.

Pierce recounts events from 1963 through 1965 at the University of Minnesota where student groups and specific professors were attacked in the press and on campus as Communist sympathizers by influential members of the Minnesota Legion. The lack of support by the university administration for academic freedom of the Student Peace Union and World Affairs Center, the campus debates between Professor Mulford Q. Silbey and Legionnaire Milton Rosen, and the involvement of local politicians, the local AAUP and ACLU are all described.

210. Radosh, Ronald. "An Interview with Eugene Genovese: The Rise of a Marxist Historian." **Change** 10(10): 31-35, November 1978.

Genovese, a Marxist historian recently elected president of the Organization of American Historians, is interviewed by Radosh on the tolerance of and freedom accorded Marxists in the academy. He disagrees somewhat with H. Bruce Franklin's contention that the late 1970s are as bad as the McCarthy period. Still, he concedes that Franklin's point is "well taken" and that the tolerance of some well-regarded Marxist academics masks a harder academic existence for the younger scholars. Furthermore, a saturated academic market makes it difficult to determine when Marxists are denied jobs because of their politics. Genovese believes that the field of history is further along in accepting Marxist scholars than other fields. Nonetheless, Marxist historians have had difficulty establishing an institutional base, particularly in the training of graduate students. This is a critical component in the legitimation and advancement of the perspective. Genovese also talks about the quality and mindset of contemporary students, and explains his rationale for publishing in a politically diverse collection of journals and magazines.

211. Slaughter, Sheila. "Academic Freedom in the Modern American University." In Philip G. Altbach and Robert O. Berdahl, editors. **Higher Education in American Society.** Rev. ed. Buffalo, N.Y.: Prometheus Books, 1987. pp. 77-105. (Frontiers of Education). ISBN 0-8797-5420-6.

Slaughter provides an historical context for academic freedom and then an analysis of fifty-nine academic freedom cases investigated during the 1970s by the AAUP. Problems in this decade are noted in areas of financial exigency, the extra-curricular civil and political liberties of professors, increasing workloads and increasing administrative control over those workloads, and a proliferation of public-private, university-industry and university-military partnerships. See entry #293 for a similar article by this author on the decade of the 1980s.

212. Stumpf, Samuel E. "Freedom and Order on Campus." **Liberal Education** 56(1): 22-27, March 1970.

Stumpf argues that each segment of an academic community (students, faculty, administration, trustees) should be accorded only those freedoms which do not conflict with the minimum requirements of order needed to keep the other segments functioning. Student-initiated campus shut-downs are cited as an example of "exaggerated and reckless expressions of freedom" that destroy order in academic communities. Stumpf calls for a consensus among those serving each function to rededicate themselves to their own primary function and clarify common objectives. This essay is based on a speech given at the 1970 meeting of the Association of American Colleges; another version appeared as "Freedom and Order on the Campus" in the Nov. 1970 issue of *School and Society* (98(2328): 401-403).

213. Whiting, Albert N. "Apartheid in American Higher Education." **Educational Record** 53(2): 128-131, Spring 1972.

The President of North Carolina Central University argues that encouraging black cultural centers or dormitories hinders the goal of integration and encourages separatism and polarization between black and white students on college campuses. Despite the proliferation of black identity groups on campuses, any attempt to "mollify" black students is argued here as being against the best interests of students. Four reasons are cited to back up this argument: unbridgeable social distances between groups only encourage xenophobic and prejudicial tendencies; black separatists often engage in "indoctrination" and intimidation of incoming black students; curricular and extra-curricular experiences are too closely circumscribed by "the Black Power frame of reference;" and conspiratorial goals to "foment strife" and resegregate are the actual aims of black campus groups -- these being groups allied with nationally and internationally organized revolutionary and fascist movements. The author concludes by arguing that special handling of minority cases (such as establishing all-black admissions boards) is very close to "a kind of Neo-South African apartheid."

214. Williamson, E. G. and John L. Cowan. "Academic Freedom for Students: Issues and Guidelines." In Lawrence E. Dennis and Joseph F. Kauffman, editors. **The College and the Student: An Assessment of Relationships and Responsibilities in Undergraduate Education by Administrators, Faculty Members and Public Officials.** Washington, D.C.: American Council on Education, 1966. pp. 252-283. LC 66-19518.

This essay presents the summary of findings from a 1964 survey of students' existing academic freedoms, with some guidelines recommended for implementing or enacting more formal sets of such freedoms. Also presented is a comparison of different methods for establishing student rights and freedoms. The authors devised six scales for use in "objective measurement of academic freedom for students," including freedom of discussing political/social issues, freedom of discussing religious/moral issues, freedom for inviting off-campus speakers (including two scales for acceptable and unacceptable speakers), freedom of mode of student expression (e.g., sit-ins or student government resolutions), and freedom to engage in civil rights activities. Surveys were sent to presidents as well as student leaders. Among findings here presented is that institutions with greater student involvement in policy making had presidents who were more enthusiastic about the benefit of this practice.

215. Wilson, Edward O. "The Attempt to Suppress Human Behavioral Genetics." **JGE: Journal of General Education** 29(4): 277-287, Winter 1978.

The author discusses opposition to the study of sociobiology from the radical left, and in particular from an organization called Science for the People and its journal of the same name. Critics charge that this science is thinly veiled racism, with little scientific merit. This author argues against most of these claims and calls for more objective scientific study on the genetic basis for criminal behavior, with independent evaluations of the results. Wilson charges that groups like Science for the People engage in tactics of politicizing science that undermine scientific freedom, encourage ideologically-oriented pseudo-science, and muddy the important distinction between ethical gathering of data and objective testing of scientific theories once data have been collected.

216. Wronski, Stanley P. "UNESCO and the Academic Community: An Analysis of the Ethics of Academic Boycotts." **Theory and Research in Social Education** 5(2): 81-96, August 1977.

Wronksi recounts a case study of a United Nations Educational, Scientific, and Cultural Organization and National Council for the Social Sciences (NCSS) co-sponsored conference on "the role of the social sciences in education for peace and human rights." The study describes the fallout at Michigan State University after a pressure group called "The Committee for an Effective UNESCO" convinced M.S.U. to withdraw their official hosting of the conference and introduced a motion at the NCSS to censure the organization for its involvement. Specific background is provided on the proponents of an academic boycott of UNESCO and on this, the only un-cancelled UNESCO meeting on a U.S. campus in 1976. The author, a past President of N.C.S.S. , accompanies this case study with a theoretical discussion of ethical and educational authority as they relate to international affairs. Also addressed are the implications of the controversy for social science educators and the NCSS.

Chapter 6

Current Issues and General Trends

217. Abrams, Kathryn, W.B. Carnochan, Henry Louis Gates, Jr., and Robert M. O'Neil. **The Limits of Expression in American Intellectual Life.** Washington, D.C.: American Council of Learned Societies, 1993. 31p. (ACLS Occasional Paper, no. 22). LC 94-175225.

Invited speakers presented papers at the 1993 annual meeting of the ACLS on the issue of whether limits on freedom of expression in artistic and intellectual discourse were justifiable or a good idea. Abrams, in an essay called "Creeping Absolutism and Moral Impoverishment: The Case for Limits on Freedom of Expression," argues that such limits are needed in order to encourage both more rigorously systematic thinking and greater respect for politically marginalized groups. Carnochan, in an essay called "Art, Transgression, Shock, and the First Amendment," discusses the issues of obscenity and artistic freedom, concluding that the quality and power of art has diminished through too much use of shock value. Gates, in "Truth or Consequences: Putting Limits on Limits" speaks against limits of expression in the arena of hate speech and obscenity in intellectual discourse. O'Neil, in "Free Expression in the Academy: Three Hard Cases that Test Easy Assumptions" presents brief vignettes on research (The Pioneer Fund's support for research with arguably racist ends), teaching (Prof. Michael Levin's lectures on race at CUNY), and a case that touches on extracurricular views and freedom of teaching (Prof. Philip Bishop's religious proselytizing in his physical education classes at the University of Alabama). O'Neil suggests that these present more substantial abrogations of academic freedoms than issues of speech codes and political correctness, and that academics should not be distracted from the hard cases.

218. Ambrose, Charles M. "Academic Freedom in American Public Colleges and Universities." **Review of Higher Education** 14(1): 5-32, Fall 1990.

This study attempts to determine how faculty and administrators define academic freedom and whether differing campus constituencies exhibit broad variations in attitudes towards academic freedom. Perceptions of academic freedom's definition are compared with the general "taxonomy" by which academic freedom has come to be defined by the courts and in professional literature. The five areas of protection identified by the author as being encompassed by standard definitions of academic freedom include: the faculty member's political or religious beliefs; his or her teaching/ classroom discussions; research/scholarship; personal conduct outside the classroom; and, institutional academic freedom. A survey was mailed to a random sample of full-time teaching faculty and to all academic administrators and department chairs within the Georgia public university system. Findings include that administrators and faculty hold similar values towards academic freedom. However, differing responses by these groups to specific case studies cited in the survey indicate important differences between perceptions or interpretations of the concept and potential actions. Among the author's concluding recommendations is a call for better clarification of roles and responsibilities among administrators and faculty.

219. Benjamin, Ernst, and Donald R. Wagner, eds. **Academic Freedom: An Everyday Concern.** San Francisco: Jossey-Bass, 1994. 105p. (New Directions in Higher Education, Number 88, Winter 1994). LC 85-644752. ISBN 0-7879-9987-3.

Academic freedom is more than just a protection for the occasional faculty member who, in the pursuit of knowledge and truth, challenges the orthodoxies of departments, institutions, and disciplines. It is also part of the infrastructure of higher education, contributing in many subtle ways to the learning enterprise and the overall mission of educational institutions. The various contributors to this edited collection focus on some of these fundamental contributions of and threats to academic freedom. The seven articles address: the constraints on teaching and learning imposed by speech codes and outcomes assessment (William W. Pendleton); the distinctions between freedom to teach and harassment (Mary W. Gray); the dangers posed by corporate and state involvement in scholarly research (Paul M. Fischer); the parallels between academic freedom and artistic expression (Carol Simpson Stern); the denial of academic freedom in the context of faculty participation in academic governance (Sheila Slaughter); the necessity of including intramural speech within the protection of academic freedom (David M. Rabban); and the mutually supportive relationship between institutional accreditation and academic freedom (Sandra E. Elman).

220. Bennett, James T. and Manuel H. Johnson. "The Future of the Modern University: Demographics, Academic Freedom and Collectivism." **The Journal of Social and Political Studies** 5(1 / 2): 149-153, Spring/Summer 1980.

The authors address threats in the 1980s to the United States higher education system. Identifying academic freedom and merit as the foundations of the American university, Bennett and Johnson cite the demographics of declining enrollment and the increase of faculty collective bargaining as direct threats to these fundamental attributes of higher education. Reduced enrollment results in economic hardships which can result in faculty dismissal and closing of academic departments. When the increasing production of Ph.D.'s is factored in, the threat to the tenure system from financial exigency and an oversupply of available instructors may be severe. Unionization poses a direct threat to merit, say these authors, in that it is a system stressing seniority over ability. Required dues payment and collective bargaining processes both are opposed to the individualism that academic freedom protects.

221. Berry, Bonnie. "The Relationship Between Infringements on the Freedom to Research and Teach and Poor Sociological Practice." **The American Sociologist** 25(3): 53-65, Fall 1994.

Focusing specifically on sociology, Berry examines many subtle infringements on teaching and research that originate both within and outside of institutions. Applied sociology is more susceptible to infringement than pure research (given that it relates to policy), is more likely to be funded, and is frequently funded by the government. Growing fiscal constraints on institutions and a more consumeristic approach to students can further erode freedom. In enrollment driven institutions, teaching behavior, standards, and expectations of students can be unfairly influenced by an institution's bottom line. Pleasing the student-consumer can loom too large in a faculty member's evaluation and, potentially, subsequent retention, tenure and promotion. This could create pressures to lower standards, curve grades, and generally "go easy" on students. While scholars cannot control political and economic constraints, they can enlist the assistance of professional organizations, such as the American Sociological Association, in examining and resisting internal constraints.

222. Bollinger, Lee C. "The Open-Minded Soldier and the University." **Michigan Quarterly Review** 32(1): 1-19, Winter 1993.

Delivered in 1992 as the Second Annual Davis, Markert, Nickerson Lecture on Academic and Intellectual Freedom, this text addresses the intolerance that the author sees within the university system. Bollinger's focus is on intellectual attitudes of faculty, administrators, and students, and on how these attitudes relate to the principle of academic freedom. Discussing the "dangers of belief" for increasing intolerance, Bollinger cites Isaiah Berlin's and Justice Oliver Wendell Holmes' similar leanings towards pluralism and tolerance. The author sees as a significant threat to academic freedom the tension between the need for commitment to belief and the impulse to intolerance.

223. Burch, David R.   **Academic Freedom: A Selected Bibliography Commemorating the Symposium on Academic Freedom.** Austin: University of Texas at Austin School of Law, Tarlton Law Library, 1987. 23p.

An unannotated guide to the literature, this selective bibliography cites books and legal articles on the following topics: the concept of academic freedom; the "modern controversies" of academic freedom in religious-affiliated institutions, and academic freedom's relation to loyalty oaths, communism and national security; student rights; secondary schools; other countries; and "academic freedom vs. society's 'right' to know."

224. Butters, Ronald R. "Free Speech and Academic Freedom." In A. Leigh De Neef and Craufurd D. Goodwin, editors. **The Academic's Handbook.** 2nd ed. Durham, N.C.: Duke University Press, 1995. pp. 81-90. ISBN 0-8223-1661-7. LC 95-16775.

Butters discusses what he sees as the vibrancy of free speech and academic freedom on current campuses. He describes how students, faculty, and administrators can help keep it that way. Butters distinguishes between the two freedoms and spells out the difference between academic freedom for students and academic freedom for faculty members. In the section on faculty, Butters takes issue with the assertions of Edward Shils in his essay "Do We Still Need Academic Freedom?" (see entry #290).

225. Cheney, Lynne V. **Telling the Truth: A Report on the State of the Humanities in Higher Education.** Washington, D.C.: National Endowment for the Humanities, September 1992. 60 p. LC 92-243131.

The Director of the National Endowment for the Humanities (NEH) discusses the politicization of scholarship and classroom teaching, citing such examples as campus speech codes and claims of undue pressure from feminist and leftist professors on students with differing political views. Cheney asserts that new theories or academic approaches to the issues of objectivity or universality in the pursuit of truth, such as poststructuralism or deconstruction, are dogmas which subvert teaching into mere indoctrination. Cheney goes on to discuss what she calls the "attack on standards" and claims that today's universities come close to requiring allegiance to a political agenda from students while allowing professors broader freedom of speech and inquiry. In a chapter on academic freedom, the author refers to the AAUP's 1915 code and its stressing of the importance of a disinterested pursuit of truth and knowledge, contrasting that with what she sees as today's more common politicized approaches to scholarship. Discussing what she sees as "Europhobic" attempts to increase the multiculturalism of high-school curricula in New York and California, Cheney also cites the AAUP's 1991 statement on the political correctness controversy as evidence of politicization of the humanities.

226. Christensen, John O. **Publish or Perish: A Selective Bibliography.** Monticello, Ill.: Vance Bibliographies, 1991. 10p. (Public Administration Series Bibliography, no. P3067). ISBN 0-7920-0787-5.

This is an annotated bibliography of books, articles and ERIC documents covering the pressure put on faculty members to publish. Criticism of this pressure, and the point of view of the professional librarian are focal points of this bibliography.

227. Dayal, Sahab. "White Collar Union-Management Relations: A Study of University Professors." **Journal of Collective Negotiations in the Public Sector** 21(3): 239-254, 1992.

The purpose of this study was to identify the collective bargaining issues and concerns that were most important to unionized faculty. Three faculty surveys were conducted during the 1980s at the same institution. Faculty were asked to rank their most important economic and professional priorities. While other research has suggested that "bread and butter" issues should predominate, the author found that academic freedom issues were rated highest by the faculty both in the professional category and in a combined ranking of professional and economic priorities.

228. DeGeorge, Richard T. "Affirmative Action and Tenure Decisions." In Steven M. Cahn, editor. **Affirmative Action and the University: A Philosophical Inquiry.** Philadelphia: Temple University Press, 1993. pp. 269-274. ISBN 1-5663-9030-3.

DeGeorge argues that while affirmative action is likely to be required for many years to come, improvements could be made to the recruitment and retention of women and minority professors. DeGeorge suggests that equal opportunity offices agree to not count as members of a target group under affirmative action guidelines those women and minority candidates who already have tenure-track positions. What this could help forestall is the "zero-sum game" of minority applicants being hired away from other university positions. The author also argues that goals or quotas, while worthwhile in the hiring process, should not be part of the tenuring process.

229. Dennis, Everette E. "Freedom of Expression, the University, and the Media." **Journal of Communication** 42(2): 73-82, Spring 1992.

The author, executive director of Columbia University's Freedom Forum Media Studies Center, discusses recent freedom of speech controversies on college campuses, including contemporary critiques of multiculturalism, political correctness and speech codes. An historical perspective is provided through reference to the University of Oregon and its long-standing tradition of support for the free speech rights of visiting speakers. These range from a 1920 visit by widely scorned pacifist Kirby Paige to a 1960s era visit by Gus Hall of the Communist Party of the U.S. The history goes on to cite the speech rights of students at the University of Oregon, who have a "free speech platform" erected in front of the student union. The author concludes by addressing the role of the press in the debate over freedom of expression on campus.

230. Dobson, Keith S.   "The Other Side of Academic Freedom is Academic Responsibility." **Canadian Psychology/Psychologie canadienne** 38(4): 244-247, November 1997.

Dobson argues that academic freedom, like other freedoms, is accompanied by responsibilities or limits.   While all individuals should be free to inquire, those engaged in teaching or research may be subject to limits because they are involving others in their inquiry. Teaching, in particular, legitimizes certain knowledge, a fact that may explain its prominence in the political correctness debate. Dobson says that legal (e.g., Constitutional), negotiated (e.g., bargaining agreements), and practical (e.g., economic factors, peer review, acceptable methodologies or theories, etc.) constraints may limit academic freedom. He similarly identifies limits on political correctness.   These should include an intolerance of dogma, limits on outside interference, the provision of a forum for debating issues and policies, and due process mechanisms for academic freedom disputes.

231. Dressel, Paul L. "The Nature and Components of Autonomy." **New Directions for Institutional Research** 7(2): 1-9, No. 26, 1980.

Institutional autonomy is an aspect of academic freedom, and no institution, public or private, is free of the expectations and needs of its students, donors, taxpayers, research grant providers, and others. To this extent, there are limitations on any institution's autonomy. Autonomy is granted with the expectation that the expected professional service will be provided and self-restraint and due process will be exercised. Dressel distinguishes between substantive and procedural autonomy. The former refers to freedom in the exercise of the basic institutional and professional mission. The institution and its members need to be granted considerable control over these matters, which can include such areas as curriculum development, degree granting, and hiring and promoting faculty.   Procedural autonomy refers to the expected oversight of the institution's fulfillment of its mission and the procedures, policies and operations implemented to achieve it. External oversight here is expected and permissible. Having made these distinctions, Dressel contends that institutional autonomy is eroding, and the remaining articles in this journal issue elaborate on that argument.

232. Elkins, Charles L. "From Plantation to Corporation: The Attack on Tenure and Academic Freedom in Florida." **Sociological Perspectives** 41(4): 757-765, Winter 1998.

Elkins argues that tenure and academic freedom have historically been at risk in Florida, which has a poor record on such matters. During the McCarthy period in the mid-1950s, the state legislature's Johns Committee searched out and fired faculty and expelled students who were considered communists or homosexuals. There was little or no due process afforded such individuals, and the committee's nine-years of activity was characterized as a "reign of terror." Elkins attributes much of this behavior to the fact that appointments to university presidencies were political appointments, and the state educational bureaucracy as a whole was a "good ole boys network." More recent policies in Florida indicate that not much has changed, says Elkins. Legislative homophobia still exists, and current attacks on tenure and academic freedom are based on criteria from the corporate world (i.e., efficiency, productivity, cost-benefit analysis). Tenure and academic freedom are considered impediments to a more market-oriented university system based on a corporate management model. Elkins concludes by observing that the corporate model may lead to higher tuition, with an accompanying decrease in access for the less affluent.

233. Epstein, Joseph. "A Case of Academic Freedom." **Commentary** 82(3): 37-47, September 1986.

Epstein recounts the case of denial of tenure to Northwestern University English Professor Barbara Foley, in large part due to her 1985 efforts with a student organization called InCAR (International Committee Against Racism) to shout down a campus speaker, Adolfo Calero (a leader of the U.S.-backed Nicaraguan Contra rebels). Officially reprimanded in 1986 by an ad-hoc faculty committee for this breach of academic freedom, Foley went on the same year to get a majority vote for tenure from her peers in the English Department. This vote was overturned by the Provost. Epstein disapproves of the activities of students and faculty on her behalf, as he feels that not tenuring Foley would support academic freedom, not violate it. (See entry #310 for the text, with commentary, of the President's decision denying tenure.)

234. Finn, Chester E. "The Campus: 'An Island of Repression in a Sea of Freedom.'" **Commentary** 88(3): 17-23, Sept. 1989.

Finn's commentary focuses on what he sees as constraints on free expression on campus that are imposed in order to promote diversity. He claims that these often have the same constraining effect on open inquiry as do more formal policies such as hate speech codes. Requirements that students take courses in race relations or cultural studies are seen here less as contributing to campus diversity and tolerance than as attempting to induce ideological conformity. Finn notes the low enrollment and high dropout rates among minority students as evidence that such "esoteric forms of affirmative action" are not helping.

235. Fogle, Pamela W. "Cold Confusion." **Currents** 17(4): 24-27, April 1991.

As Director of News and Information Services at the University of Utah, Fogle was involved from the beginning when in 1989 University of Utah electrochemists B. Stanley Pons and Martin Fleischmann announced that they had produced nuclear fusion at room temperatures (a claim later widely discredited). Fogle discusses the tensions between the researchers' legal need for secrecy because of pending patents, and the demands for openness by both news services and the academic peers of the scientists. Conflicts can arise, as they did in this case, between the needs for peer review and factual reporting and the proprietary rights of academic institutions and scientists. Fogle asserts that ongoing research on the topic of cold fusion must continue very quietly to avoid further controversy that might stifle the scientific process.

236. Fuentes, Carlos. "Free Trade in Ideas." **Academe** 75(5): 24-26, September-October 1986.

Fuentes, the famous Mexican novelist, recounts his long history of being refused entry into the United States under provisions of the McCarran-Walter Act of 1952. He was first denied entry into the United States in 1961, when he was to appear on television in a foreign policy debate over the Alliance for Progress. Though subsequently granted a visa at the time *The Death of Artemio Cruz* was published, it was nonetheless restrictive both in duration and in location (i.e., New York only). While Fuentes was refused visas on later occasions, his lawyers were ultimately able to obtain waivers from the McCarran-Walter restrictions. However, they were never able to find out the official reasons why he was blacklisted, despite requests made under the Freedom of Information Act. Nonetheless, Fuentes is sure that he was excluded for political reasons, despite the Helsinki Agreement of 1975 that mandated "free passage" of persons and ideas. The exclusionary clause, though waived in some cases, continues to impede the free exchange of people and ideas. Ultimately, it is the United States that suffers, says Fuentes.

237. Glazer, Nathan. "Levin, Jeffries, and the Fate of Academic Autonomy." **Public Interest** 120: 14-40, Summer 1995.

Glazer reviews the free speech/academic freedom cases of Michael Levin and Leonard Jeffries at the City College of New York and argues that academic autonomy and scholarly principles were sacrificed in the handling of the cases. Both Levin and Jeffries had generated controversy with public and allegedly racist statements they had made regarding blacks (Levin) and Jews (Jeffries). The university brought some sanctions against both professors, offering competing sections of Levin's course (taught by less controversial faculty) and reducing Jeffries' term as chair of the Black Studies department. These actions prompted both faculty members to sue the university and win free speech cases in court. According to Glazer, however, the university acted exactly the opposite of how it should have acted were it motivated by support for scholarly inquiry and academic freedom. The university undermined Levin, whose controversial positions were an outgrowth of his scholarly inquiry in his field. Glazer contends that Levin should have been supported; instead, his academic freedom was compromised. By contrast, the university minimally and belatedly sanctioned Jeffries, despite the fact that he had no scholarly output and his statements could not withstand scientific or scholarly scrutiny. In letting these cases be decided as free speech cases, the university abrogated its responsibility to make qualitative judgements on faculty members' scholarly contributions toward the pursuit of truth. Ultimately, Levin's academic freedom and the university's autonomy were sacrificed.

238. Gleberzon, William. "Academic Freedom and Holocaust Denial Literature: Dealing with Infamy." **Interchange on Education** 14(4)/15(1): 62-69, 1983/1984.

Gleberzon recounts a 1982 controversy at the University of Toronto's main library over the classification of Holocaust denial literature under the classification for studies on the Holocaust. From a student-led campaign for reclassification as fiction, this spread to calls from the Toronto Jewish community and the B'Nai Brith for the same. Canadian criminal legislation on hate speech might cover this material, though a suit was never brought. Larger issues have to do with whether the request for reclassification poses an attack on academic freedom, and whether academic freedom should be limited by social responsibility. Gleberzon holds that lies should not be defended in the name of academic freedom, and that reclassification of these books as fiction would not infringe on academic freedom.

239. Glicksman, Maurice. "Institutional Openness and Individual Faculty Academic Freedom." **Academe** 72(5): 16-18, September-October 1986.

Freedom of research entails both the freedom of the faculty member to select his or her research interest, and the responsibility to make those research results available. The distribution of research results allows for the critique and evaluation of one's research and may also eliminate the needless duplication of research effort. These are the mechanisms by which knowledge is advanced. Having stated the rights and obligations of academic research, Glicksman here presents hypothetical cases of restrictions a university may place on the research and publications of its own faculty members, including: banning the dissemination of corporate-sponsored research, restrictions placed on private research material, and classified research. Defense-related and corporate-sponsored research may both come with publication restrictions for national security and marketplace reasons, respectively. Glicksman argues that it may be appropriate for institutions to restrict a faculty member's rights to enter into restrictive research agreements. These undermine the institution's broader commitment to the free publication and circulation of knowledge.

240. Gottfredson, Linda S. "The New Challenge to Academic Freedom." **Journal of Social Distress and the Homeless** 5(2): 205-212, April 1996.

Gottfredson argues that, unlike in earlier decades, academic freedom is now threatened more by those within universities than by those outside. After giving a couple of historical examples of external interference in academic freedom, Gottfredson discusses her and a colleague's recent academic freedom case. Their freedom was compromised by some colleagues and administrators within the institution who sought to delegitimize their research (i.e., racial differences in intelligence; affirmative action policy) and funding sources (i.e., the Pioneer Fund). Delegitimizing their research led to Gottfredson initially being denied promotion; denial of her funding source effectively hampered her research, thus compromising her academic freedom by indirect means. Gottfredson argues that academic freedom principles and policies are useless if faculty and institutions do not defend them. Relying upon external sources of support to defend academic freedom, while sometimes effective, also risks the reintroduction of outside political forces into an internal, professional matter. If faculty do not protect and defend academic freedom, says Gottfredson, they may lose it.

241. Gouran, Dennis S. "Academic Freedom and the Management of Higher Education: An Administrative Perspective." **ACA Bulletin** 73: 82-91. Aug. 1990.

Academic freedom is here defined in terms of its limits, as "the right to do that which a faculty member finds appropriate to scholarly inquiry and instruction, so long as it is not legally proscribed, does not constitute an explicit violation of institutional policy or a prior agreement to perform designated responsibilities and observe specified standards of conduct, and can be defended as having demonstrable educational significance." Two administrative problems associated with academic freedom are: first, protection of the principle from threats, whether external or internal; and second, the consequences of exercising academic freedom. The second problem examines abuses of academic freedom such as unreasonable teaching standards, grading practices, or inappropriate or irrelevant course content or scholarship by faculty members.

242. Haber, B. "Why Not the Best and the Brightest? Equal Opportunity vs. Academic Freedom." **Equal Opportunity Forum** 8(12): 11-15, October 1981.

According to Haber, academic freedom and peer review are often used to exclude women from teaching positions in higher education. Peer review is the process of making professional judgements about the qualifications, competence and scholarship of current or prospective colleagues. It is considered a necessary part of an academic's freedom. Haber argues, however, that male academics use the concept as protection against their biased decision-making in the hiring and firing of women. Higher education remains a "good old boy" network, says Haber, and those perpetuating the bias hide behind academic freedom and peer review. In the process, women remain underrepresented in many departments and universities. Peer review can also be used to punish academics who undertake "unpopular" or "unfashionable" research. Consequently, the peer review process becomes the mechanism by which the academic freedom of some faculty is denied. Haber also argues that universities avoided compliance with equal employment opportunity guidelines in the 1970s because federal investigators were largely unfamiliar with academia and wary of infringing on academic freedom.

243. Hackney, Sheldon. "The NEA Under Attack: Resisting the Big Chill."
     Academe 76(4): 14-17, July-August 1990.

The "Big Chill" referred to by Hackney is the "Helms amendment to a National Endowment for the Arts appropriation bill" (p. 15). This amendment was a response to controversies generated by the art of Robert Mapplethorpe and Andres Serrano. Senator Jesse Helms proposed that the NEA be prohibited from funding work that is obscene, that denigrates religious beliefs, or that denigrates various social groups (e.g., race, sex, age). However, the crucial question is: who decides which works of art are "offensive to the sensibilities of large numbers of taxpayers" (p. 16) or "without any redeeming literary, scholarly, cultural or artistic value" (p. 17)? As Hackney points out, there will always be works on the "frontier of the permissible." In fact, this "frontier" changes over time; banned works can and have become more acceptable. Ultimately, says Hackney, "the best protection we have found for democracy is an unregulated market in expression" (p. 17).

244. Harwit, Martin. "Academic Freedom in 'The Last Act.'" **Journal of American
     History** 82(3): 1064-1082, December 1995.

Harwit was Director of the National Air and Space Museum in Washington D.C. at the time of the planning for a controversial exhibit called "The Last Act: The Atomic Bomb and the End of World War II." In response to pressure from conservative lawmakers and such interest groups as the American Legion, the Smithsonian cancelled he exhibition in favor of an exhibit stripped of its historical context. Harwit resigned in response to this decision, because he felt it violated the curators' academic freedom. Discussion is included about exhibitions, how they are developed and written, and how the outside pressure brought to bear on the institution affected the process.

245. Hart, Kathleen. "Is Academic Freedom Bad for Business?" **Bulletin of the Atomic Scientists** 45(3): 28-34, April 1989.

In 1982, Professor David Noble publicly opposed the creation of the for profit Whitehead Institute for Biomedical Research at MIT as being an inappropriate 'sale' of public intellectual resources to a private corporation. In 1984 he was denied tenure and in 1986 he sued, saying that his outspoken condemnation of the Institute was central to this decision. Noble's case received support from a Ralph Nader-sponsored academic freedom monitoring organization called the National Coalition for Universities in the Public Interest. Hart explores ways in which corporate sponsored research and closer university-industry ties limit academic freedom in the name of profit making.

246. Hawkesworth, Mary. "The Politics of Knowledge: Sexual Harassment and Academic Freedom Reconsidered." In Malcolm Tight, editor. **Academic Freedom and Responsibility.** Milton Keynes: Society for Research into Higher Education/Open University Press, 1988. pp. 17-30. ISBN 0-3350-9531-3.

The author argues against the position that developing and implementing sexual harassment policies could infringe on academic freedom. After outlining the forms that sexual harassment can take in higher education, and some of the institutional responses made by American universities, Hawkesworth calls into question the traditional academic ideal of universalized, ahistorical, and objective truth as being the sole object of cognitive inquiry or academic research. Knowledge can never be value-free, this author argues. Requiring a reconsideration of implicit sexist biases within various disciplines can be threatening to the epistemological assumptions on which much research is founded. Sexual harassment policies question sexist power relations within the classroom as well as within disciplinary socialization processes and within cognitive practices. In this manner these policies undermine prohibitions against open inquiry and thereby support and foster rather than infringe on academic freedom. See Tight (entry #461) for a description of the full volume of essays.

247. Heins, Marjorie. "Academic Freedom and the Internet." **Academe** 84(3): 19-21, May-June 1998.

Heins discusses the implications of a 1996 Virginia law prohibiting all state employees from accessing, downloading, printing or storing "any communications having sexually explicit content" (p. 19). This applied to faculty, research assistants and librarians in universities as well, raising concerns about infringements on the freedom of academics to engage in research without state preapproval (a condition of the new law). The law was challenged in a court case, Urofsky v. Allen. The plaintiffs in this case argued that state agency approval raised the specter of political pressure limiting certain scholarly viewpoints. They also argued that there is no way of knowing in advance when information in the arts, humanities, social sciences, or health might run afoul of such guidelines. In fact, Heins recounts a number of instances, brought up in court, where the Virginia law negatively affected the academic freedom of faculty. Ultimately, the plaintiffs won the case. Heins reviews some of the prior Supreme Court decisions that provided support for viewing academic freedom as a "special concern of the First Amendment" (p. 21).

248. Hirsch, Jennifer. "Sexual Harassment vs. Academic Freedom & Due Process." **Women In Higher Education** 3(11): 4-5, November 1994.

According to Hirsch, the desire to end sexual harassment has led some colleges and universities to overreact to alleged incidents of harassment. They have not always observed due process in the consideration of such charges, nor have they always protected legitimate professional speech or behavior. Hirsch reviews three cases in which a university's haste in acting against an accused professor led to procedural mistakes and, in a couple of cases, to a lawsuit by the professor. The AAUP's position is that universities must protect the free exchange of ideas, and that sexual harassment should be defined as "targeted" harassment that restricts the opportunities of individuals. Sexual discrimination is the root of sexual harassment.

249. Iles, Alastair T., and Morton H. Sklar. **The Right to Travel: An Essential Freedom for Scientists and Academics.** Washington, D.C.: American Association for the Advancement of Science, 1996. 1 v.(various paging). LC 96-083157.

This report not only argues for the essential importance of the right to travel for scientific and scholarly work, but also documents the existing state of this right in human rights law and in various countries around the world. The three main chapters of the report itself look at human rights law, restrictions imposed by the United States government, and restrictions imposed by foreign governments. There is also a useful introductory chapter that defines the right to travel and explains its scholarly importance, as well as a concluding chapter with recommendations. Appended are relevant Presidential executive orders, Congressional legislation, relevant parts of the Helsinki Agreement, the Universal Declaration of Human Rights (relevant Articles), the United Nations Study of the Right to Leave and Return, and other documents related to the freedom to travel.

250. Jones, Anthony. "Stars and Bras: A Report from the Trenches." **Academe** 76(4): 18-23, July-August 1990.

While dealing with the more general topic of artistic freedom in academic settings, Jones recounts the details of three controversies at the School of the Art Institute of Chicago. The first revolved around a student art work of the late mayor Harold Washington, a work that was considered disrespectful and offensive by some members of the community. With the assistance of city police, offended city alderman confiscated the art work as a threat to public order. A suit was filed on the student's behalf by the American Civil Liberties Union. As part of the Institute's response to the event, another exhibition was organized for minority students. One of the art works ("What is the Proper Way to Display the U.S. Flag?") at that exhibition precipitated the second controversy. Perceived by some as being disrespectful of the flag, this art work led to massive demonstrations. A student artist's decision to re-display the above-mentioned art work at a graduating class exhibition prompted the third and final controversy. The Institute's president decided that the work would "disrupt the educational process" and, in keeping with the Exhibitions Policy, decided to not show it. Some student artists protested the decision. Jones concludes by suggesting that art is becoming more political, which assaults the sensibilities of those with contrary views of art.

251. Jones, U. Lynn. "See No Evil, Hear No Evil, Speak No Evil: The Information Control Policy of the Reagan Administration." **Policy Studies Journal** 17(2): 243-260, Winter 1988/1989.

Changes in classification policy from the Carter to the Reagan eras are here outlined, with an overview of the expansion of the scope of classification under Reagan. More information classified at the highest possible level for the longest possible time was the general trend under Reagan, who eliminated automatic declassification. Also covered are Reagan administration efforts towards limiting communication by federal employees with the press, and towards controlling the speech and writings of both current and former government officials through prepublication review and expansion of the Espionage Act to allow prosecution of peace-time government leakers of information. Relations of the Reagan Administration with Freedom Of Information Act requests, the press and academia are all addressed, including the control in export of technical information through the Export Administration Act. The author criticizes these efforts at information control as ineffective in achieving the Reagan Administration's expressed goals and finds a greater need for balance between national security concerns and freedom of expression.

252. Kadish, Sanford H. "The Theory of the Profession and Its Predicament." **AAUP Bulletin** 58(2): 120-125, June 1972.

The rights and obligations of the professoriate rest on an implicit theory of the profession articulated in various AAUP policies and documents. The root of this theory is that faculty must be granted freedom and autonomy in their research and teaching because their acquisition and transmission of knowledge benefits society. However, three recent developments call this theory into question. First, collective bargaining and faculty strikes negate the faculty's claim to be serving society at large and not their self interest. Second, the supposed neutrality of higher educational institutions is compromised by 1) university involvement in partisan government-sponsored research, and 2) reactions to such involvement that champion social activism, social reform and social justice. Third, students' consumeristic attitudes toward the educational "product" and their desire for involvement in academic decision-making undermine faculty claims to "primary responsibility" over these and related domains. Kadish concludes with observations on how the profession might begin to resolve these contradictions.

253. Kaplan, Craig, and Schrecker, Ellen, eds. **Regulating the Intellectuals: Perspectives on Academic Freedom in the 1980s.** New York: Praeger, 1983. 260p. ISBN 0-0306-3943-3.

This edited collection focuses on institutional, economic, employment, and legal perspectives on academic freedom. A common thread throughout is the argument that colleges and universities are both dependent upon and a reflection of the broader, unequal society. This impinges on the content and process of higher education and inevitably affects the extent of academic freedom. Political and economic pressures from outside the university, as well as from trustees and some faculty, can affect what is taught and who is allowed to teach. Furthermore, the fiscal crisis in higher education has served to limit students' equal access, to favor the more utilitarian disciplines (e.g., business, engineering) and research (e.g., defense), to limit critical education, to increase the influence of corporations, and to constrict career opportunities for social science and humanities scholars, particularly minorities and women. The accompanying growth of part-time teaching entails further constraints on academic freedom.

254. Kennedy, Donald. "Academic Freedom, Academic Duty." **Academic Duty.** Cambridge: Harvard University Press, 1997. pp. 1-22. ISBN 0-674-00222-9. LC 97-13210.

Kennedy's focus is on the responsibilities or academic duties incumbent upon faculty enjoying academic freedom. These ethical and professional obligations are part of the "bargain" of academic freedom, yet are not as frequently discussed or as clearly delineated. This chapter, and in fact the entire book, discusses these academic duties in the context of contemporary higher education, with numerous examples drawn from Kennedy's experience as president of Stanford University. By fulfilling these obligations, faculty can help institutions of higher education regain the public trust and fulfill their obligations to their students and to the community.

255. Kirshstein, Rita J., Nancy Matheson, and Zhongren Jing. **1993 National Survey of Postsecondary Faculty, NSOPF-93: Institutional Policies and Practices Regarding Faculty in Higher Education.** NCES 97-080. Washington, D.C.: United States Dept. of Education. National Center for Educational Statistics, 1996. 94p.

This volume presents findings from a 1992-1993 survey of higher education institutional policies regarding faculty and instructional staff. Some of the tenure findings included: 71% of institutions with full time permanent instructional faculty and staff had tenure systems, but that between 1987 and 1992 about one half of higher education institutions took some steps to lower the percentage of tenured faculty. Also, 83% of those institutions with tenure systems placed some kind of limits on the maximum amount of time that one could remain in a tenure track position.

256. Klotz, Irving M. "'Misconduct' in Science: Quis Custodiet Ipsus Custodes." **Academic Questions** 6(4): 37-48, Fall 1993.

Klotz sees a threat to academic freedom in recent legislative watchdog reports of the National Academy of Sciences inquiry into scientific fraud and misconduct, published in 1992 as *Responsible Science: Ensuring the Integrity of the Research Process* (ISBN 0-3090-4591-6). Klotz argues that science is better served by peer review than by legislative oversight, bolstering his claim by drawing on debates among historians of science regarding alleged fraud by Newton and Galileo. He also cites Arkansas and Louisiana laws that promote the teaching of creation science as further examples of science "established by legislative fiat."

257. Kreiser, B. Robert. "AAUP Perspectives on Academic Freedom and United States Intelligence Agencies." **Journal of College and University Law** 19(3): 251-257, Winter 1993.

Kreiser raises the question of what should be the relationship between higher education and intelligence agencies, specifically with regard to sponsored research. The AAUP position on academic freedom is that it is a common good, and that institutions should try to avoid compromising the integrity of professors in their free and open search for truth. However, some requirements of research on behalf of intelligence agencies (e.g., concealing the source of support; misrepresenting interests and objectives of the research; submitting findings to agencies for prior approval of dissemination) run counter to principles of academic freedom. As such, they could harm the credibility of academics and undermine trust in their professional integrity. The AAUP recommends, in various policy documents, full disclosure of individual and institutional relationships with outside funding agencies.   This includes intelligence agencies. The goal should be to find a balance between the legitimate needs of external agencies and the academic's commitment to free inquiry and the unfettered advancement of knowledge.

258. Kurland, Jordan E. "Six Months of Experience with Accuracy in Academia."
      PS 19(2): 286-290, Spring 1986.

      Associate General Secretary of the AAUP, Kurland here reports on the history of Accuracy in Academia, founded in order to "combat the dissemination of misinformation" and liberal bias in higher education. The reasons behind the AAUP's opposition to their activities are spelled out.   Specific cases that Accuracy in Academia has associated itself with are traced, along with the AAUP's responses in each case.   The AAUP advises faculty members who find themselves under questioning or monitoring by AIA. A 1985 Committee A report condemning AIA is reprinted here as well.

259. Lawrence, Malcolm.   "Accuracy in Academia: Is It a Threat to Academic Freedom?" **Vital Speeches of the Day** 52(2): 44-49, November 1, 1985.

      The President of Accuracy in Academia denies that his organization threatens academic freedom, calls for formation of campus chapters and explains the liberal bias that his organization investigates and opposes in higher education. Criticism from the mainstream media and the AAUP is answered, with the text of an AIA document released in response to the official AAUP statement on AIA (see entry #345). Quotes from students from around the country who support AIA efforts and documented cases of bias or liberal political advocacy in courses and classrooms are provided.

260. Leik, Robert K. "There's Far More Than Tenure on the Butcher Block: A Larger Context for the Recent Crisis at the University of Minnesota." **Sociological Perspectives** 41(4): 747-755, Winter 1998.

      To understand the growing attacks on tenure, says Leik, one needs to appreciate the broad social context in which these occur. An ongoing fiscal crisis has led to calls for university accountability. This has created competition for scarce public funds and an increased emphasis on financial and economic criteria in university decision-making. Consequently, institutions become more oriented toward the market and the bottom-line, which affects the content and process of education. In this market model, students are viewed as consumers, and education is subtly redefined as job training. Furthermore, universities are increasingly "micro-managed" by non-academicians, thus reducing the decision-making role of academics. Within universities, units or departments are encouraged to pay their own way via enrollments, which can negatively affect programmatic decisions. Similarly, "cash cow" programs may get preference over less cost-effective ones in a university focused on the bottom line. The increasing privatization of universities can also narrow research agendas and increase tuition costs. For these and other reasons, says Leik, the traditional research university is in crisis.

261. Lester, Julius. "Academic Freedom and the Black Intellectual." **Black Scholar** 19(6): 16-26, November 1988.

The author, tenured at the University of Massachusetts at Amherst, was a professor in that college's Department of Afro-American Studies from 1971 until 1988, when the department terminated their relationship. He then transferred to the Department of Judaic and Near Eastern Studies. At issue in this transfer was Lester's published referrals to James Baldwin as an anti-Semite. Lester describes his ongoing relationship with his former department, chronicling what he describes as an atmosphere of intolerance for divergent views. His essay is rebutted by another in this same issue of *Black Scholar*, called "Don't Believe the Hype," which also reproduces university documents related to the case. Both essays refer to an essay by James Baldwin called "Blacks and Jews," reprinted here.

262. Levine, Lawrence W. "Clio, Canons and Culture." **Journal of American History** 80(3): 849-67, December 1993.

A revised version of the author's 1993 presidential address before the Organization of American Historians, this essay discusses recent expansion of the historian's "canon" to make multi-cultural issues more widely researched and published on. Addressing the claim by some critics of contemporary historical research that the European and Western traditions are being either attacked or ignored by sectarian or overly-politicized scholars, Levine gives an historical overview of the gradual expansion of the history curriculum over the past 150 years.

263. Lewis, Lionel S. **Scaling the Ivory Tower: Merit and Its Limits in Academic Careers.** New Brunswick, N.J.: Transaction Publishers, 1998. 238p. ISBN 1-5600-0958-6.

Originally published in 1975, this book was reissued with a new introduction by the author. Lewis addresses how merit relates to such higher education issues as teaching and publication, professional evaluation and letters of recommendations, academic culture, appointment and recruitment, and academic freedom. Throughout, Lewis notes ways in which the principle of merit, though claimed to be at the root of academic practices, actually has little to do with academia. In a chapter devoted to "The Bearing of Merit on Academic Freedom," Lewis examines dismissals from 1916-1970, finding evidence that most dismissals do not hinge on issues of competence but are in fact due to violations of academic freedom.

264. Lippman, Matthew, and Dennis R. Judd. "Intellectual Repression in Higher Education." **Thought & Action: The NEA Higher Education Journal** 2(1): 41-62, Winter 1986.

Lippman and Judd argue that there has always been intellectual and ideological repression in higher education, but that the agents and interests served have changed over time. The earliest colleges were primarily a training ground for clerics, so faculty and tutors were constrained by the religious control and mission of the institution. Over time, as colleges and universities became more secularized, economic and industrial interests gained more influence over these institutions. As the authors put it, "business ideology or patriotic zeal replaced religious conformity" (p. 50) as the sources of ideological repression. Currently, according to Lippman and Judd, corporations and the government exert undue influence over higher education. Corporate executives increasingly dominate boards of trustees, while curricula and "applied" research reflect a growing dependence on corporate donations. The government exerts growing influence over research agendas through its support of military research on campus. All of these influences constrain intellectual freedom. What has remained constant over time, say the authors, is the "utilitarian" nature of higher education in its service to powerful interests.

265. Lyons, Beauvais. "Artistic Freedom and the University." **Art Journal** 50(4): 77-83, Winter 1991.

The relationship of academic freedom to the visual arts is here examined. Lyons cites cases from the McCarthy era through the present in which community standards were brought to bear on peer-reviewed and/or university-sponsored exhibitions or theatrical performances. Typical moral and political grounds for censorship are discussed. The mission of the university to be a laboratory for critical inquiry and the principle of institutional autonomy are both violated when freedom of the arts is compromised.

266. Marchant, Gary. "Political Constraints: Military Funding & Academic Freedom." **Science for the People** 20(1): 27-33, January/February 1988.

Marchant discusses encroachments on the academic freedom of scientists pursuing research that is either funded by or of interest to the military. Forced withdrawal of papers, pre-publication review clauses in grant contracts, threatened withdrawal or review of security clearances, the use of export control laws to restrict scientific communication, and travel restrictions on foreign scholars are all examples of the adverse impact of increased military spending on higher education. The military also controls the political activities and possible dissent of scientists receiving military funding through enticement via lucrative grant funding or consulting arrangements. Specific examples of all of these practices are provided by Marchant.

267. Markie, Peter J. "Affirmative Action and the Awarding of Tenure." In Steven M. Cahn, editor. **Affirmative Action and the University: A Philosophical Inquiry.** Philadelphia: Temple University Press, 1993. pp. 275-285. ISBN 1-5663-9030-3.

While affirmative action may be justifiable in initial appointment, it should not play a role in the awarding of tenure. Responses to lack of opportunity or equality that focus on preferential treatment as a primary response can result in numerous types of problems, here outlined.

268. McPherson, Michael S. "Public Purpose and Public Accountability in Liberal Education." **New Directions for Higher Education** no.85: 83-92, Spring 1994.

McPherson identifies a growing conflict between two legitimate values related to higher education: the need for academic freedom and institutional autonomy, and the public demand for accountability. Both public and private colleges and universities have been granted significant autonomy, in part, because of their pursuit of knowledge and truth and their guardianship of democracy. However, in the current period of fiscal constraints on public and private institutions, boards of trustees and legislators are demanding more accountability for how funds are being expended. The public's skepticism may be further fueled by academic structures and processes that reward faculty for their publications and successful grants and not for their teaching. However, reducing the mission of liberal education to its measurable and utilitarian benefits may distort the university's mission of free inquiry. McPherson makes some suggestions for changing the academic reward structure to reward teaching, to place more emphasis on the quality of publications, and to adopt common teaching evaluations. To make such changes effective, colleges and universities would have to cooperate in adopting similar policies, while being mindful of antitrust laws and protecting autonomy.

269. Menand, Louis. "The Future of Academic Freedom." **Academe** 79(3): 11-17, May-June, 1993

The first in a series called "Academic Freedom and the Future of the University," this essay reconsiders academic freedom in the light of both external and internal pressures against the concept. One example of external pressure given is a 1991 report from NEH director Lynne Cheney, called "Telling the Truth" which called for controlling professors with offensive views. As internal pressure, Menand cites a trend towards skepticism among academics regarding the possibility of an objective search for truth, one of the traditional philosophical grounds for supporting academic freedom. And the wide freedom of inquiry afforded to the tenured specialist in a narrow field can at the same time be exclusive enough to limit the distribution of that freedom to untenured or independent scholars, or to students at an institution with a speech code in place. Menand suggests that current "politically correct" sorts of pedagogical approaches are a retreat to some of the earliest assumptions about higher education noted by Metzger in his history of academic freedom as superseded by Darwinism and the rise of the modern research institution -- the concept that ideas can be proved on the basis of their moral advantage rather than on the basis of scientific inquiry. But the author ends with a reminder that John Dewey himself did not believe in truth as an absolute, or that facts were value-free, and what seems like a recent attack on the principle of a disinterested pursuit of knowledge is not so radical after all.

270. Menand, Louis, ed. **The Future of Academic Freedom.** Chicago: University of Chicago Press, 1996. 239p. ISBN 0-2265-2004-8.

This collection of essays reprints a series of articles originally published in the *AAUP Bulletin*, after presentation at the national meetings of the Association. Divided into three sections on "What Does Academic Freedom Protect?;" "The Problem of Hate Speech;" and "The Ethics of Inquiry," this book throughout responds to polemics against academia, political correctness and other such controversial topics of the 1980s and 1990s. Many of these nine essays are abstracted and entered under the author. Essays here are by Louis Menand (see entry #269); Richard Rorty (see entry #29); Thomas L. Haskell; Cass R. Sunstein; Henry Louis Gates Jr.; Joan W. Scott (see entry #31); Ronald Dworkin (see entry #12); Evelyn Fox Keller; and Edward W. Said.

271. Moran, Gordon. **Silencing Scientists and Scholars in Other Fields: Power, Paradigm Controls, Peer Review, and Scholarly Communication.** Greenwich, Conn.: Ablex, 1998. 187p. (Contemporary Studies in Information Management, Policy, and Services). ISBN 1-5675-0342-X.

Moran investigates the varied ways that open intellectual inquiry can be and often is suppressed. Case studies are presented of suppression of information and/or debate in a number of different fields, ranging from art history to bioethics, from librarianship to AIDS research. Moran addresses the gap he sees between a rhetoric of academic openness and a reality of secrecy and silence in academia. Through chapters on such issues (among others) as peer review, data falsification, whistleblowing, the degeneration of academic debate into public scandal, political correctness pressures, and lack of proper or full indexing/citation of sources, Moran makes the case that the silencing of scholars and scholarship is a widespread phenomena. A final chapter on "Silencing Scholars in the Electronic Age" addresses the impact that peer-reviewed electronic publishing or government- and internetprovider-sponsored censorship can have on open scholarship and dialogue on the Internet.

272. Morton, Donald. "Multiple Submissions and the Institutional Power/Knowledge Network." **New Literary History** 28(3): 495-500, Summer 1997.

Morton argues that an author should be free to submit manuscripts to as many journals as s/he wishes, and then choose one from among those accepting the text for publication. The author argues that the issue is less one of professional ethics than one of the relative political power imbalance between writers on the one hand, and the largely unchallenged power of journal editors and editorial boards on the other hand. Morton disagrees with *PMLA* editor Domna Stanton (see entry #295) that the only problem at issue in single submissions is the unethically slow response to manuscript submissions of editors.

273. Moynihan, Daniel Patrick. "State versus Academe." **Harper's** 261(1567): 31-40, December 1980.

Moynihan, a Senator from New York State, addresses increasing federal influence and control over the internal affairs of universities. Examples include: Dept. of Labor access to previously confidential records of university hiring and tenure decisions; increasing federal aid with a corresponding increase in federal regulation over such issues as curricula, student enrollment, and faculty selection. Moynihan notes increasing federal control over private institutions as well. The negative influence on academic self-governance of acts of Congress and Executive orders from the late 1950s through the late 1970s is also here examined.

274. Mulcahy, Richard P. "A Full Circle: Advocacy and Academic Freedom in Crisis." In Patricia Meyer Spacks, editor. **Advocacy in the Classroom: Problems and Possibilities.** New York: St. Martin's Press, 1996. pp. 142-160. ISBN 0-3121-6127-1.

Mulcahy compares a 1934 AAUP investigation at the University of Pittsburgh (Pitt) into the Ralph E. Turner affair with some contemporary cases, including that of Stephan Thernstrom at Harvard. Pitt was censured by the AAUP for dismissing Turner over his anti-religious commentaries. Thernstrom was publicly condemned for "racial insensitivity" by students who found his courses on ethnic and racial minorities offensive. The Harvard administration permitted at least tacit support for what Mulcahy sees as inappropriate student attempts to dictate course content. In both cases Mulcahy sees evidence of the dangers of politicizing the university; both cases are cited as evidence for a need for a neutral university as the foundation of academic freedom.

275. Nelson, Cary, editor. **Will Teach for Food: Academic Labor in Crisis.** Minneapolis: University of Minnesota Press, 1997. 308p. (Cultural Politics, vol. 12). ISBN 0-8166-3033-X.

This collection of essays focuses in large part on the (ultimately unsuccessful) unionizing efforts on the Yale Campus during the 1995-1996 academic school year, when a "grade strike" by graduate assistants was called in response to the administration's refusal to negotiate holding a union vote for graduate assistants. Part I presents a "Yale Strike Dossier" which includes essays originally presented by student activists at a 1996 Graduate Employee and Students Organization-sponsored Yale symposium. Other papers in this section place the Yale events in larger political, racial, or pedagogical contexts. In Part II, which is called "Academic Workers Face the New Millennium," essays present other case studies related to graduate student unions and the widespread use or abuse of part-time and adjunct faculty. An essay here by Ellen Schrecker addresses the question "Will Technology Make Academic Freedom Obsolete?" forecasting the potential impact on academic freedom of such educational trends as distance learning and the increasing use of videotaped lectures.

276. Nordin, Virginia Davis. "Autonomy, Academic Freedom, and Accountability: The University, the Individual, and the State." In Judith P. Swazey and Stephen R. Scher, editors. **Whistleblowing in Biomedical Research: Policies and Procedures for Responding to Reports of Misconduct, Proceedings of a Workshop, September 21-22, 1981.** Washington, D.C.: Superintendent of Documents, 1982. pp. 23-40. LC 82-600605.

The author describes the governance structure of universities and how Federally-mandated Institutional Review Boards could work effectively to regulate campus biomedical research on human subjects. Nordin concludes that IRBs probably could not function effectively in university settings because of traditions and values of institutional autonomy and faculty academic freedom. Yet use of human subjects in research must be ethical and responsible, and if internal governance mechanisms can't protect them, government intervention will be necessary.

277. Ollman, Bertell. "Academic Freedom in America Today: A Marxist View." **Monthly Review** 35(10): 24-46, March 1984.

Also published as a chapter in a 1983 compilation edited by Craig Kaplan and Ellen Schrecker (*Regulating the Intellectuals*, entry #253), this essay addresses the role of the university in the American capitalist economy. Ollman claims that under the conditions imposed by capitalism, the practice of academic freedom acts more as a "policing mechanism" than as an assurance of the freedoms of radical professors and students. Ollman outlines a three-tiered system of academic repression coming from the government, from administrators, and from departmental faculty. The wide gap between the stated ideal of academic freedom and the actual practice of preserving a narrowly regulated status quo nevertheless allows for a certain amount of the exercise of critical thinking and progressive trends which expand the boundaries of what can be studied. Ollman concludes by predicting an increase in the numbers of radical teachers along with a rise in the amount of academic repression.

278. O'Neil, Robert M. "The AAUP at 75: Three Academic Freedom Challenges." **Academe** 77(1): 32-33, January/February 1991.

Director of the Thomas Jefferson Center for the Protection of Free Expression, O'Neil sees three major tests of current AAUP policies. One relates to the prominence in scientific fraud cases given to whistle-blowers and the lack of due process for the accused; another relates to hate speech codes and their potential for compromising academic freedoms; and the last is the threat to federal funding of the arts through the National Endowment for the Arts and the National Endowment for the Humanities.

279. O'Neil, Robert M. **Free Speech in the College Community.** Bloomington, Ind.: Indiana University Press, 1997. 257p. ISBN 0-2533-3267-2.

O'Neil addresses a wide range of topics here. In a chapter on speech codes, the author addresses what such codes can accomplish, how many institutions have instituted them, what is wrong with speech codes, and alternatives to their use. Discussing the speech rights of university professors, O'Neil cites the court cases of Michael Levin and Leonard Jeffries at CUNY. Other chapters present such issues as off-campus speakers invited to address students (citing the case of Khalid Abdul-Muhammad), email and the Internet, freedoms of student organizations and the student press, artistic freedom on campus, academic research, religious speech on public campuses and free speech on private campuses.

280. Park, Robert L. "The Muzzling of American Science." **Academe** 75(5): 19-23, September-October 1986.

The free exchange of ideas is critical to the research process and the advancement of knowledge, says Park. But concern about the security aspects of unregulated technology transfer, such as to the Soviet Union, raises an important question: "in our attempts to impede technology transfer to the Soviets, do we endanger our own technological enterprise" (p. 19)? Park's position is that while the export of strategic goods may appropriately be restricted, the underlying science should be kept free. In the mid-1980s a number of scientific scholarly associations protested government restrictions on the exchange of unclassified information. While the government relented and conceded the value of free scholarly exchange, the door was left open for legislative restrictions. Park reviews an historical list of such legislation, including the Atomic Energy Act, the Invention Secrecy Act, the Arms Export Control Act of 1976, the Export Administration Act of 1985, and the Defense Authorization Act of 1984.

281. Phillip, Mary-Christine. "Academic Freedom & Black Thought." **Black Issues in Higher Education** 10(26): 12-15, February 24, 1994.

Through interviews and an overview of events, Phillip reviews the controversy involving Professor Tony Martin at Wellesley College. A Professor ot Africana studies, Martin has been criticized for requiring students in one of his courses to read a Nation of Islam book alleging connections between Jews and the slave trade. Because of the negative reactions he received from the college president and others inside and outside of the university, Martin wrote a book presenting his view of events. This book, entitled *The Jewish Onslaught: Dispatches from the Wellesley Battlefront*, further contributed to the controversy. A number academics interviewed questioned whether African American scholars can write on the issue of race and still retain their academic credibility. Martin and others also argued that challenging the academic status quo, as Martin had done, can place one's career and academic freedom in jeopardy. Others interviewed suggested that the Nation of Islam book is extremist and unscholarly, and that Martin's book is polemical. Throughout, the article raises questions about academic freedom, the obligations of scholarly inquiry, and possible constraints on research topics.

282. Ramsey Colloquium. "The Inhuman Use of Human Beings: A Statement on Embryo Research." **First Things** 49: 17-21, January 1995.

The Colloquium, sponsored by the Institute on Religion and Public Life, is a group of Jewish and Christian theologians and scholars. This essay, signed by 26 academics, decries the 1994 report of the National Institutes of Health Human Embryo Research Panel that endorsed government funding for the creation of human embryos for research purposes. The authors argue that as embryos are human beings, they should not be produced as raw material for scientific research. The potential gains in knowledge and medical advances come at too high a cost. The authors hold that such a program would violate the Nuremberg Code restricting medical research as well as the 1975 Helsinki Declaration of the World Medical Association affirming the paramount interests of the research subject over the interests of science and society.

283. Relyea, Harold C. "National Security Information Policy After the End of the Cold War." In Peter Hernon, Charles R. McClure, Harold C. Relyea, editors. **Federal Information Policies in the 1990s: Views and Perspectives.** Information Management Policy and Services. Norwood, N.J.: Ablex, 1996. pp. 165-182. ISBN 1-5675-0282-2.

Changes in the official secrecy practices of Federal agencies and departments since the end of the Cold War are reviewed and new policies analyzed in this essay. Security classification practices since 1940, Clinton-led efforts at declassification and the attendant controversies are outlined. Changes in the volume and cost of classifying, in the procedures for classifying, and in the procedures for permitting access to materials are all detailed here. An extensive bibliography is also provided.

284. Rice, Patricia Ohl. "Academic Freedom and Faculty Status for Academic Librarians: A Bibliographical Essay." Eric Doc. No. ED 246917. 18 p. August 1984.

The author surveys documents from library literature which argue in favor of granting librarians academic status, where those arguments are based either in whole or in part on the concept of academic freedom. Thirteen items are identified and reviewed. Included are the 1946 American Library Association statement in support of tenure for librarians, a number of essays from a 1976 book edited by L.C. Branscomb entitled *The Case for Faculty Status for Academic Librarians*, and articles from professional journals in the 1960s and 1970s. A concluding section discusses the state of professional literature on the topic, noting persistent failures of librarianship to distinguish between academic and intellectual freedom as well as an inconsistency in attitudes towards tenure among members of the academic library profession.

285. Sacken, Donald M. "Taking Teaching Seriously: Institutional and Individual Dilemmas." **The Journal of Higher Education** 61(5): 548-564, September/October 1990.

Recent reform efforts in higher education have focused, in part, on improving the effectiveness and accountability of teaching. However, doing so poses problems for administrators and faculty. Sacken cites a couple of recent lawsuits in which faculty claimed that their teaching methods were part of their overall academic freedom. Courts seem disinclined to accept this, supporting the idea that faculty and administrators have the expertise and responsibility to evaluate a colleague's teaching, particularly a probationary colleague. Still, while courts may grant such latitude, higher educational institutions may feel obliged to tackle the evaluation of teaching. Sacken discusses many of the difficulties confronting such an effort. Teaching effectiveness is invariably tied to outcomes assessment, which is itself controversial. Furthermore, it is difficult to specify the "core characteristics" of good teaching; there are many ways to be a good teacher. Student evaluations are a part of teaching evaluation, but are insufficient in and of themselves. Administrators and faculty are generally not trained in pedagogy, and therefore may not be comfortable in evaluating colleagues. Sacken recommends multiple measure of teaching effectiveness, as well as variability across disciplines and programs. Incentives and disincentives can be linked to performance. Ultimately, evaluation "should be primarily developmental" (p. 559).

286. Schell, Eileen E. **Gypsy Academics and Mother-Teachers: Gender, Contingent Labor, and Writing Instruction.** CrossCurrents, New Perspectives in Rhetoric and Composition. Portsmouth, N.H.: Boynton/Cook, 1998. 158p. ISBN 0-8670-9441-9.

Focusing on the increasing use of part-time instructors in academe, Schell highlights women teachers of first-year undergraduate composition. The threat this practice poses to tenure is outlined in a feminist critique of what Schell sees as a growing exploitation of poorly-paid, part-time adjunct faculty, a "contingent labor" role disproportionately filled by women. The increasingly "permanent" nature of what was once perceived as a temporary work force has institutionalized working conditions marked by little or no on-the-job training, little job security or opportunity for professional advancement, and no health insurance. Schell's argument that women's experiences under such working conditions differ significantly (and in worse ways) than men's is statistically supported by a number of research studies. After charting the history of women writing instructors, Schell cites a number of "gendered myths" about part-time teachers that she deflates through a process of interviewing and surveying non-tenure track women writing faculty. Schell calls for changes in administrative policies for employing part-timers, and calls on professional organizations, unions, faculties, and others to take action in support of strategies for change. Schell concludes by offering four solutions: the "conversionist" solution, whereby contingent positions are converted to full time tenure track positions; the "reformist" solution, a process of professionalizing the working conditions of contingent faculty; the "unionist/collectivist" solution of collective bargaining; and the "abolitionist" solution which does away entirely with the teaching of freshman comp due to its uneven quality and status and its exploitation of a broad and growing class of workers.

287. Schrecker, Ellen. "The Chilling Case of Kate Bronfenbrenner." **Academe** 84(4): 8-9, July/August 1998.

Testifying in a town meeting sponsored by Congress, Bronfenbrenner found that her critical remarks about the illegal anti-union activities of Beverly Enterprises Inc. led to her being sued for defamation by the company. Schrecker briefly reviews the details of the case, then focuses on the chilling effect such a lawsuit could have on faculty. The case against Bronfenbrenner was ultimately thrown out because she was protected by testimonial immunity. However, similar comments by Bronfenbrenner in other venues, not protected by immunity, could generate a valid suit. The fact that the suit was undertaken at all, in addition to the time and money required to fight it, could deter faculty whose research touches on controversial public issues. To avoid such potential controversy and legal proceedings, scholars may censor themselves and gravitate toward less controversial topics. Another troubling aspect of the case, says Schrecker, was the company's request under the discovery process to see Bronfenbrenner's research notes. Had the court granted such a request, it would have made it "harder for scholars like Bronfenbrenner to carry out their work" (p. 9). The AAUP's friend-of-the-court brief argued that the discovery process threatened academic freedom, and that the best corrective to research errors is "countervailing speech."

288. Schwab, Jessica D. "National Security Restraints of the Federal Government on Academic Freedom and Scientific Communication in the United States." **Government Publications Review** 17(1): 17-48, January/February 1990.

Schwab examines the history and current state of conflict between academic freedom and national security, addressing such means of restriction as: export regulations, classification of information, control over travel and visits by foreign scholars, control over issuance of contracts, and pre-publication review of results. An appendix provides a partial list from 1980 through 1988 of restrictions on academic and scientific freedoms imposed in the name of national security.

289. Sheinin, Rose. "Academic Freedom and Integrity and Ethics in Publishing." **Scholarly Publishing** 24(4): 232-247, July 1993.

The author links academic freedom necessarily with academic integrity. Sheinen discusses how breaches in academic integrity impact academic freedom, particularly in the area of scholarly publishing, addressing in particular a 1990 incident in Canada, the "Gordon Freeman affair" in which a Chemistry Professor bypassed peer review processes to publish a methodologically suspect study of cheating by female undergraduates. A number of breaches of integrity are discussed in reference to this case. Sheinen concludes by calling on all universities to draft academic freedom statements and codes of integrity for research and publication.

290. Shils, Edward. "Do We Still Need Academic Freedom?" **American Scholar** 62(2): 187-209, Spring 1993.

Since the founding of the American Association of University Professors in 1915, and for many decades since, tenure has been a necessary condition for protecting academic freedom. Threats to this freedom came from many quarters, including community members, boards of trustees, university administrators, and governmental officials. In the face of these changing threats, tenure allowed faculty to pursue truth at the highest levels of inquiry without fear of losing their jobs. According to Shils, however, academic freedom is now generally accepted as a necessary condition for higher education. Threats from outside interests are, for the most part, no longer a problem. The AAUP is less concerned with protecting academic freedom than with promoting the well being of its members, and faculty have more latitude in their behavior than ever before. Overall, academics have unprecedented freedom from traditional threats. However, according to Shils, the new threat to academic freedom comes from within the academy in the form of affirmative action, positive discrimination, and cultural diversity. The pursuit of truth and excellence at the highest scholarly levels now often takes a back seat to these new priorities in hiring and in curricula. To the extent that it does, academic freedom is not protected.

291. Shulman, Seth. "Stopping Star Wars." **Science for the People** 18(1): 10-15, January/February 1986.

Shulman recounts the growing number of professors and graduate students pledging not to seek or accept Strategic Defense Initiative (SDI) funding. Over 2,400 professors and 1,700 graduate students signed, with over 56% of faculty at the fourteen top physics departments signing on. The text of the pledge is reproduced as is an excerpt on "Star Wars and Academic Freedom" by Tufts professor Sheldon Krimsky outlining the threats to academic freedom posed by SDI funding.

292. Slaughter, Sheila. "Academic Freedom and the State." **The Journal of Higher Education** 59(3): 241-262, May/June 1988.

The growing fiscal crisis among public institutions and the increasing competitiveness of a global marketplace have led to attempted reforms of higher education. These reforms have included more accountability, tighter funding, higher standards, and more support for utilitarian and competitiveness-oriented curricula and research, among others. Many universities have sought to compensate for lost funding by offering more programs and services to businesses, from whom they receive increased support. This growing dependent relationship, both with business and with government-sponsored defense research, threatens to alter curricular offerings and constrain academic freedom. Within universities, those who control the funding have increasing influence over academic programs and research. University-industry-government partnerships serve to redirect funding and limit autonomy and intellectual diversity within the university. A narrowing of what is considered legitimate and valuable knowledge has followed., with a concomitant narrowing of academic freedom.

293. Slaughter, Sheila. "Academic Freedom at the End of the Century: Professional Labor, Gender and Professionalization." In Philip G. Altbach, Robert O. Berdahl and Patricia J. Gumport, editors. **Higher Education in American Society.** 3rd ed. Amherst, N.Y.: Prometheus Books, 1994. pp. 73-100. (Frontiers of Education). ISBN 0-8797-5905-4.

Slaughter reviews forty-seven academic freedom cases investigated during the 1980s by the AAUP, comparing her findings with an earlier study that focused on the 1970s (see entry #211). Issues of labor restructuring, centralization of decision-making, gender biases, and failures of faculty to maintain professional autonomy are all identified as trends in the 1980s. While (as in the 1970s) financial exigency played the largest role in dismissals of tenured faculty in the 1980s, a broad undermining of the tenure system was also caused in part by new administrative labor-relations techniques such as (among others): program restructuring, increased use of part-timers, heavier teaching loads. In another difference from the 1970s, sex discrimination for the first time became an AAUP category of academic freedom cases. Specific sex discrimination cases are cited.

294. "Stanford Documents." **Partisan Review** 55(4): 653-674, Fall 1988.

Reprinted here are Sidney Hook's "Open Letter to the Stanford University Faculty Senate" dated January 20, 1988; news items and other letters to the editor of the Stanford Daily and the Peninsula Times of Palo Alto; and a final essay by Hook called "Educational Disaster at Stanford University." These documents related to controversy over the replacing of Stanford's course in Western Culture with a course called "Culture, Ideas and Values." Covered here are protests by minority students and the influence of and role played by the Black Student Union and its chair Bill King in getting the University to replace what was seen as a racially biased course with what Hook describes as a "politically diluted course in sociology."

295. Stanton, Domna C. "Editor's Column on Multiple Submissions." **New Literary History** 28(3): 487-493, Summer 1997.

Reprinted from vol. 109 (1994) of *PMLA*, this essay recounts a survey conducted by the *PMLA* staff and editorial board of the editorial policies of fifteen journals in modern language and literature. Stanton presents findings on the issue of whether or not journals accepted articles previously submitted elsewhere for publication. These findings give context to the decision of the editorial board of *PMLA* "not to review articles that are under consideration" elsewhere. Issues of the professional ethics of writers and editors are addressed. Companion articles in this issue take issue with the Stanton piece (see entry #272).

296. Steneck, Nicholas H. "Whose Academic Freedom Needs to be Protected? The Case of Classified Research." **Business & Professional Ethics Journal** 11(1): 17-32, Spring 1992.

The author discusses the dilemma that conducting classified research on university campuses poses for academic freedom. Citing as a case study the 1991 criticism of Rochester Institute of Technology professorial involvement in CIA-funded research, Steneck explores three differing current university policy approaches to cooperation with secret government research. He suggests a way to reconcile conflicting views that alternatively see this sort of research as either clearly at odds with a free exchange of ideas central to the professor's and institution's commitment to academic freedom or vital to national interest, widely sanctioned by public policy, and a valuable source of support for faculty, staff, and equipment. "Avoidance, separation and regulation" are cited as the three typical approaches to classified research taken by university administrators. The pros and cons of each are explored. Steneck concludes by recommending acceptance of a certain degree of secrecy or control over publication, but also stresses the need for institutions to arrive at collective and openly discussed policy approaches for dealing with researchers who wish to engage in classified research. The author calls on the government to refrain from a knee-jerk mistrust of institutions where such research is conducted (citing a 1982 AAUP statement on "Federal Restrictions on Research"). He also calls on universities to provide the same trust and latitude to individual researchers conducting classified research as they do to researchers not so involved.

297. Streharsky, Charmaine Judy. "Freedom of Inquiry versus Public Responsibility: Some Philosophical Perspectives." **Journal of the Society of Research Administrators** 18(1): 49-54, Summer 1986.

Streharsky discusses the conflict between the principles of academic freedom and the need for public accountability in spending public funds on higher education. Potential exists for abridging freedoms of individual researchers to pursue unfettered research at universities, themselves independent from governmental control. Examples of this include federal spending on research targeted at specific public, governmental, or military objectives. The Strategic Defense Initiative is one such example discussed here.

298. Strohm, Paul. "Convocation on Current Threats to Academic Freedom." **Academe** 72(1): 41-45, January-February 1986.

The AAUP sponsored a conference attended by representatives of the organizations that originally endorsed the *1940 Statement of Principles on Academic Freedom and Tenure*. The purpose of the conference was to discuss current threats to academic freedom, of which four threats are identified: Accuracy in Academia; government restrictions on academic freedom; irregular faculty appointment and post-tenure review; and academic freedom in church-related institutions. Accuracy in Academia is the conservative watchdog group that has classroom recruits looking for "errors" in faculty teaching. Government restrictions seem to apply primarily to imposed limits on disseminating information gathered from government-sponsored research. The growth of non-tenure-eligible appointments is seen as a undermining academic tenure and freedom, while post-tenure review is viewed as unnecessary in light of salary and promotion evaluations. Finally, church-related institutions are now more like non-sectarian institutions in their adherence to AAUP principles. However, interesting issues remain, such as the relationship between theologians and bishops, who have different and potentially conflicting roles and functions.

299. Strohm, Paul. "The 1990 Wolf Trap Conference: Academic Freedom and Artistic Expression." **Academe** 76:4. 7-13, July-August 1990.

Strohm, the editor of *Academe*, opens this special issue of the journal with an overview of a three-day conference held from April 29-May 1, 1990. Issues covered include: the politicization of the arts, the concept of institutional neutrality, the breadth and scope of protections that can viably be sought for the arts. A concluding statement issued by conference participants deals with curtailing artistic expression at academic institutions and ways for supporting policies that discourage restrictions on public presentations of art. Other articles in this special issue on censorship in the arts are based on presentations made at this conference.

300. Strossen, Nadine. "Academic and Artistic Freedom." **Academe** 78(6): 8-15, November-December 1992.

301. Strossen, Nadine. "Academic Freedom and Artistic Freedom." **Academe** 79(1): 30-37, January-February 1993.

An adaptation of an address to the annual AAUP meeting by the president of the American Civil Liberties Union, this two-part essay focuses on four threats to artistic freedom in the United States: threats from the Supreme Court, from other government agencies, from private organizations, and from public opinion. The first installment opens with a broad overview of recent attacks on free speech, and details sources of such attacks in religious fundamentalism, such as the Iranian death threat against Salman Rushdie and Pat Buchanan's declaration of "religious war" at the opening of the 1992 Republican Party Convention. Constraints on the First Amendment which follow from Supreme Court decisions are also detailed here. The second installment touches on governmental entities whose actions curtail academic and artistic freedom, such as: the Obscenity Unit of the Justice Department and its attempts to harass creators and distributors of constitutionally protected, but sexually oriented materials; a 1991 Congressional bill called the Pornography Victims Compensation Act, sponsored by Senator Mitch McConnell of Kentucky who acknowledged that the bill's purpose was to bankrupt purveyors of sexually explicit material; state and local governmental efforts in Ohio (against a Cincinnati exhibition of photographs by Robert Mapplethorpe), Illinois (against student art work displayed at the Art Institute of Chicago), and Florida (against 2 Live Crew, a rap music group). Detailing the pressure against artistic expression brought by private pressure groups, Strossen discusses the efforts of the Christian Coalition, the Eagle Forum, Concerned Women of America, and the American Family Association. Finally, public opinion polls from 1991 are cited to illustrate attitudinal trends opposing artistic and expressive freedoms.

302. "Symposium: Academic Freedom at Century's End." **Academic Questions** 10(4): 16-74, Fall 1997.

Included here are brief essays by a variety of contributors on contemporary issues in academic freedom. Most of the articles revolve around the existence and extent of political correctness on campus and its effect on the expression of diverse viewpoints. However, many of the essays do revisit some classic writers and issues in the academic freedom literature; these include Sidney Hook and his distinction between heresy and conspiracy, as well as the AAUP's *1940 Statement of Principles on Academic Freedom and Tenure*. The contributors come from a variety of disciplines and political perspectives and include Mary Lefkowitz, Mickael Berube, Irving Louis Horowitz, David Riesman, John Silber, and C. Vann Woodward, among others.

303. Tehranian, Majid, editor. **Restructuring for Ethnic Peace: A Public Debate at the University of Hawaii.** Honolulu, Hawaii: University of Hawaii, Spark M. Matsunaga Institute for Peace, 1991. 187p. ISBN 1-8803-0903-3.

This volume brings together presentations made at seven public forums held in 1991concerning problems of ethnic and racial tensions on the University of Hawaii campus. The first of these forums focused on academic freedom rights. Short papers from four University of Hawaii professors discuss the 1990 campus controversy over a series of student newspaper articles and letters to the editor which focused on issues of Hawaiian history and the place that settler- and missionary-led genocide had in destroying native island culture. The topics of some of the other campus forums here recounted include racism, colonialism, affirmative action, and "The Search for Ethnic Peace in Hawaii." Appendices provide a chronology of events and reprint original documents from the controversy. Included are pieces by a native Hawaiian administrator (also a presenter at the first forum) named Haunani-Kay Trask and "A Statement on Racism in Academe" issued by the Faculty of the Philosophy Department.

304. Thomson, Judith Jarvis, et al. "Academic Freedom and Tenure: Corporate Funding of Academic Research." **Academe** 69(6): 18a-23a, November-December 1983.

In light of the growing role of corporate-sponsored research on campus, a subcommittee of the AAUP's Committee A (Academic Freedom) investigated the nature and extent of its impact on academic freedom. The findings and recommendations are discussed in this report. Because of shrinking state support since the late 1970s, corporate research support has become more important. This raises a number of potential risks. Faculty may slight pure research for applied research that is of interest to corporate sponsors. Also, faculty may spend more time consulting for corporate sponsors at the expense of their campus-based teaching and research. Close corporate ties may also affect recruitment and evaluation of graduate students and junior faculty. Universities may also have conflicts of interest if their retention, tenure, promotion and salary decisions inappropriately favor those faculty who generate large research income for the university. Further concern related to potential restrictions and delays in disseminating research results from corporate-sponsored research. The committee was also concerned that a corporation might restrict, through control of research funds, the researcher's choice of a research topic. Suggested guidelines and principles governing corporate-funded research are discussed.

305. Trachtenberg, Stephen Joel. "What Strategy Should We Now Adopt to Protect Academic Freedom?" **Academe** 82(1): 23-25, January/February 1996.

President of George Washington University, Trachtenberg recounts numerous attacks on tenure and the academy in the professional literature, popular press, and TV of the early 1990s. The author outlines a strategy for an "active defense" of academic freedom based on three principles: 1) award tenure as a contract that runs 30-35 years with retirement at age 65; 2) pursue education and outreach to the American public regarding the benefits of tenure (not just its abuses); and 3) support fixed-term teaching contracts as a replacement for the awarding of tenure.

306. Trow, Martin. "Defining the Issues in University-Government Relations: An International Perspective." **Studies in Higher Education** 8(2): 115-128, 1983.

Using a comparative perspective, Trow investigates the growing financial dependence of universities on governments, and the potential loss of institutional freedom or autonomy. The threat to institutions comes not from a limited or external budgetary source, but from the governmental use of budgetary support to influence the "core elements of university autonomy." These elements can include appointments, promotion, performance assessment, curricular content, instruction, and academic standards. The best protection of university autonomy, says Trow, is provided by the expertise of the faculty, and the freedom that necessarily must accompany that. Having multiple sources of budgetary support is beneficial as well. However, as public university systems expand, only elite institutions are likely to be accorded an optimal degree of freedom. Others may be more subject to the control that accompanies the accountability movement, the democratization of higher education, and budgetary constraints on public funds. The key challenge for universities is to preserve their autonomy while trying to accommodate fiscal constraints, manpower needs, "the research and development needs of industry and government," and the career goals of students/consumers.

307. Tyrrell, R. Emmett Jr. "A Bizarre Province: Preliminary Findings from **The American Spectator's** Amnesty in Academia Campaign." **American Spectator** 24(11): 16-18, November 1991.

Tyrrell recounts and analyzes the initial data collected by Amnesty in Academia, an organization founded "to monitor human rights violations on campus." Recounting the hundreds of calls placed to the AIA Hotline, this essay also addresses methods by which cases will be resolved. AIA will pursue some cases through court challenges and others through mediation teams sent by the organization to universities. The charge is made that politically-correct authoritarians at a variety of institutions have dismissed fourteen professors and intimidated numerous students. Specific cases are outlined.

308. University of Massachusetts at Amherst. W.E.B. DuBois Dept. of Afro-American Studies. "Don't Believe the Hype: Chronicle of a Mugging by the Media – A Documentary History of the Debate Between the W.E.B. DuBois Department of Afro-American Studies and Julius Lester." **Black Scholar** 19(6): 27-43, November 1988.

Signed by the W.E.B. DuBois Department of Afro-American Studies, this article rebuts one by Julius Lester, called "Academic Freedom and the Black Intellectual." Reproduced here are University of Massachusetts at Amherst documents related to the termination of Julius Lester's (a tenured professor) relationship with the Dept. of Afro-American Studies. Included are: the departmental position on Lester's claim that James Baldwin was an anti-Semite; a chronicle of the events leading up to Lester's transfer to the Dept. of Judaic and Near Eastern Studies; a letter from the Dept. to the Dean of Humanities and Fine Arts; an open letter from the Dept. to "Colleagues, Friends and Members of the University Community;" and the text of a "Special Report of the Faculty Senate Rules Committee." The Rules Committee found that while Professor Lester was not expelled by his department, he did not request a transfer. Therefore, according the this Faculty Senate Committee, "there is no evidence of any direct threat to academic freedom in connection with Professor Lester's transfer."

309. Veraldi, Lorna. "Academic Freedom and Sexual Harassment." **Contemporary Education** 66(2): 74-76, Winter 1995.

Veraldi starts by citing the 1994 case of the University of New Hampshire Sexual Harassment Appeals Board ruling that Professor J. Donald Silva was guilty in his teaching of "repeated and sustained comments and behavior of a sexual and otherwise intrusive nature." Comments made during classroom lectures and in the university library were at issue in this case, and in a few others cited by Veraldi. This author charges that sexual harassment policies are written too broadly and thereby impinge on academic freedom. Veraldi also finds an element of gender discrimination implicit in the idea that women in particular must be protected from 'adult' language, or that they necessarily are more offended by sexual comments and innuendos.

310. Weber, Arnold R., with comments by Edwin J. Delattre and Robert Royal and by Peter Suedfeld. "Decision in the Matter of Professor Barbara C. Foley." **Academic Questions** 1(1): 65-85, Winter 1987/1988.

This is a reprint with commentary of Northwestern President Weber's 1987 decision to uphold Provost Raymond W. Mack's denial of promotion and tenure to Professor Foley, despite a unanimous vote in favor of tenure and promotion from the faculty committee. Foley was involved in a 1985 disruption of the campus talk of Adolfo Calero, a Nicaraguan Contra rebel leader. A faculty committee determined that this incident violated academic freedom. Foley charged that Mack's denial of tenure violated her academic freedom. The Northwestern President quotes extensively from AAUP policy statements, as well as from transcripts of hearings on the Calero incident and tenure appeal. In two pieces of accompanying commentary (called "Comment (I)" and "Comment (II)"), the Northwestern decision is lauded, and an increasing threat to academic freedom from professors who misuse the principle is decried.

311. Winks, Robin W. "Government and the University in the United States." In John W. Chapman, editor. **The Western University on Trial.** Berkeley, Calif.: University of California Press, 1983. pp. 184-197. ISBN 0-5200-4940-3.

Specific ways that the United States government interferes with institutional autonomy are here addressed, including cumbersome administrative and accounting needs associated with compliance with government regulations, affirmative action, privacy/confidentiality laws regarding student and personnel records, censorship or pre-publication review of federally funded projects. Threats to the diversity of types or institutions of higher education in the United States, and threats to the political neutrality of these institutions are among the results of increasing government interference in higher education.

312. Woolf, Patricia K. "Integrity and Accountability in Research and Publication." **Scholarly Publishing** 24(4): 204-213, July 1993.

Woolf addresses abuses of scientific and academic freedom and calls on scientists to protect these "privileges" of freedom by rooting out and issuing sanctions against cases of scientific fraud and research misconduct. Included here are ethical guidelines for publication of research.

Chapter 7

Academic Freedom and the Culture Wars

313. Abcarian, Gilbert. "Ideology and Alienation: Conservative Images of the Liberal Academic Establishment." **Educational Theory** 19(2): 111-128, Spring 1969.

Abcarian analyzes politically conservative negative images of the academy, calling these images the bureaucratic, philosophic, political, and professional. He discusses these right-wing indictments of academia along with a prescriptive academic model proposed by what the author calls the "Anti-Establishment Conservatives." Key figures whose views are argued against here include: William F. Buckley, M. Stanton Evans, and E. Merrill Root. According to Abcarian, indictments of academia by the right (here analyzed) include charges that the liberal establishment professes "objectivity" or use of the scientific method while practicing indoctrination; that there is no free marketplace of ideas in American universities; that those professors and students who resist liberalism are ostracized in an environment that nonetheless professes a dedication to diversity. Elements of the academic model being pushed by the right in Abcarian's view include the claim that the university's primary responsibility is to transmit or perpetuate the cultural heritage of the United States; that the intellectual climate of universities must be one that fosters morality; that the ultimate commitment of higher education must be to principles of truth, principles to be affirmed and supported rather than questioned.

314. Altman, Andrew. "Liberalism and Campus Hate Speech: A Philosophical Examination." **Ethics** 103(2): 302-317, January 1993.

The author argues that there is a basis in the political philosophy of liberalism for a narrow prohibition of hate speech. Accepting that hate speech can cause psychological harm to those at whom it is directed, but accepting that speech codes cannot be viewpoint neutral, Altman does not contend that regulation is justified solely on the basis of harm. Instead, he argues, using speech act theory, that some forms of hate speech wrong people by treating them as moral subordinates. The aim in regulating such speech should not be to prohibit speech causing psychological harm, but to prohibit speech which, regardless of its content, engages in such "speech-act subordination."

315. Aronowitz, Stanley.   "Academic Freedom: A Structural Approach."
      Educational Theory 35 (1): 1-13, Winter 1985.

Aronowitz discusses both economic and ideological factors in the current crisis in higher education. The economic downturn has led educational policymakers to address what they see as the "overproduction" of educated labor. Consequently, state-supported liberal arts institutions, which had opened up in the last two decades in response to pressures from working adults, women, and blacks, are under attack. Similarly, liberal arts curricula are criticized as not being "functional" or instrumental in the labor market. The worsening economic situation has also created pressure on college students to seek out vocational curricula, thus further damaging the liberal arts. Politically, a growing neoconservatism has attacked the liberal arts as a haven for radical faculty, whose academic freedom and jobs are thereby threatened.   The declining job market for many academics further undermines academic freedom and encourages conformity because of the pressure to obtain and keep tenure-track faculty positions.   Consequently, critically-oriented faculty are pressured to accommodate themselves to the more mainstream expectations of their departments. This narrowing of intellectual diversity runs counter to popular conceptions of the university as a pluralistic institution providing a marketplace-of-ideas.

316. Astin, Alexander W.   "Values, Assessment, and Academic Freedom: A
      Challenge to the Accrediting Process. **NCA Quarterly** 67(2): 295-306, Fall
      1992.

Part of this article addresses the contradictions between universities' explicit and implicit values and goals. Astin suggests that many universities effectively define excellence in terms of either their reputation or their resources, rather than in terms of the development of their students. The other part of the article, however, examines the political correctness (PC) debate on campus and its impact on academic freedom. While Astin argues that campus speech codes do in fact inhibit free speech, he also contends that 1) such speech codes are rare and 2) the conservative critics of political correctness are not driven by a desire to promote critical thinking and free speech. Rather, they are seizing an opportunity to challenge liberal academic reform, particularly on such policies as affirmative action and the curriculum.   For Astin, however, it is important to remember that academic freedom is a necessary condition for the pursuit of truth. The freedom to express and discuss diverse views is our strength.

317. Aufderheide, Patricia, ed. **Beyond PC: Toward a Politics of Understanding.** St. Paul, Minn.: Graywolf Press, 1992. 239p. ISBN 1-55597-164-4. LC 92-2513.

Included in this edited collection are reprinted articles, essays, and book chapters reflecting various perspectives on the political correctness (PC) debate. Focusing on higher education, most contributions address the debate over speech codes and free speech, the multiculturalization of the curriculum (and the alleged concomitant demise of the classics of Western culture), the lowering of academic standards, identity politics, and related topics. The contention of the PC critics is that speech codes limit the speech of both students and faculty, and that the multiculturalization of the curriculum narrowly redefines what knowledge should be taught, thus limiting the academic freedom of faculty and students. The academic "search for truth" is constrained by the ideological constraints of political correctness. Furthermore, the classics and great works of Western literature and culture (the "canon") are given less prominence in the curriculum, resulting in a lowering of curricular quality. Other contributors argue that the critique of PC on campus is a media-inspired myth, and that the broadening of the curriculum is appropriate and modest in its effect. Notable contributors include Nat Hentoff, Ruth Perry, Sara Diamond, George Will, Mortimer Adler, Molefi Asante, Michael Berube, Todd Gitlin, Patricia Aufderheide, and Dinesh D'Souza, among others.

318. Balch, Stephen H. and Herbert I. London. "The Tenured Left." **Commentary** 82(4): 41-51, October 1986.

The authors charge that university campuses are where most of the political extremists in the United States are located. Evidence cited for this claim includes: a 1984 Carnegie Foundation for the Advancement of Teaching survey of the political orientation of faculty members; new left-leaning scholarly journal titles (such as *Dialectical Anthropology*) and the influence and writings of Marxist and leftist scholars (such as Bertell Ollman and Frederic Jameson); new partisan or politically-oriented courses in such areas as Economics and Black Studies; the proliferation of peace studies programs; and a politicization of scholarly associations. Balch and London see in all of this a rise in "adversarial education" in which class, racial, and socio-cultural differences and resentments are emphasized and even encouraged. Academic freedom is threatened by a parceling out of higher education resources with little regard for intellectual merit. The authors contend that academic freedom in its current form actually serves those groups which are the most vocal, assertive, or sizable.

319. Berman, Paul, ed. **Debating P.C.: The Controversy over Political Correctness on College Campuses.** New York: Laurel, 1992. 338p. ISBN 0-4405-0466-X.

According to Paul Berman, the political correctness debate began in 1990 when neoconservatives charged that campus leftists, both faculty and students, were radicalizing the curriculum and creating an atmosphere of intolerance on campus. The political correctness (pc) debate revolves around three major and related issues. First, critics of political correctness argue that college campuses are becoming dominated by a radical multiculturalism that promotes ethnic separatism and is socially divisive. Second, and related to the first point, the classic works of Western literature (the "canon") are allegedly being devalued and replaced by radical, multicultural works that are not only of less enduring quality, but also critical of Western culture. Third, critics argue that campus groups fighting racial, ethnic, and gender bias are passing speech and behavior codes that deny the free speech and academic freedom of many students and faculty. Berman's edited collection presents a cross-section of participants and positions in this debate. Major sections address an overview of the debate, the canon, speech codes, a case study of the University of Texas, public schools and multiculturalism, and other, diverse views.

320. Burris, Val, and Sara Diamond. "Academic Freedom, Conspicuous Benevolence, and the National Association of Scholars." **Critical Sociology** 18(3): 125-142, Fall 1991.

Burris and Diamond examine the network of neoconservative foundations (e.g., Mellon-Scaife Family Trusts, John M. Olin Foundation, Adolph Coors Foundation, Lynde and Harry Bradley Foundation) and think tanks (e.g., Heritage Foundation, American Enterprise Institute, Madison Center for Educational Affairs) that provide an ideological support structure for the National Association of Scholars (NAS). The authors describe these foundations and organizations and the thrust of their political activities since the mid-1980s. Particular focus is given to their activities in the area of higher education, where they have fought against multiculturalism, affirmative action, and political correctness. According to Burris and Diamond, the NAS and its supporters have tried to portray themselves as true supporters of academic freedom, higher standards and intellectual diversity on campus, in contrast to what the neoconservatives characterize as the repressive and antidemocratic tactics of liberal, left and radical faculty. The authors argue that this is part of a strategy of the neoconservatives to capture the intellectual and moral high ground in campus debates over policy, access, and curriculum. Burris and Diamond contend that these neoconservative groups support "private monied interests" at the expense of publicly supported education.

321. Chait, Jonathan. "Bad Examples: Political Correctness and Academic Freedom." **Reason** 25(7): 58+, December 1993.

Chait reviews the controversy surrounding Professor David Goldberg of the Sociology department at the University of Michigan. Goldberg came under fire by students for what they considered to be racial and gender insensitivity reflected in his teaching. Specifically, Goldberg used examples in his statistics class that debunked liberal beliefs on certain matters of race and gender. Students were offended and complained to university officials and to Goldberg's department head. In recounting the events, Chait observes that Goldberg's academic freedom was not well defended. He argues that these events, in combination with an earlier controversy over another instructor's race relations class, had a chilling effect on faculty members' willingness to teach certain courses.

322. Coleman, James S. "The Sidney Hook Memorial Award Address: On the Self-Suppression of Academic Freedom." **Academic Questions** 4(1): 17-22, Winter 1990/1991.

Coleman charges that threats to academic freedom come less from administrators or universities than from fellow faculty members. These threats come through spoken or unspoken taboos on what sorts of questions may legitimately be researched by professors or asked by students. Examples cited include genetic bases for racial differences in intelligence and the possible sources of homosexuality in biology or genetics. The author focuses less on policy issues here than on subtle pressures towards conformity that lead academics into "self-suppression" of research questions. Coleman calls for recasting our understanding of the hierarchies of academic rights and values, with the value of free inquiry held higher than the value of equality.

323. Cox, Phil. "The Disputation of Hate: Speech Codes, Pluralism and Academic Freedoms." **Social Theory and Practice** 21(1): 113-144, Spring 1995.

The author disputes the propriety of speech codes, on philosophical and pluralist grounds. The typical arguments in favor of speech codes are found lacking. Even if such codes could pass constitutional muster, it would be better for universities, and a more effective response to the problem were institutions to not engage in negative efforts to punish offensive speech but instead find positive ways to promote tolerance, civility and diversity.

324. Csorba, Les, III. **Academic License: The War on Academic Freedom.** Evanston, Ill.: UCA Books, 1988. 329p. ISBN 0-937-04711-2.

This is an edited collection of essays, most of which appear to have been originally presented at an Accuracy in Academia annual conference. The majority of the essays are critical of a perceived leftist ideological bias in universities. A common theme is that many of the radical leftists of the 1960s have become administrators and tenured faculty members in today's universities and colleges. In their new positions, these leftists are imposing their ideological biases on administrative decisions, curriculum development, and classroom instruction. Rather than presenting the prescribed curriculum in a balanced manner, many faculty members are indulging their own political biases. This constitutes, say the critics, academic license, which is an abuse of academic freedom. In other cases, leftist faculty are developing curricula, such as Peace Studies or Women's Studies, with a distinct leftist perspective. A number of the essays review particular cases in which conservative students and faculty members were allegedly denied their academic freedom or freedom of speech by leftist faculty and administrators. These include cases at Dartmouth, Fordham, University of Southern California, Stanford, State University of New York at Farmingdale, George Washington University, and the University of Colorado at Boulder, among others. A couple of the essays reflect opposing viewpoints.

325. Davidson, Cathy N. "'PH' Stands for Political Hypocrisy." **Academe** 77 (5): 8-14, September-October, 1991.

Davidson argues that political correctness is not a threat to intellectual freedom and free speech, and that college and university campuses are as intellectually diverse as one might hope. However, neoconservatives have cynically used the charge of political correctness to promote their conservative agenda for higher education, which includes opposition to affirmative action and support for a curriculum that "promotes capitalist and Judeo-Christian values" (p, 10). Davidson considers it "political hypocrisy" for conservatives to conceal their political interests under the guise of supporting unbiased objectivity and academic freedom. She believes this is a greater threat to the intellectual life of campuses than political correctness, a threat fabricated by conservatives and the media.

326. Dey, Eric L. and Sylvia Hurtado. "Faculty Attitudes Toward Regulating Speech on College Campuses." **Review of Higher Education** 20(1): 15-32, Fall 1996.

Using data from a 1992-1993 survey of college teaching faculty, the authors examined the variables that influenced or were correlated with faculty support for campus policies regulating speech. Among some of the findings were: most faculty were found to support prohibiting hate speech but not to support banning outside speakers with extreme views. Conservative, rather than liberal professors were more likely to support prohibitions on racist or sexist speech.

327. Diamond, Sara. "Readin', Writin', and Repressin.'" **Z Magazine** 4(2): 44-48, February 1991.

Diamond analyzes the efforts of the right-wing National Association of Scholars to influence public higher education policy, organize conservative faculty, and effect conservative change on college campuses in the United States. Publisher of *Academic Questions*, the NAS was founded in 1987 by Stephen H. Balch and Herbert I. London. Diamond traces the history of the NAS to other conservative and neo-conservative thinkers and organizations. Citing NAS activity at the University of Texas in opposition to diversity and multiculturalist coursework, Diamond also discusses an NAS member survey designed to gather information about left-leaning professors, courses, and administrative practices.

328. Dickman, Howard, editor. **The Imperiled Academy.** New Brunswick, NJ: Transaction Publishers, 1993. 281p. ISBN 1-5600-0097-X.

This edited compilation addresses cultural and academic disputes surrounding issues of political correctness, relativism and postmodernism, multiculturalism, racial preferences, and feminism. Concerns outlined in these essays include claims that the traditional role and proper mission of the university is being undermined by postmodernist, anti-objectivist, and relativist studies and by efforts to set boundaries on acceptable campus speech. Parallels of current pluralist trends are found in Isaiah Berlin's work; historical sources of current political correctness moralism are found in the doctrinal demands of America's early church-affiliated schools. A unifying theme throughout is that, to the detriment of higher education, the campus movements of the 1960s have gained strength and institutional support. These essays are presented in direct opposition to the trend of "this new variant of intolerance and ideological orthodoxy sweeping the universities." The book includes essays by Daniel Bonevac, Stanley Rothman, Seymour Lipset, Eric Mack, Lino Graglia, Alan Kors, Joseph Hamburger, Jerry Martin, and Fred Sommers.

329. D'Souza, Dinesh. **Illiberal Education: The Politics of Race and Sex on Campus.** New York: The Free Press, 1991. 319p. ISBN 0-02-908100-9. LC 90-47055.

D'Souza's work is primarily a critique of political correctness on college campuses and its effect on curricula, freedom of speech, tolerance for diverse opinions, admissions requirements, and scholarship. He is particularly critical of what he sees as a growing liberal consensus that constrains intellectual freedom on campus and hinders the achievement of excellence. This is reflected in campus speech codes, in preferential admissions, in a devaluation of the classics of Western literature and scholarship (the "canon"), and in the ascendancy of postmodern literary criticism, multiculturalism, and Afrocentrism. These developments serve to limit the academic freedom of both faculty and students, and a number of cases are discussed, including those of Stephan and Abigail Thernstrom.

330. D'Souza, Dinesh, Christina Holl Sommers, Charles Murray, Christopher Hitchens. "Forbidden Thoughts: A Roundtable on Taboo Research." **American Enterprise** 6(1): 65-72, January/February 1995.

This essay presents the transcript of a discussion among iconoclastic academics all engaged actively in controversial research or political writing. Pressures to not pursue certain lines of inquiry have been experienced by all present, whether from feminists (against Sommers), from socialists (against Hitchens), or from social scientists (against Murray and D'Souza). The authors decry hypocrisy and intolerance in academia, as well as a lack of moral accountability among scholars. The experiences of being a maverick academic and a perceived overzealousness in the reactions of politically correct opponents mark the careers of all four.

331. Fish, Stanley. **There's No Such Thing As Free Speech, And It's A Good Thing, Too.** New York: Oxford University Press, 1994. 332p. LC 93-15347. ISBN 0-19-508018-1.

This collection of essays ranges widely over such topics as free speech, campus speech codes, the literary "canon" wars, affirmative action, reverse racism, critical legal studies, the new historicism, and literary theory, among others. However, a number of the essays deal with the biases of language and ideology that often limit our understanding of intellectual and academic freedom. Many of Fish's insights deal with subtle constraints on free speech, competing definitions of legitimate knowledge, and limitations of the marketplace-of-ideas. Across these topics, he reiterates the unavoidable social construction of knowledge and the implicit assumptions or biases of seemingly neutral categories (e.g., free speech, merit, reason, fairness, the marketplace-of-ideas).

332. Giroux, Henry A. "Teaching in the Age of 'Political Correctness.'" **The Educational Forum** 59(2): 130-139, Winter 1995.

Anti-politically correct conservatives argue that leftist and radical academics are undermining standards of excellence by promoting open admissions, multicultural curricula, and affirmative action. Conservatives argue further that these radical academics attack academic freedom by politicizing the curriculum. That is, their teaching is supposedly guided by a desire to promote radical social change, rather than by a desire to seek the truth. This has led to censorship of the curricular classics (the canon), as well as censorship of certain types of speech (hate speech). However, Giroux counters these arguments by suggesting that all knowledge is socially selected and transmitted. One must necessarily see the connection between social and political power and the curricular knowledge that is considered legitimate. True intellectual freedom entails a full and open examination of the connections of power and knowledge. The cultural conservatives, by contrast, take for granted the origin and value of their knowledge, focusing only on its transmission. This serves to oppress students, deskill teachers and fossilize knowledge.

333. Hentoff, Nat. "Speech Codes on the Campus and Problems of Free Speech." **Dissent** 38: 546-549, Fall 1991.

The author, citing speech codes at Stanford University and the University of Buffalo Law School, discusses the chilling effect they have on students and faculty who are choosing more often to self-censor their public comments. The views of students and faculty interviewed by Hentoff at a variety of institutions are here quoted.

334. Himmelfarb, Gertrude. "Academic Advocates." **Commentary** 100(3): 46-49, September 1995.

Discussing the case of the City College of New York's 1992 removal of Leonard Jeffries from his chairmanship of the Black Studies Department and his subsequent reinstatement, Himmelfarb holds that the substitution of professor as advocate for professor as truth-seeker is the most important academic freedom principle at issue here. Postmodernist objections to objectivity, and an increasingly politicized classroom work together to undermine scholarship, according to Himmelfarb. With no ideal truth or knowledge there are no safeguards "against willful ignorance and deception."

335. Huer, Jon. **Tenure for Socrates: A Study in the Betrayal of the American Professor.** New York: Bergin & Garvey, 1991. 211p. LC 90-38827. ISBN 0-89789-244-5.

Provocatively written, this book argues that academic freedom and tenure are currently being wasted by those faculty who supposedly need them. Huer divides academics into those from "functional" disciplines (e.g. accounting), and those from "academic" disciplines (e.g. sociology). The functional disciplines deal primarily with the learning and teaching of facts and therefore are in no need of academic freedom and tenure. By contrast, the academic disciplines should be pursuing "truth" and questioning orthodoxy, which could potentially place their jobs at risk. Consequently, they are in need of academic freedom and tenure, which allows them the security to pursue these larger social truths. The problem, however, is that faculty in these academic disciplines mostly ignore their obligations to pursue truth. Instead, they develop expert knowledge in narrow and obscure academic specialties that are not part of the pursuit of truth. So, Huer argues, they do not deserve or need academic freedom and tenure. He proceeds to discuss the distinction between facts and truth, the potential value of Marxism in a capitalist society and culture, the dangers of professors becoming professionals (i.e., seeing oneself as a commodity; emulating the functional disciplines; becoming orthodox in their views), and other encroachments on the pursuit of truth (e.g., tenure as an economic sinecure).

336. Hunter, James Davison. "Education." In James Davison Hunter. **Culture Wars: The Struggle to Define America.** New York: Basic Books, 1991. pp. 197-224. ISBN 0-465-01534-4. LC 91-70065.

Hunter's chapter on the culture wars in education deals with both K-12 schooling and higher education. Within higher education, the culture wars often center "on what the boundaries of academic freedom should be," boiling down to a "battle to define the content of knowledge and truth" (p. 214). In effect, these are struggles over the curriculum, with both sides arguing that the other is politicizing what is taught. Conservatives argue that many universities are secular humanist institutions and that a growing multiculturalist curriculum undermines traditional values and the classic curriculum. This perspective provides support not only for challenges to the progressivist agenda, but also for parochial and Evangelical colleges, which vary in their accommodation of secular trends. The reassertion of traditional values led some religious colleges and seminaries in the 1980s and early 1990s to purge professors who did not adhere to the values and religious orthodoxy of the institution. By contrast, progressives argue that the curriculum is inherently political and they are simply advocating for more inclusiveness and diversity within it.

337. Kimball, Roger. **Tenured Radicals: How Politics Has Corrupted Our Higher Education.** Rev. ed. Chicago: Elephant Paperbacks, 1998. 246p. LC 98-11100. ISBN 1-56663-195-5.

Kimball examines the culture wars in American higher education, contending that the traditional canon of Western scholarship and literature, most notably in the humanities, is being replaced by anti-Western, deconstructionist, postmodernist, post-structuralist, and multiculturalist theory and literature. This academic revolution is being championed by "tenured radicals" who are denying what Kimball argues is the best of what has been written and thought in Western culture. As a result, politics and ideology dictate what is considered legitimate knowledge in higher education, thereby constraining both the academic's freedom to teach and the student's freedom to learn. According to Kimball, this has led to the degradation and corruption of higher education.

338. Kors, Alan Charles, and Harvey A. Silverglate. **The Shadow University: The Betrayal of Liberty on America's Campuses.** New York: The Free Press, 1998. 415p. LC 98-8728. ISBN 0-684-85321-3.

After reviewing the legal and philosophical underpinnings for free speech and academic freedom, Kors and Silverglate document their growing denial on college campuses. The authors trace the origins of this movement to the political philosophy of Herbert Marcuse. Marcuse argued that formally equal freedoms (such as free speech) in a fundamentally unequal society served to reinforce the existing inequalities and power relations. This analysis provides a rationale for denying free speech for some if it will promote the equality of those less powerful. Kors and Silverglate argue that campus speech codes and the restrictive climate of political correctness grow out of this perspective. They discuss a large number of cases of the denial of free speech and academic freedom, both of students and faculty. Additional chapters discuss 1) the official campus equating of multiculturalism with "group identity" (and the corresponding minimization of individual identity, conscience and autonomy), and 2) infringements upon the due process rights of students, among other topics.

339. Korwar, Arati R. **War of Words: Speech Codes at Public Colleges and Universities.** Nashville, Tennessee: Freedom Forum First Amendment Center, 1994. 56 p.

This study examines the range of public college and university regulations governing speech and conduct and provides a state-by-state breakdown of 14 types of speech rules organized "generally in order of their progressive offensiveness to the First Amendment" (p. 22). Korwar includes sexual harassment policies in his listing, but does not analyze them. The author examined student handbooks and codes of conduct from all accredited and publicly funded colleges and universities in the 50 states and D.C. which offered at least a bachelor's degree. The results are charted, and state totals are provided for each type of rule. Korwar summarizes the views of both proponents and opponents of campus hate speech codes, provides an overview of the relevant case law affecting such rules, and proposes alternative methods for combatting the problems of racism, prejudice and hate crimes on college campuses.

340. Lewy, Guenter. "Academic Ethics and the Radical Left." **Policy Review** 19: 29-42, Winter 1982.

Lewy addresses the issue of political advocacy and bias in the classroom by radical professors. Denying the claim by some on the left that U.S. higher education serves to indoctrinate students according to the interests of a capitalist ruling class, Lewy charges that an increasing percentage of left or liberal academics pursue political agendas in their classrooms. Citing critiques of objectivity in the hard and social sciences, a lack of codes of professional conduct, and the necessity of examining the ideology of certain candidates for appointment, tenure, and promotion, Lewy calls on academics to pursue self-governance more effectively so as to avoid the damage that would occur from the interference of outside forces.

341. Messer-Davidow, Ellen. "Manufacturing the Attack on Liberalized Higher Education." **Social Text** 36: 40-80, Fall 1993.

The author charges that the right has invented its attack on higher education in order to effect "radical cultural change." In addressing debates over political correctness and academic theories of post-structuralism, feminism, and Marxism, Messer-Davidow puts these debates in the context of a history of the American conservative movement. The influence of cultural conservative thinkers and foundations is detailed here. Included in Messer-Davidow's analysis are such figures as M. Stanton Evans, Stephen Balch, Paul Weyrich, and William F. Buckley (among others); and foundations such as Olin, Coors, Bradley, and Scaife. Particularly effective has been establishment of policy-oriented think tanks, training institutes, and grass-roots organizations in higher education, including the Intercollegiate Studies Institute, the Madison Center for Educational Affairs, the Leadership Institute, the National Association of Scholars, the Center for Individual Rights, and the Washington Legal Foundation, and such Heritage Foundation projects as the Bradley Scholars and Salvatori Center for Academic Leadership. Funding sources and activities of these organizations are detailed, as are the statements, publications, and policy decisions of Reagan and Bush-era appointees such as Lynne V. Cheney (NEH Chairman). Connections are drawn between right wing foundations granting funds and organizations leveraging changes in higher education. The author's "field research in conservative organizations" concludes that there are three main areas of attack on higher education: the manufacture of conservative victim stories; the push to revise curricula to emphasize conservative values; and a new focus on legal and grass-roots change through direct mail, electronic bulletin boards (such as the *National Review* "Town Hall" system), and cable television (such as the Free Congress Foundation's syndicated "National Empowerment Television"). The author concludes by calling on progressive academics to engage more in activism and less in debate.

342. Mohl, Raymond A. "The Culture Wars and the Universities." **Educational Forum** 58(1): 15-21, Fall 1993.

Mohl suggests that the universities are embroiled in a battle over academic values (the "culture wars") and that academic freedom and the creation of new knowledge are at risk. Citing Lynne Cheney's *Telling the Truth*, a National Endowment for the Humanities report, Mohl points to a stream of conservative books contending that universities have become politicized and are suppressing academic freedom. While he agrees that they are politicized, Mohl counters that it is the conservatives doing the politicization. Behind such books as Allan Bloom's *The Closing of the American Mind* and E. D. Hirsch's *Cultural Literacy*, cultural conservatives are reasserting that Western culture should be the shared body of knowledge. At the same time, they are opposing new topics and lines of inquiry in academia that may help generate new knowledge, expand what is considered legitimate knowledge, and challenge received wisdom. For Mohl, the academic values of freedom of inquiry and the creation of new knowledge must be defended against political intervention.

343. National Association of Scholars. "Sexual Harassment and Academic Freedom." [Online]. (Web address: http://www.nas.org/statements/harass.htm). (Accessed: April 14, 1999).

In this position statement, the NAS contends that while sexual harassment is impermissible, efforts to combat it have often infringed on academic freedom. Campus anti-harassment policies can reflect a number of problems: 1) "harassment" is vaguely defined; 2) opinions and attitudes can be prohibited, inhibiting free speech; 3) the occurrence of harassment is subjectively defined; 4) mid-level administrators are often in charge of the entire process, from investigation to punishment; 5) an investigation can be a "pretext" for ideological attacks; 6) groups are sometimes penalized for the acts of individuals; and 7) sanctions often look like "thought reform." To correct these problems, the NAS recommends: 1) precise definitions of sexual harassment; 2) a statute of limitations on charges; 3) due process and the adequate right of defense for those accused; 4) punishment for knowingly false accusations; and 5) forceful action against "proven harassers."

344. Nyden, Paul J. "Labor and the Defense of Academic Freedom." In Marvin J. Berlowitz and Frank E. Chapman, Jr., editors. **The United States Educational System: Marxist Approaches.** Minneapolis: Marxist Educational Press, 1980. pp. 105-113. LC 80-12394. ISBN 0-930656-12-1.

Drawing upon his own experiences as a professor fired from the University of Pittsburgh, Nyden talks about the ways that Marxist or radical faculty members can defend their academic freedom. They should be fully aware, says Nyden, that powerful economic and class interests have significant influence in universities. This is reflected in the corporate dominance of many Boards of Trustees, in the growing number of corporate-funded professorships, and in government and corporate-funded research. For protection, progressive faculty can and should forge alliances with communities and working people, particularly trade union and civil rights organizations. A broad base of community support may help ensure that a progressive faculty member is less likely to be fired for his or her political ideas. Vigorous community response, and the accompanying bad publicity, may deter university administrations considering such firings. Beyond developing community support, radical faculty need to be top scholars who are active in professional associations and publish their work. Nyden also suggests that a progressive research agenda, which takes seriously the issues and concerns of working people, may further enhance a professor's community support.

345. "On 'Accuracy in Academia' and Academic Freedom." **Academe** 71(5): 1a, September-October 1985.

This report represents the AAUP's response to and position on Accuracy in Academia, a watchdog group looking for faculty who, they allege, disseminate misinformation. The AAUP considers Accuracy in Academia, an offshoot of Accuracy in Media, a threat to academic freedom. The organization attempts to recruit individuals to report on what faculty say in their classes. Faculty disseminating "misinformation" would be notified and asked to correct their errors. Otherwise, the organization would publish their errors. The AAUP's position is threefold. First, the classroom must be protected as a place for the free and open expression of ideas, including "new or unpopular theories." Spies in the classroom would discourage the free exchange of ideas, both for students and faculty. Second, the AAUP considers Accuracy in Academia presumptuous and "arrogant" to say that it can determine which ideas are "correct." That is the job of university trustees and faculty colleagues engaged in peer evaluation. Third, it appears to the AAUP that Accuracy in Academia is most concerned with promoting its own rather narrow and sectarian political agenda. As always, the AAUP adheres to its *1940 Statement of Principles on Academic Freedom and Tenure* and related guidelines.

346. Parenti, Michael. "The Myth of the Liberal Campus." **Humanist** 55(5): 20-23, September/October 1995.

Parenti disputes the claim of conservatives that most American universities are places where reactionary leftist views predominate. Evidence is provided to the contrary that anti-capitalist views were historically suppressed in higher education, that left-leaning professors have often been fired in the years since World War I, and that university administrations engaged in repressive tactics in response to protests of the 1960s.

347. Riley, Gresham. "The Cost of Speech Codes." **Academe** 79(4): 26-30, July/August 1993.

Riley is a former President of Colorado College. He sees the consequences of restricting student hate speech as a license to eventually suppress other unpopular speech. Riley argues that false ideas, even those that offend, must be allowed a forum and must be countered by arguments.

348. Root, Michael. "The Open Classroom and Its Enemies." In Patricia Meyer Spacks, editor. **Advocacy in the Classroom: Problems and Possibilities.** New York: St. Martin's Press, 1996. pp. 84-95. ISBN 0-3121-6127-1.

Root claims that classroom teaching and dialogue is less open now than in the past, due to the dogmatic political advocacy efforts of some in academia. He disagrees with such conservative critics as William Bennett and Allen Bloom that conservative values should be advanced by colleges and universities. But the ideal of neutrality in arts and sciences is a myth; academic freedom should therefore be expanded to protect partisan research and teaching. Dogmatism rather than partisanship is the enemy of the open classroom, which should be committed not to value-neutrality but to critical debate.

349. Schmidt, Benno. "The University and Freedom." **Educational Record** 73(1): 14-18, Winter 1992.

Focusing mainly on the issue of speech codes on campus, Schmidt laments a current trend toward lack of faith in the power of free expression to counteract offensive speech. From his perspective, there are well-meaning but misguided groups on numerous campuses who are willing to proscribe speech toward the end of furthering an enforced sense of civility and community. As Schmidt argues, to attempt to further "civility, mutual respect, and harmony" by suppressing offensive speech "is both futile and an inversion of the values that underlie the academic mission" (p. 16). By prohibiting offensive speech, such codes violate the First Amendment distinction between offensive speech and fighting words. Consequently, they can have a "chilling effect" on free expression on campus.

350. Sunstein, Cass R. "Liberalism, Speech Codes, and Related Problems." **Academe** 79(4): 14-25, July/August 1993.

The author argues in favor of speech codes as not intruding on freedom of speech and pluralism in academia. Safeguarding the exchange of ideas may require restricting any "low-value" speech which subverts the educational mission of the university. Sunstein discusses codes at Stanford and the University of Michigan as well as US Supreme Court and Minnesota Supreme Court decisions relating to speech codes.

351. Sykes, Charles J. "Academic License." In Charles J. Sykes. **Profscam: Professors and the Demise of Higher Education.** New York: Regnery Gateway, 1988. pp. 133-150. ISBN 0-8952-6559-1.

In his critique of higher education, Sykes accuses faculty of diluting the curriculum, avoiding undergraduate teaching, and pursuing trivial research agendas for careerist purposes. He argues that the increasing power of professors has turned academic freedom into a "bureaucratic dogma" that protects faculty from accountability. Furthermore, the protection of faculty rights has been at the expense of students' rights. While academic freedom was originally intended to foster the free exchange of ideas in the classroom, it now gives faculty license to propagandize and indulge their biases. Because classrooms are considered "inviolable" under the current conception of academic freedom, faculty bias goes unchecked, says Sykes.

352. Trow, Martin. "The Threat From Within: Academic Freedom and Negative Evidence." **Change** 17(4): 8-9, 61-64, September/October 1985.

Trow identifies what he sees as a significant, contemporary threat to academic freedom on campus: the harassment of teachers, researchers and guest speakers by students and others who disagree with the viewpoints expressed. This "threat from within" is illustrated by the protests, heckling and disruption of guest lectures by Milton Friedman and Jeane Kirkpatrick at the University of California at Berkeley. The disruption of Kirkpatrick's lecture led her to cancel a second lecture and an accompanying question and answer session. Trow argues that academic freedom requires us to set an even higher standard than the First Amendment's free speech guarantees. This standard obliges members of the university community to allow diverse points of view to be presented, including those with which we disagree. By heckling and disrupting the speech of others, protesters were not meeting that higher standard, though they may have been indulging their own First Amendment rights. Underlying the support for diverse views and academic freedom is the belief that a scholarly approach to knowledge and truth requires us to consider negative evidence.

353. Williams, Jeffrey, ed. **PC Wars: Politics and Theory in the Academy.** New York: Routledge, 1995. 340p. LC 94-3735. ISBN 0-415-91072-2.

Included in this edited collection are separately authored chapters discussing the origins, manifestations, and consequences of the anti-political correctness movement. The chapters are divided into three sections: the campaign against PC; the trouble with theory; and othering the academy. As Joan Wallach Scott succinctly points out in her essay ("The Campaign Against Political Correctness: What's Really At Stake"), the PC debate is really over what counts as legitimate knowledge within the academy. Scott and other contributors argue that the anti-PC movement is attempting to discredit contemporary, critical theories such as postmodernism, poststructuralism, deconstructionism, and multiculturalism. By labeling such perspectives as extremist, opposed to objective truth, and nihilistic, the anti-PC movement delegitimizes the teaching, research and writing of faculty from these theoretical perspectives. This poses a threat to their academic freedom and, as a result, could limit the diversity of ideas in the academy. Articles in the last two sections focus more on the theoretical and cultural developments that provide a broad context for the PC debate.

Chapter 8

Academic Freedom and Religion

354. Ashbury, Beverly A. "The Role of Campus Ministers in Protest and Dissent." **Liberal Education** 56(2): 317-327, May 1970.

Ashbury calls on Judeo-Christian campus ministers to consider their responsibilities in terms not of office or order, but in terms of modes or roles of ministry. This instrumental rather than institutional approach to ministry is one which focuses on whether ministerial action in the context of student protest legitimates either the status quo or revolutionary violence. Considering in turn the preaching, prophetic, and governance modes of ministry, the author considers how ministers of various Judeo-Christian faiths can call on these common traditional roles in service on campuses where protest and dissent are rampant.

355. Cafardi, Nicholas P., editor. **Academic Freedom in a Pluralistic Society: The Catholic University.** Pittsburgh: Duquesne University, 1990. 78 p. LC 91-196934.

This volume presents the proceedings of a symposium held at Duquesne University in 1989. Papers were presented by the Presidents of Duquesne and Catholic University of America (Dr. John E. Murray, Jr. and Rev. William Byron) and other professors and clergy members. Topics addressed focused on the relationship between the Catholic Church and its teachings on the one hand and, on the other, the concepts and practices of academic freedom on campuses of Catholic universities. John Silber, President of Boston University, gave a presentation on "Academic Freedom: A Secular Perspective" in which he addressed the limits on academic freedom in secular universities. Responses by panel discussion participants are also here reproduced.

356. Cramer, Jerome. "Academic Freedom and the Catholic Church." **Educational Record** 67(2-3): 30-37, Spring/Summer 1986.

Cramer recounts the background of a dispute between Catholic University and tenured professor of moral theology Charles Curran, a dispute which pitted academic freedom against obedience on the part of Catholic educators to the Vatican. Curran's longstanding views on homosexuality, divorce, and birth control put him at odds with church authorities. Concerns are here outlined over the autonomy of boards of trustees of Catholic institutions and a "Proposed Schema for a Pontifical Document on Catholic Universities" requiring all teachers of theology at Catholic universities to get a "mandate" from a local bishop who might in effect have the power to fire professors.

357. Curran, Charles E. "Academic Freedom and Catholic Institutions of Higher Education." **Journal of the American Academy of Religion** 55(1): 107-121, Spring 1987.

Curran briefly discusses the historical development of U.S. Catholic higher education that led to academic freedom being endorsed in the 1960s at Catholic institutions of higher education. He addresses threats from Papal legislation to academic freedom on Catholic campuses, and argues that the Catholic Church should recognize and encourage academic freedom at Catholic institutions of higher education as something for the good of the Church.

358. Curran, Charles E. "Academic Freedom: The Catholic University and Catholic Theology." **Academe** 66(3): 126-135, April 1980.

At the outset of the article, Curran defines academic freedom in traditional terms and then explains how Catholic universities and colleges came to embrace this conception of academic freedom in the 1960s. Contributing factors included the enrollment growth within these institutions, the expansion of graduate education, the move to administrative oversight by Boards of Trustees, the availability of government monies for research, and the hiring of lay faculty, among others. Curran then confronts a more difficult issue: the freedom of theological faculty in catholic universities. Some bishops or church authorities suggest that the role of theologians is to defend the "teaching of the hierarchical magisterium" (p. 133). Others see theology's role as interpretive, thus requiring more freedom, including the freedom to responsibly dissent from the Church's non-infallible teachings. However, in 1979 Pope John Paul II issued *Sapientia Christiana* regulating pontifical universities. This document does not guarantee academic freedom, says Curran, since such universities and their theological faculty are viewed as upholding the Church's teaching function. If this and related documents are interpreted narrowly, the academic freedom and autonomy of Catholic faculty and universities are at risk.

359. Davis, Gary. "Academic Freedom and the Teaching of Religion." **Improving College & University Teaching** 32(2): 76-80, Spring 1984.

After a brief review of the German roots of academic freedom and the principles of academic freedom developed by the AAUP, Davis addresses the permissible restrictions on academic freedom allowed in religious institutions. The AAUP's *1940 Statement of Principles on Academic Freedom and Tenure* continues the organization's "1915 Declaration of Principles" in allowing that 1) "religion is a subjective study that requires faithful interpreters" and 2) "religiously-supported institutions have a fair right to require religious conformity from faculty members" (p. 78). Davis considers both of these positions wrong. First, he rejects the assumption that one must subjectively experience the faith, or for that matter any subject, in order to study or interpret it.   Second, Davis rejects the proposition that a religious institution can extend the right of academic freedom to some of its faculty members, but not to those teaching on areas of religious doctrine. This indicates a lack of commitment to free inquiry, and a lack of appreciation for the role of self-criticism in the search for truth. Furthermore, other disciplines explore and research religious beliefs and practices. By attempting to block certain questions from being asked, "intellectual understanding is distorted" (p. 80). For these reasons, Davis argues that the American Academy of Religion should ask the AAUP to "repudiate" the statement permitting church-related institutions to abridge the academic freedom of some faculty.

360. Easton, Loyd D.   "Church-Affiliated Colleges and Academic Freedom." **Religion in Life** 26(4): 544-549, Autumn 1957.

Easton argues that the best measure of an institution's "Christian character" is its commitment to academic freedom, not its doctrinal requirements regarding faculty selection, teaching or study. A brief overview of AAUP statements from 1915, 1925, and 1940 addresses the place of religious belief in AAUP policy recommendations. Open inquiry is justified on the basis of Christian doctrine as expounded by George A. Coe, Reinhold Neihbur, and Daniel Day Williams (see entry #374).

361. Hinson, Keith.   "University Independence Sparks Renewed Tensions." **Christianity Today** 41(2): 81, February 3, 1997.

The academic freedom and autonomy of many Baptist-affiliated colleges and universities has been an issue of late, as many of these schools have made efforts to become more independent. In this process, these schools have had to revisit their relationships with their state Baptist conventions. Historically, these conventions not only have provided financial support to the schools, but also may have had input into policies or appointments to the Board of Trustees. Hinson reviews how some universities and their state Baptist conventions have renegotiated and compromised on some of the key issues.

362. Hoye, William J. "The Religious Roots of Academic Freedom." **Theological Studies** 58(3): 409-428, September 1997.

Hoye makes the case that the conceptual roots of academic freedom go back further than the Enlightenment, back to the origins of the idea of the university in the Middle Ages. Hoye begins by addressing three famous Enlightenment cases in turn, those of Christian Wolff's 1723 expulsion from the Prussian University of Halle; Immanuel Kant's conflict in the late 18th century with Frederick the Great; and Johann Gottlieb Fichte's dismissal in 1799 from the University of Jena. In each case it was the state rather than the church that encroached on academic freedom for reasons of theology. Medieval Christianity of the 13th century is cited by Hoye as being the source of what was then called "scholastic freedom" or "scholastic liberty." As an early paradigm for freedom of thought, religious thinkers developed pedagogical methods for encouraging doubt.

363. Hunt, John F. and Terrence R. Connelly, with Charles E. Curran, Robert E. Hunt, and Robert K. Webb. **The Responsibility of Dissent: The Church and Academic Freedom.** New York: Sheed and Ward, 1970. 224p. ISBN 0-8362-0039-X.

This book examines the relationship between the authority of the Catholic Church and the autonomy of Catholic University in Washington, D.C. in a 1968 case of professorial dissent from papal teaching on birth control. Threatened with suspension by the Board of Trustees, the 21 professors who had signed a public dissent from a papal encyclical on birth control were exonerated by a Faculty Inquiry Board which found that the professor's dissent was both tenable with Catholic theology and with their educational responsibilities. The Inquiry Board ruled further that the Board of Trustees had denied the academic due process of the professors. All relevant documents are reproduced here, including the initial dissent, the trustee's reaction, and the faculty inquiry. The authors, who represent legal counsel for the professors, conclude with a chapter outlining academic freedom and due process recommendations that they feel could improve the situation.

364. Kliever, Lonnie D. "Religion and Academic Freedom: Issues of Faith and Reason." **Academe** 74(1): 8-11, January/February 1988.

Kliever makes the claim that study of religion has a place in academia, but only if four criteria are adhered to: that such study be pluralistic, comparative, interdisciplinary, and objective. In discussing the growing politicization of religious belief, and the effects fundamentalism can have on the role religion plays on universities, Kliever addresses the "limitations clause" of the AAUP *1940 Statement of Principles on Academic Freedom and Tenure* as being potentially dangerous to academic freedom. Rather than treating religion as the one "permissible exception" to institutional commitment to academic freedom, the author instead asserts that religious education should be considered the "test case" of such commitment.

365. Kurland, Jordan E. "Charles E. Curran: Theology Professor at Risk." **Academe** 72(5): 43-44, September-October 1986.

Kurland reviews the past and current difficulties faced by Father Charles Curran at Catholic University. A theologian," Curran was almost denied tenure in the late 1960s for his liberal views. Most recently, he was under investigation by the Vatican's Sacred Congregation for the Doctrine of the Faith for his "writings and teachings on moral theology, particularly on issues relating to life, sex, and marriage" (pp. 43-44). Curran was notified that he would no longer be allowed to teach Catholic theology because of his dissenting positions. Curran received support from both the Catholic Theology Society of America and the College Theology Society, whose joint statement questioned the "academic integrity" of Catholic colleges and universities.

366. Logan, Samuel T., Jr. "Academic Freedom at Christian Institutions." **Christian Scholar's Review** 21(2): 14-17, December 1991.

Logan, President of Westminster Theological Seminary, suggests here that Christian institutional policies regarding academic freedom should carefully define and affirm freedom in the context of the mission of the institution. Rather than being affirmations of a negative freedom "from" this or that, these policies should make it clear that freedom is a means to the institutions' higher purpose. Logan takes issue with the stated academic freedom policies of the AAUP, the Association of Theological Schools, and the Middle States Association of Colleges and Schools. In all of these cases, freedom is defined as an end in and of itself.

367. Marsden, George M. "The Ambiguities of Academic Freedom." **Church History** 62(2): 221-236, June 1993.

One of the academic freedom cases that led to the founding of the AAUP was a 1913 case of dismissal on religious grounds of John Mecklin from Lafayette College. That case is outlined here as a case study in how attitudes towards religion came to be shaped in American concepts of academic freedom. Free inquiry leading to scientific truth and social progress is hindered, in this traditional conception of academic freedom, by prejudice and religious belief. Marsden asserts that religious based schools should ignore contemporary pressure to abandon faith-based teaching. While abuses of academic freedom by early 20th century religious higher education did occur, a place must be made in today's higher education for academic viewpoints based on religious faith.

368. Marsden, George M. "Liberating Academic Freedom." **First Things** 88: 11-14, December 1998.

Marsden discusses what he sees as the AAUP's historical disdain for religious institutions, questioning the validity of the claim that higher education should be neutral on religious or ideological grounds. Marsden argues that secular institutions are inferior in both quality of education and in academic freedom, given that religious institutions have remained largely free from outside influence from government or secular special interests.

369. May, William W.   "Academic Freedom in Church-related Institutions." **Academe** 74(4): 23-28, July-August, 1988.

May addresses some of the difficult issues involved in reconciling academic freedom with the possible doctrinal constraints imposed by church-related institutions. He reviews AAUP and accrediting agency statements on academic freedom in such institutions and reports on interviews with some Presidents and chief academic officers. The AAUP's *1940 Statement of Principles on Academic Freedom and Tenure,* as well as a 1970 interpretive comment, give "reluctant permission" for church-related institutions to limit academic freedom. Such limitations must be clearly stated "at the time of appointment." In his interviews with Presidents and chief academic officers, May examines some of the more difficult issues, philosophies, and policies at such institutions. Many of the interviewees expressed support for academic freedom and the exploration of knowledge. Some supported teaching and discussion that ran counter to church doctrine, though others drew the line at publishing contrary opinions. The most difficult cases involved faculty whose beliefs had changed over time, to the point where they no longer shared the values and beliefs of their institution. In such instances, the interviewees hoped that the faculty member would either honor his or her obligation to the institution and its values or resign.

370. Orsy, Ladislas M. "Academic Freedom and the Teaching Church." **Thought: A Review of Culture and Ideas** 43(171): 485-498, Winter 1968.

Academic freedom is a basic requirement for any school of theology. This view is defended here, through theology. What appear to be conflicting interests between the Catholic Church and the theological university are actually not in conflict. The roles of Canon Law, of the Episcopate, of the individual Bishop, and the roles of individual theologians are all spelled out as they relate to freedom in theological research and teaching.

371. Sanchez, Jose M. "Cardinal Glennon and Academic Freedom at Saint Louis University: The Fleisher Case Revisited." **Gateway Heritage: Quarterly Journal of the Missouri Historical Society** 8(3): 2-11, Winter 1987/1988.

Sanchez recounts the 1939 case of dismissal of the Director of the Department of Bacteriology at the Saint Louis University School of Medicine, Moyer Fleisher. The author studied the AAUP files and conducted interviews with those who knew the people involved. The AAUP investigated the incident and censured the school for the dismissal. Fleisher supported a lecture by a visiting unfrocked priest who was lecturing in support of the anticlerical Loyalist forces fighting against Franco in the Spanish Civil War.

372. Stimpson, Catharine R. "The Farr Case: The Next Chapter in the History of Academic Freedom?" **Change** 25(4): 70-71, September/October 1993.

Cecilia Concha Farr was a feminist scholar and Mormon teaching in the English department at Brigham Young University. After a third-year review, she was terminated from her position, allegedly for being a bad scholar. Stimpson briefly reviews the facts of the case and suggests that Farr was really fired for her efforts at reconciling feminism and Mormonism and for some of her public positions on controversial issues, such as abortion. Objective review of her teaching evaluations and scholarly productivity suggest that she ranked higher than many junior faculty who were retained. Stimpson suggests that there was a lack of understanding of and an antipathy towards Farr's feminist perspective. The larger question is also raised: is it possible for academic freedom to coexist at an institution that requires religious orthodoxy?

373. Walton, Clarence C. "Academic Freedom at the Catholic University During the 1970s." **Catholic Historical Review** 76(3): 555-563, July 1990.

Former President of Catholic University from 1969-1978, Walton claims that never during his time there was any professor's claim to academic freedom "ever challenged or curtailed." The main focus of this article is on events surrounding and following the 1969 signing by 20 professors of a statement in opposition to a Papal encyclical which condemned contraception. Also covered here are controversies regarding Walton's overriding of the faculty election of Roland Murphy as Dean of the School of Sacred Theology. Activities of Father Charles Curran, and Chancellor Patrick Cardinal O'Boyle throughout these episodes are also detailed.

374. Williams, Daniel Day. "Christian Freedom and Academic Freedom." **Christian Scholar** 36(1): 11-22, March 1953.

The author expounds a Protestant philosophy of freedom as a context for exploring issues of academic freedom and its protection. Distinguishing various meanings of freedom, Williams arrives at four fundamental premises regarding Christian freedom: that human freedom is based on metaphysical order, that full realization of freedom requires a life of service, that human beings are capable of and responsible for misusing freedom, and that freedom depends on a higher standpoint from which judgement of all things is possible. That freedom to learn and teach must be defended is related back to this standpoint in which faith and responsibility are conditions of true freedom.

375. Zagano, Phyllis. "Sectarian Universities, Federal Funding, and the Questions of Academic Freedom." **Religious Education** 85(1): 136-148, Winter 1990.

Zagano's article revolves around a single question: does a sectarian university necessarily infringe on academic freedom and, therefore, render itself ineligible for federal funding? The question seems especially relevant in light of some recent academic freedom disputes at Catholic universities, most notably the case of Charles Curran at Catholic University of America. According to Zagano, the federal government's only restrictions in providing funding are that the institution be accredited and that it comply "with the relevant laws." Federal law would prohibit support to catechetical education, such as that provided at theological institutions. Other than that, Catholic universities should be eligible to receive funding. Furthermore, the federal government and the American Association of University Professors grant such institutions the right to expect faculty to adhere to matters of faith, particularly in connection with teaching on ecclesiastical matters. Therefore, according to Zagano, academic freedom in these institutions remains an "internal matter."

Chapter 9

Tenure—Defense, Critiques and Alternatives

376. Baratz, Morton S. "Academic Tenure and Its Alternatives." **National Forum** 60(2): 5-8. Spring 1980.

The former General Secretary of the AAUP addresses the key attributes and purposes for the tenure system and argues against commonly proposed alternatives: lengthening pre-tenure probationary periods, limiting the period of tenure, and/or replacing it with fixed-term renewable contracts. Baratz concludes that the current system is better than any of the alternatives.

377. Beazley, Hamilton, and John Lobuts, Jr. "Ransomed Teaching, Indentured Research, and the Loss of Reason." **Academe** 82(1): 30-32, January-February, 1996.

Critics of higher education often suggest that it is inefficient and that it needs to adopt a business model of operation. Part of this reform would entail doing away with tenure, which restricts the ability of administrators to manage the institution most efficiently (e.g., move or eliminate personnel). Beazley and Lobuts argue, however, that doing away with tenure will be at the expense of academic freedom and that this will be reflected both in ransomed teaching and indentured research. Without tenure, professors will be inclined to teach only those ideas that will not get them in trouble with administrators, trustees, and corporate donors. Similarly, researchers will feel pressured to research topics, and obtain findings, that are compatible with the needs of corporate and government funding sources. In fact, this is already a danger. Without the protection of tenure, there will be no academic freedom, and the search for truth will be seriously compromised.

378. Breneman, David W. **Alternatives to Tenure for the Next Generation of Academics.** Washington, D.C.: American Association for Higher Education, 1997. (Working Paper Series; Inquiry #14). 16p.

Financial uncertainty and the need to meet market demand may be forcing universities to investigate and consider new employment relationships with faculty. Breneman attempts to explore alternatives to tenure, to discuss their possible advantages for universities and faculty, and to specify the conditions needed to implement these new relationships. Term contracts, with lengthy appointments and higher salaries in lieu of tenure, may benefit faculty in a tight academic labor market. There would be more movement in academic positions, thus creating more opportunity for new faculty. Additionally, Breneman proposes that universities should make these non-tenure track appointments attractive by offering higher salaries for them. Faculty could choose between a tenure track appointment, at lower pay, or a term contract at higher pay. This would provide more academic opportunity, higher salaries and, for universities, some flexibility in reallocating personnel based on the demand for courses of study. The costs involved in the higher salaries for some faculty would be offset by the money saved through eliminating unproductive faculty. While the most selective colleges and universities may want and need to adhere to a more traditional tenure track model, other institutions could gradually evolve toward Breneman's model of more variety in the types of appointments. Some challenges or obstacles to implementing such an employment practice are discussed.

379. Burgan, Mary, and Milton Greenburg. "Considering Tenure." **Educational Record** 76(4): 34-37, Fall 1995.

While both Burgan and Greenburg defend the value of tenure at a general level, they disagree significantly on its usefulness as currently constituted. For Burgan, academic freedom and tenure are at risk under the educational efficiency movement, which minimizes the role of faculty in "interactive," futuristic classrooms and replaces full-time with part-time faculty. As she sees it, politics and economics will increasingly dominate the decision-making process in dealing with faculty. Tenure and academic freedom must be defended more than ever. Greenburg, on the other hand, sees tenure as an obstacle to improvement in higher education. It is, in effect, a lifetime job. It also constitutes an effective barrier against the advancement of women and minority faculty, since most tenured faculty are white males between the ages of 35 and 55. Greenburg offers alternatives to tenure that, he contends, could protect academic freedom while eliminating the negatives of tenure. These suggestions include elevating the status of non-tenure track appointments, creating a national commission to investigate and defend academic freedom, easing "financial exigency" requirements for university administrations, setting a faculty code of conduct, varying tenure standards with institutional mission, and avoiding specific tenure timetables, among others.

380. Byrne, J. Peter. **Academic Freedom Without Tenure?** Washington, D.C.: American Association for Higher Education, 1997. (Working Paper Series; Inquiry #5). 17p.

Byrne explores the pros and cons of uncoupling tenure and academic freedom, and mechanisms by which the latter might be protected without the former. In the current climate in higher education, universities may find advantages to doing away with tenure. These would include replacing substandard faculty and reallocating faculty positions to meet demands of the educational market. But how would institutions protect academic freedom if they did eliminate tenure? Byrne suggests that a number of conditions need to be met. First, universities would have to define what was meant by academic freedom. Second, they would have to have a rigorous and fair faculty evaluation procedure. Third, faculty contracts would need to be longer in the absence of tenure. Fourth, universities would need a fair "internal-appeals mechanism to challenge adverse personnel decisions on the ground that they violate the faculty member's academic freedom" (p. 7). Fifth, peer review would have to be central to decision-making on faculty reappointments. Sixth, "faculty decision makers need enhanced job security to promote their independence from institutional preferences" (p. 13).

381. Cadwallader, Mervyn L. "Reflections on Academic Freedom and Tenure." **Liberal Education** 69(1): 1-17, Spring 1983.

The author argues that tenure is not a necessary condition for exercising academic freedom, here defined narrowly as "the freedom to inquire and teach critically." Cadwallader identifies this freedom within his concept of teaching as a "fourth branch of government." Tenure works best in research settings, where after a probationary period, tenure accrues to scientists and scholars primarily to protect them from each other. Tenure would work better in a teaching setting if it were preceded by an apprenticeship and focused on the refining of teaching techniques.

382. Carr, Robert K. "The Uneasy Future of Academic Tenure." **Educational Record** 53(2): 119-27, Spring 1972.

Carr weighs the cases for and against tenure. Recounted as forces against the tenure system are: the knowledge explosion, and the inability of aging professors to keep up with changes in their fields; tightening of the job market and growth in the numbers of Ph.D. candidates; dissatisfaction of students with teaching methods and course relevance. Carr argues that the tenure system could be strengthened if such steps were taken as: being more conservative with respect to tenure appointments; using existing internal means to get rid of incompetent teachers so as to diminish the threat of outside interference in university autonomy; encouraging early retirement. The conclusion here is that tenure should not be abolished, just improved.

383. Chait, Richard P. and Andrew T. Ford. **Beyond Traditional Tenure.** San Francisco: Jossey-Bass, 1982. 291p. ISBN 0-8758-9519-0.

The authors present a systematic survey of alternatives to the tenure track system by examining case studies of several institutions, drawing conclusions about the strengths and weaknesses of various models and offering their own recommendations for "auditing" and improving human resources management regardless of the policy in place. Among the institutions without tenure examined and evaluated are: Hampshire College, Evergreen State College, and the University of Texas at Permian Basin. Institutions with tenure and non-tenure dual track systems examined include: Webster College and Coe College. Extended probationary periods are examined by looking at: University of Rochester, University of Georgia, and University of Tulsa. Some institutions have suspended the "up or out" rule and declare professors tenurable but without conferring a permanent position until a slot opens up. These include: Union College, Hartwick College, and Albion College. The pros and cons of tenure quotas are examined as they exist at Colgate University, CUNY, and the New Jersey State Colleges. Schools with fairly sound traditional tenure policies are also examined, including: St. Olaf College, the College of Letters & Science at the University of Wisconsin-Madison, and Harvard Graduate School of Business Administration. The Harvard Business School's policy is offered by Chait and Ford as a model statement on promotion and tenure and the full text of the policy is included here.

384. Chemerinsky, Erwin. "Is Tenure Necessary to Protect Academic Freedom?" **American Behavioral Scientist** 41(5): 638-651, February 1998.

Critics of tenure have proposed two alternatives for protecting academic freedom: the First Amendment, and long-term contracts. Chemerinsky looks closely at both alternatives and concludes that neither will protect academic freedom adequately. Faculty are already protected by the First Amendment, says Chemerinsky, and will only lose additional protection if tenure is eliminated. Without tenure, the burden falls on the faculty member to initiate a claim against the university and to demonstrate that the termination was a response to Constitutionally protected speech. Furthermore, the First Amendment would allow for a broader range of reasons for terminating faculty, potentially encroaching on their academic freedom. The second alternative to tenure, long-term contracts, is also inadequate, says Chemerinsky. J. Peter Byrne's proposal, in particular, says that speech must be of "major public concern," that it must be "scholarship" and not "advocacy" (a difficult distinction), and that it not lead to external misunderstandings. Overall, this gives too much discretion to university officials and provides less procedural and substantive protection than tenure.

385. Colorado Commission on Higher Education. **Tenure Report.** Denver: The Commission, Feb. 1997. 21p. LC 97-145210.

The Colorado Legislature's Joint Budget Committee asked the Commission to report on the appropriateness of tenure at public higher education institutions, on the various forms of post-tenure review in place state-wide, on the proper balance between full- and part-time faculties, and on the proper balance between teaching and research. Among the recommendations proposed here are: that contractual agreements and salary be explicitly linked with annual merit review based on clearly established professional and ethical responsibilities; that such reviews occur also for tenured faculty (every seven years or more frequently) and that such reviews include both peer and student evaluations; that remedial procedures be established and called on in all cases of weak performance; that Colorado higher education institutions establish multiple appointment tracks including variable-term appointments as well as part-time and non-tenure track positions.

386. De Pasquale, Sue, et al. "Tenure Under Scrutiny." **Johns Hopkins Magazine** 49: 16-31, September 1997.

Noting a national trend of attacks on tenure, De Pasquale looks at tenure at Johns Hopkins University. She interviews faculty and administrators for their views of tenure, its necessity for the protection of academic freedom, and mechanisms for the ongoing evaluation of faculty. Interviewees disagreed as to whether tenure was needed to protect academic freedom, and whether it provided a balance of power between administrators and faculty. The elimination of tenure and academic freedom could, according to some faculty, limit lines of research inquiry. An increasing reliance on external funding might exacerbate this problem. Johns Hopkins has tenure, though its probationary period is for 10 years, longer than the norm at other institutions. Furthermore, the ultimate decision on recommendations of tenure is made by a Faculty Council, which is made up of faculty from all over campus. The committee's diverse make-up can help guarantee that scholarly and academic competencies are rigorously and fairly evaluated. This is particularly important at a university like Johns Hopkins, which places a premium on research productivity. Some interviewees argued that this tenure system makes it difficult to keep junior faculty and encourage good teaching. Finally, faculty disagreed as to whether there were "deadwood" tenured faculty, and whether post-tenure review was needed to eliminate them.

387. Finkin, Matthew W. "The Assault on Faculty Independence." **Academe** 83(4): 16-21, July-August 1997.

In defense of tenure, Finkin identifies and responds to six rhetorical techniques used by critics, most notably C. Peter Magrath and Richard Chait. First, he argues that the Constitution's protections of free speech are not sufficient for protecting academic freedom. Second, the fact that there are many part-time and adjunct faculty without the protection of tenure, does not negate the importance of tenure for the scholarly mission of those who do have it. Third, it is an "invidious comparison" to suggest that since many private sector employees serve "at will," so should faculty. Fourth, Chait's suggestion that "more alternatives" to tenure should be devised begs fundamental questions: how does the current system not serve the end of guaranteeing academic freedom, and can alternatives make that guarantee? Fifth, tenure should not be viewed as some individual property right that can be bartered away simply because some administrators and faculty may think it is mutually beneficial (e.g., trading tenure for salary). It serves larger institutional and social ends by guaranteeing freedom and independence of thought in the pursuit of knowledge. Sixth, academic freedom is not possible without guarantees and safeguards for independence of thought and judgement. Tenure helps ensure this, while many reforms, such as those endorsed by Chait, do not. According to Finkin, safeguarding faculty independence is the fundamental issue that confronts the profession, just as it was in 1915.

388. Finkin, Matthew W. **The Case for Tenure.** Ithaca, N.Y.: ILR Press, 1996. 211p. ISBN 0-8014-3316-9. LC 96-16788.

According to Finkin, academic freedom and tenure are currently under attack in the name of accountability, efficiency, and flexibility, with a number of states considering laws to abolish tenure. In response to these attacks, and in defense of the value of tenure, Finkin has assembled classic and contemporary writings that explore academic freedom and tenure and the legal and procedural foundations that protect them. The book comprises eight chapters exploring various key issues. These include an opening chapter on the meaning of tenure, as well as subsequent chapters on probation, dismissal and due process, the economics of tenure, tenure and resource allocation, tenure and retirement, post-tenure review, and the new criticism. Chapters can include excerpts from AAUP Committee A reports on particular institutions, excerpts from the scholarly literature, organization reports, and commentaries from Finkin that attempt to crystallize the issues and evidence. The Committee A reports are selected to illustrate the value and importance of AAUP guidelines in such areas as financial exigency and due process. Throughout, this is a sophisticated treatment of major issues in academic freedom and tenure, with consideration given to contrary points of view.

389. Finkin, Matthew W. "Tenure After the ADEA Amendments: A Different View." **New Directions for Higher Education, no. 65.** 17(1): 97-111, Spring 1989.

Finkin responds to a number of proposals to do away with tenure and replace it with alternatives such as post-tenure review or fixed long-term appointments. The specific proposals Finkin addresses were made in response to the Age Discrimination in Employment Act (ADEA). This legislation uncapped the mandatory retirement age and, according to some commentators, created a burden on higher educational institutions. Tenure, which had been guaranteed until retirement (barring dismissal for cause), is now indefinite, thus constraining educational institutions in their efforts to reallocate resources and guarantee faculty performance. Finkin responds to these various proposals and suggests that they either 1) do not meet the statutory requirements of the ADEA (i.e., to avoid age discrimination), or 2) pose a threat to academic freedom. In either case, such proposals are not recommended. Finkin suggests that other policies, such as early retirement incentive programs, can induce some senior faculty to retire early and allow institutions some flexibility in reallocating resources. Such programs would not threaten academic freedom or run afoul of the ADEA.

390. Finkin, Matthew W. "Tenure and the Entrepreneurial Academy: A Reply." **Academe** 84(1): 14-22, January/February 1998.

Finkin's "reply" is to a work by David Breneman (entry #378), who argues that tenure is economically dysfunctional for contemporary institutions of higher education and should, therefore, be replaced. Tenure limits institutional flexibility in the current academic environment, Breneman argues, and depresses both academic salaries and the labor market. To wean faculty from tenure and to address the above-mentioned problems, Breneman proposes, among other things, offering higher salaries to new faculty in exchange for giving up tenure. Finkin challenges Breneman's assumption that tenure is a "property right" of faculty that can be bartered away without any consideration except the faculty member's perceived self interest. Tenure was conceived not as a property right, says Finkin, but as a mechanism to ensure academic freedom and the social good. Finkin argues that Breneman offers no mechanism for guaranteeing academic freedom in the absence of tenure. Without tenure, says Finkin, faculty in the entrpreneurial university would again be subject to the potential prejudices and narrow self-interest of administrations, industry, and communities.

391. Hamilton, Neil W. "Peer Review: The Linchpin of Academic Freedom and Tenure." **Academe** 83(3): 15-19, May/June 1997.

According to Hamilton, the right to "professional academic freedom" has been accompanied by the obligation on the part of the professoriate to govern itself through peer review. Through this process, the faculty evaluate the professional competence and ethical behavior of their current and potential colleagues. Once these probationary faculty have demonstrated their ability to develop and disseminate knowledge, they are ensured, through tenure, of the professional freedom to pursue these goals. At that point, the burden of proof for dismissing faculty falls upon the university, which must carefully adhere to due process in such procedures. However, tenure does not mean lifetime employment, and faculty must continually ensure that their members adhere to the ethical obligations of their positions. Hamilton asks rhetorically if the professoriate has shown the ability and willingness to police itself. The small number of cases of loss of tenure each year, along with survey reports of more widespread ethical abuses, suggests to Hamilton that the professoriate is not willing to do this. The public's loss of trust in the professoriate can be restored, Hamilton says, through the education of faculty on the obligations of academic freedom and peer review. Hamilton also supports effective post-tenure review.

392. Hohm, Charles F., and Herbert B. Shore. "The Academy Under Siege: Informing the Public About the Merits of Academic Tenure." **Sociological Perspectives** 41(4): 827-832, Winter 1998.

If tenure is to be protected in the current social climate, it must be better explained to the general public. This explanation needs to go beyond the usual, though correct, argument that tenure protects academic freedom. First, the public must be made aware of the lengthy and demanding process by which faculty are recruited, retained, and tenured. Second, tenure allows faculty to teach and publish freely in their area of expertise. It also allows some security in this endeavor, which is a trade-off for professors' generally lower salaries. Third, society benefits by tenure because faculty will not be pressured to teach or research only "safe" topics. Fourth, American universities benefit by tenure, which is part of the process that has made our institutions of higher education the world's best. It encourages long-term planning, faculty loyalty, and faculty involvement in governance in such areas as teaching, research, and curricular matters. Tenure results in high standards and excellence in these areas. The authors conclude by suggesting that American businesses could benefit by adopting tenure.

393. Jackson, Frederick H., and Robin S. Wilson. "Toward a New System of Academic Tenure." **Educational Record** 52(4): 338-42, Fall 1971.

Jackson outlines a scheme for incremental tenure, providing renewable term appointments of gradually increasing increments at each rank up through associate professorship. Details related to contract renewal, possibly increased potential for litigation, and impact on retirement compensation are all spelled out. The authors make a case for a national commission to be organized around the issue of wholesale revision of the tenure system.

394. Leslie, David W. "Redefining Tenure: Tradition Versus the New Political Economy of Higher Education." **American Behavioral Scientist** 41(5): 652-679, February 1998.

A growing financial crisis in higher education and public demands for accountability have altered faculty work and eroded traditional supports for tenure. Universities now must find ways of balancing the "competing values of academic freedom and efficiency." Currently, some 50% of faculty positions are non-tenure track, including a growing percentage of part-time faculty appointments. Numerous institutions have also instituted multiyear contracts (e.g., Florida Gulf Coast University), post-tenure review (e.g., Minnesota), or longer probationary periods. Leslie reviews the court cases and common practices related to tenure, suggesting that tenure is whatever institutions want it to be, provided that the process is fair, consistent, and mindful of academic freedom. He suggests that, currently, tenure is awarded based on short-term priorities and weighting of faculty skills and does not allow for evolving institutional or faculty needs and interests. The goal is to allow for the evolution of faculty work beyond tenure, while still protecting tenure. As an example, Leslie proposes having faculty regain tenure within each rank, based on the expectation that different ranks might have a different array and weighting of faculty responsibilities. If alternative, flexible ways of defining faculty jobs are not found, tenure may continue to be eroded.

395. Lewis, Lionel S. "Academic Tenure: Its Recipients and Its Effects." **Annals of the American Academy of Political and Social Science** 448: 86-101, March 1980.

The author undertook an examination of the tenure dossiers of 115 individuals awarded tenure in 1967 and 1968 in order to compare the differing requirements for tenure and to examine the effects of tenure on its recipients. Lewis describes inconsistencies in the criteria applied for granting tenure, and notes that ten years after tenure was awarded, over one-third of tenure recipients were at a rank less than Full Professor. Yet little evidence is found by the author to support the claim of some that intellectual productivity declines after tenure is granted. On the other hand, Lewis also finds little to suggest that tenure protects idiosyncratic or dissenting professors.

396. Licata, Christine M. **Post-Tenure Faculty Evaluation: Threat or Opportunity?** Washington, D.C.: Association for the Study of Higher Education, 1986. 107p. (ASHE-ERIC Higher Education Report, no. 1). ISBN 0-9133-1728-4.

This report discusses whether post-tenure evaluation poses a threat to AAUP policy statements or to the principle of tenure; how different segments of the academic community perceive its purpose; findings from a 1984 survey of the status of post-tenure evaluation; and recommendations for further study. According to the model mapped out here, post-tenure review need not violate the principle of tenure as long as the review is not used as the sole basis for dismissal.

397. Mann, William R. "Is the Tenure Controversy a Red Herring?" **Journal of Higher Education** 44(2): 85-94, February 1973.

Mann discusses the issue of financial exigency in higher education as it relates to attacks on the tenure system and proposals for alternatives, such as freezing new hires, ranks, and salaries; abolishing tenure; requiring faculty to submit to secondary tenure review. Mann concludes that these arguments address only the symptoms of a deeper problem, one that should be addressed from within the current tenure system. Proposals for dealing with financial exigency include: job restructuring, encouraging enrollment of atypical students, promotion of outside income-producing activities for faculty, encouraging early or phased retirement, and flexibility in ranking to allow reappointment at lower ranks.

398. Miller, John Perry. "Tenure: Bulwark of Academic Freedom and Brake on Change." **Educational Record** 51(3): 241-45, Summer 1970.

This essay recounts both positive and negative aspects of tenure. Miller suggests two ways to minimize tenure's "unfortunate effects": establishing some non-tenured professorships, and developing a system of incentives to encourage tenured faculty to accept early retirement.

399. Oldenquist, Andrew. "Tenure: Academe's Peculiar Institution." In Steven M. Cahn, editor. **Morality, Responsibility and the University: Studies in Academic Ethics.** Philadelphia: Temple University Press, 1990. pp. 56-75. ISBN 0-8772-2646-6.

Oldenquist addresses the conflicting values of meritocracy and scholarly community in defending the institution of tenure. He argues that a department should pursue a qualified course of being "ruthless before tenure and protective thereafter," and that faculties and departments have strong obligations (though of differing sorts) to the untenured and tenured alike. Academic departments at their best are communitarian rather than adversarial; hence tenure is a better job protection scheme than a union.

400. O'Toole, James. "Against Tenure." **National Forum** 60(2): 8-9, Spring 1980.

O'Toole criticizes the AAUP for ignoring the down side of the tenure system and its effects on women and minorities, its reduction in the mobility and salaries of tenured professors, and its creation of disincentives to reform of higher education. O'Toole calls tenure an anachronism and charges that the AAUP, in its fixation on the tenure system, is in danger of dying out and is unresponsive to the real needs (jobs, higher salaries, teaching reform) of up and coming professors. Likening the AAUP to a labor union seeking job protection for its members, the author finds "cognitive dissonance" in the fact that most faculty members would not describe their primary aim as being job security and would balk at the comparison with unionists.

401. O'Toole, James. "Tenure: A Conscientious Objection." **Change** 10(6): 24-31, June/July 1978.

Comparing the tenure system with alcoholism, the author calls for "abstinence" by American academics. The author, who renounced his tenured status at the University of Southern California, claims that tenure is unnecessary, discourages innovation, limits professors' mobility and bargaining power, distorts normal career growth, exacerbates bureaucratization, increases "credentialism," and is inimical to academic freedom. He calls for a major university (any major university) to set the precedent of abolishing tenure and calls also on his tenured colleagues to renounce their tenured status. His argument is answered by William Van Alstyne in "Tenure: A Conscientious Objective" (see entry #410). Both articles are reprinted and expanded upon as essays in a monograph entitled *Tenure: Three Views*.

402. Park, Dabney, Jr. "A Loyal AAUP Member Says 'Down With Tenure.'" **Change** 4(2): 32-37, March 1972.

Park argues that the tenure system works against the interests of non-tenured faculty, limits the educational quality of institutions, inhibits academic freedom, and generates conflict between the academic "haves" and the "have nots." Park calls for renewable term contracts, with periodic performance review, and application of academic due process for all faculty, whether tenure track or not.

403. Perley, James E. "Problems in the Academy: Tenure, Academic Freedom, and Governance." **Academe** 81(1): 43-47, January-February 1995.

Written during his presidency of the AAUP, this article presents Perley's assessment of a hostile environment for academics and a growing hostility by nonacademics towards tenure. Listing numerous examples of negative media coverage of tenure and attempts by state legislatures to eliminate programs or schools, the author identifies three broad trends as being behind recent attacks on tenure: budgetary cutbacks at all types of educational institutions, cutbacks in instructional and personnel budgets at private institutions, and attempts to increase institutional efficiency through such measures as: reorganization or consolidation of academic units; increasing faculty workload; personnel displacement, including the hiring of adjuncts; reduction in programmatic redundancy in state-wide public education; and turning to nonacademics to assess the failures of the academy and propose solutions. Perley argues that tenure is far from an impediment to removing incompetent professors, but rather a protection ensuring that ours remains the "best educational system in the world."

404. Perley, James E. "Reflections on Tenure." **Sociological Perspectives** 41(4): 723- 28, Winter 1998.

Perley, past president of the AAUP, reviews a number of critiques of and proposed alternatives to tenure. The critiques include the arguments that tenure protects "deadwood" faculty, that tenure plus the uncapping of mandatory retirement has harmed younger prospective faculty, and that tenure is not needed to protect academic freedom since the 1st Amendment does it. Perley counters there are no data supporting the widespread existence of deadwood faculty. Nor are there data supporting the argument that faculty are retiring later, and that this has depressed the academic job market. On the contrary, university policies of replacing full-time faculty with part-time and adjunct faculty account for the depressed job market, says Perley. Relying on the 1st Amendment to resolve academic freedom issues will lead to lengthy and costly court cases, which would favor the Boards of Trustees over faculty. Alternatives to tenure, such as post-tenure review, ignore the fact that faculty are already evaluated annually for pay raises. Many of the new management alternatives for higher education are inappropriately drawn from the world of business. Perley argues for the collective defense of historic academic and professional standards.

405. Shils, Edward. "Academic Freedom and Permanent Tenure." **Minerva** 33(1): 5-17, Spring 1995.

Shils holds that permanent tenure is not necessarily a guarantee of academic freedom. Sanctions can be wielded against tenured teachers whose views or activities offend their superiors. Also, appointment to positions of permanent tenure can in some few cases do damage to the well being of the institution. Yet tenure should not be done away with. Shils argues that most infringements on academic freedom are infringements on the extra-academic civil rights and liberties of an individual academic. Arguments in favor of retaining the system of tenure need to be strengthened; the increasing use of political criteria in making retention and promotion determinations should be curtailed.

406. Smith, Bardwell L. "Academic Freedom, Tenure, and Countervailing Forces." In Bardwell L. Smith, editor. **The Tenure Debate.** San Francisco: Jossey-Bass, Inc., 1973. pp. 201-222. ISBN 0-8758-9148-9. LC 72-6058.

Smith details how faculty self-determination has declined since 1915, despite the institution of tenure. A brief historical overview of tenure and academic freedom in the years since 1915 is followed by a section on present threats to academic freedom. In a final section on tensions between accountability and autonomy, the author notes five examples which show where improvement is needed: long-term planning must begin to enhance diversity; governing boards must be strengthened in their attention to and sympathy for issues of academic freedom; a variety of models for increasing institutional accountability should be tried; curricular expansion should not come at the expense of curricular coherence; and attention to teaching must be increased.

407. Stichler, Richard N. "Academic Freedom and Faculty Responsibility in Disciplinary Procedures." **Academe** 83(3): 20-22, May-June 1997.

Stichler suggests that recent attacks on tenure are an outgrowth of public perceptions that incompetent tenured faculty members are not subject to removal from their positions. The implicit social pact, tracing back to the founding of the AAUP, seems to be that professors should be granted tenure to ensure the academic freedom necessary for the pursuit of truth in teaching and research. In return, there is an expectation on the part of the public that the professoriate will police itself and remove incompetent or unethical tenured faculty. Stichler argues, however, that very few tenured faculty are removed from their positions for incompetence. This fact fuels public perceptions that tenured positions are appointments for life, and that faculty protect each other. Professional associations have the ability to censure unethical conduct by members, but they have no power over one's employment. To ward off attacks on tenure by forces outside of the university, faculty need to come up with mechanisms and the will to identify and remove incompetent tenured faculty.

408. Tucker, Allan and Robert B. Mautz. "Academic Freedom, Tenure and Incompetence." **Educational Record** 63(2): 22-25, Spring 1982.

The authors assert that tenure is necessary to academia, and also to the broader welfare of society. They dispute claims that tenure will always remain a "bulwark of incompetency" and call for redefining the conditions for granting, denying, and withdrawing tenure. Ways in which the concept of academic freedom has expanded since 1913 and also since 1968 are addressed as background to the 1980s disputes over the institution of tenure.

409. Van Alstyne, William. "Tenure: A Summary, Explanation, and 'Defense.'" **AAUP Bulletin** 57(3): 328-333, September 1971.

Critics of higher education suggest that it needs to be made more accountable and efficient. Furthermore, they see tenure as a major obstacle to achieving these goals and consider it nothing more than "lifetime employment for the incompetent and irresponsible." In defense of tenure, Van Alstyne argues that it does not guarantee lifetime employment, but rather guarantees that termination be for adequate cause after due process has been provided. He also notes that probationary faculty go through an extensive six-year review before tenure is awarded. This gives faculty and institutions an adequate basis for determining if an ongoing appointment is warranted. The protections of "adequate cause" and "due process" help ensure that faculty will feel secure in their jobs and free to pursue their scholarly interests without fear of political interference. Van Alstyne also points out that faculty may still be removed not only for cause, but also for programmatic changes and financial exigency. Thus, institutional flexibility is not diminished. Once tenure has been awarded, however, the burden of proof in termination proceedings falls upon the institution. Finally, Van Alstyne addresses the seeming inconsistency between academic freedom for the tenured and untenured. He notes that AAUP guidelines also provide for due process in the nonrenewal of probationary or untenured faculty.

410. Van Alstyne, William W. "Tenure: A Conscientious Objective." **Change** 10(9): 44-47, October 1978.

Van Alstyne responds here to an article by James O'Toole called "Tenure: A Conscientious Objection" (see entry #401). Van Alstyne sees O'Toole's strongest two points as: tenure is unnecessary since our legal system now protects academic freedom, and tenure disrupts a marketplace of mobility among academics who would be better off in different positions but are stuck in unsuitable yet secure positions. Both articles are reprinted and expanded upon as essays in a monograph entitled *Tenure: Three Views*.

411. Westhues, Kenneth. **Eliminating Professors: A Guide to the Dismissal Process.** Queenston, Ontario: Kempner Collegium Publications; Lewiston, N.Y.: Edwin Mellen Press, 1998. 218p. ISBN 0-7734-8210-5.

Westhues maps out what he sees as the typical method by which institutions of higher education get rid of tenured professors who bear certain "marks of undesirability." The author dubs such a professor as PITA (for "pain in the ass") and recounts as a case study his own experiences of harassment at the hands of administrators at the University of Waterloo. Numerous case studies from other universities, from social science research on "workplace mobbing" and from non-educational workplaces provide evidence of a common five-stage human resource process for recognizing an "undesirable" employee and working to get rid of him or her. A process of ostracizing and harassment generally leads to a culminating incident that merits an official response from the institution. A final afterward provides a filmography of movies that dramatize the process of elimination described in this book.

412. Wiener, Jon. "Tenure Trouble." **Dissent** 45(1): 60-64, Winter 1998.

Wiener addresses arguments that market forces should play a larger role in higher education personnel issues, and that tenure should be done away with in favor of more flexible, cost-effective ways to educate college students. Richard Chait, tenured at Harvard, opposes tenure and his arguments against it are disputed here. While Chait claims that academic freedom can be protected without tenure, Wiener cites cases that call this claim into question. Cases cited include the 1993 Bennington College decision by new President Elizabeth Coleman to abolish tenure, and the 1996 fight at the University of Minnesota where the regents with the help of Chait drafted a plan (not implemented) to permit laying off of untenured faculty. The biggest threat to academic freedom that Wiener sees is the increasing use of adjunct and part-time instructors.

Chapter 10

Academic Freedom in Other Countries

413. Abbott, Frank. "Academic Freedom and Social Criticism in the 1930s." **Interchange** 14(4)-15(1): 107-123, 1983-1984.

During the Depression of the 1930s, a debate arose in Canada over academic freedom and the proper role of the academic. Traditionally, the academic's pursuit of truth had been justified by philosophical and religious traditions, as well as by institutional history. However, the Depression gave rise to social and political activism on the part of some faculty. These efforts to bring about radical social change went beyond the limits of academic freedom and the dispassionate pursuit of truth, according to critics. Many politicians, businessmen and conservative academics took the position that faculty were free only to teach the truth, not to engage in politics or criticism of the existing social order. Abbott illustrates these points by reviewing the controversies involving Frank Underhill, Frank Scott, and King Gordon. All three were attacked by the above-mentioned constituencies for their progressive positions on social and political issues. Abbott suggests that most Canadian faculty were inclined toward the traditional view of scholarship, not toward "partisan politics." Still, few activist faculty lost their jobs. Ultimately, the defense of academic freedom in Canada was based on the argument that civil liberties should be extended to teaching. In that period, the concept of academic freedom offered little protection.

414. **Academic Freedom in Indonesia: Dismantling Soeharto-Era Barriers.** New York: Human Rights Watch, 1998. 117p. LC 98-87242. ISBN 1-56432-186-X.

Coming after the resignation of President Soeharto in Indonesia, this report attempts to identify the legacy of infringements on human rights and academic freedom and to suggest remedies. Under Soeharto, neither students nor faculty were free. Faculty underwent ideological screening before they were appointed, and their subsequent teaching and research activities were closely monitored and controlled by the government. Dissidents were arrested, books were banned, and speakers were often prohibited from speaking. Student activity and expression was controlled, and the military spied on and actively intervened in campus affairs. A large portion of this report recounts the historical development of these restrictions on freedom. Recommendations are provided for the purpose of giving meaning and substance to Indonesian legal rhetoric supporting academic freedom.

415. "Academic Freedom in South Africa: The Open Universities in South Africa and Academic Freedom, 1957-1974." **Minerva** 13(3): 428-65, Fall 1975.

This essay recounts the period immediately following the 1957 National Party Government's racial segregation of universities, when the University of Cape Town and the University of the Witwatersrand in protest published a joint statement of academic freedom principles called "The Open Universities in South Africa." This article reaffirms the core beliefs contained in the 1957 statement while recounting changes in or extensions of those beliefs. Also described are the main legislative, political and educational events between 1957 and 1974 related to South African academic freedom; the differences in governance and financing that have evolved between largely "White" universities and those "Black" universities created in 1957 are highlighted. Both documents rely on a definition of academic freedom that includes the "four freedoms that should be accorded to all universities: who can teach, what may be taught, how it shall be taught and who may be admitted." This essay is divided into two parts, covering the right of universities to decide who may teach and who may be admitted to study; and, freedoms of expression related to the right of universities to decide what may be taught and how it shall be taught. Extensive bibliographic notes on legislation and South African higher education make this an excellent introduction to the confluence of apartheid and higher education and the dire effects that racist ideologies can have on academic freedom. An appendix reprints a 1972 letter from University of the Witwatersrand Vice-Chancellor G.R. Bozzoli to then-Prime Minister John Vorster calling on him to respond favorably to legitimate student grievances at "segregated universities for Black and Brown South Africans" before violence erupts of the sort that broke out in Kent, Paris, and Tokyo.

416. **Academic Freedom Under the Soviet Regime: A Symposium of Refugee Scholars and Scientists Who Have Escaped from the USSR, on the Subject 'Academic Freedom in the Soviet Union as a Threat to the Theory and Practice of Bolshevik Doctrine.'** Munich: Institute for the Study of the History and Culture of the USSR, 1954. 32p. LC 55-417.

This volume presents the proceedings of a conference held at the UN Plaza (New York) in April of 1954, presented under the auspices of the American

Committee for Liberation from Bolshevism and organized by former Soviet scholars. In three sessions devoted to pure sciences, social sciences, and history and literature, émigré scholars representing different disciplines and Soviet republics presented papers on a lack of academic freedom in the Soviet Union. In presentations and panel discussions, the role (or lack) of academic and scientific freedoms is addressed in such disciplines as geology, genetics, engineering, jurisprudence, economics, and literature.

417. Aldous, Peter. "An Industry-Friendly Science Policy: A Restructuring of Britain's Research Councils, Aimed at Making Academic Research More Useful to Industry, Is Now Taking Hold - and Unease is Growing in Some Disciplines." **Science** 265(5172): 596, July 19, 1994.

Under Prime Minister John Major, British research councils, which award research funds, were reorganized to increase the relevance of university research to industry. While some academic researchers found a number of the reforms useful, others found them a threat to their freedom to pursue basic research in areas of their choice. Some academics alleged that the engineering and physics research council was making funding decisions based upon, in part, the existence of a "user" for the research. This would seriously jeopardize basic research at the expense of applied research. Furthermore, the fear was that this criterion for funding would spread to other research councils, posing a broad threat to British scientific research. Finally, academic researchers were afraid that competition for research funds would intensify if industrial researchers could receive funding.

418. Ben-David, Joseph and Randall Collins. "A Comparative Study of Academic Freedom and Student Politics." **Comparative Education Review** 10(2): 220-249, June 1966.

The authors describe the main sources of conflict concerning academic freedom and examine national differences between such conflicts and their solutions. Among the sources of friction are the potential involvement of the university in wider societal conflict, the definition of the group and scope of activities over which academic freedom is extended, and the divisions of power between administrators, faculty and students. An international comparison of different organizational models for higher education notes that professional schools tend to be of two types: elite systems set up under widely accepted and stable institutional models (19th century England, France, United States); and elite systems set up as deliberately pioneering or reform-oriented institutions (18th century Austria, Prussia, Russia; or 20th century Eastern and Southern European or Latin American institutions). Differing pressures occur in each type of system and in each country. This essay also reprinted in Seymour Martin Lipset, editor. *Student Politics*. New York: Basic Books, 1967. pp. 148-195. (Student Movements Past and Present, v. 1). LC 67-23817.

419. Bessant, Bob. "Privatisation and Academic Freedom." **The Australian Universities' Review** 29(2): 11-15, 1986.

Though ostensibly modeled on British and Scottish universities, the early Australian universities lacked faculty involvement in self-governance on academic matters. Instead, university councils and state governments held inordinate decision-making power and influence in university governance. According to Bessant, this had a negative affect on faculty teaching and research. The academic freedom case of Sydney Sparkes Orr, as well as the unprecedented growth of Australian universities in the 1950s and 1960s, helped to mobilize the academic community and elevate issues of academic freedom. The Murray Report of the 1950s further helped to support the freedom of academics in their teaching and research, and to support their rightful involvement in academic affairs. According to Bessant, however, recent threats to academic freedom and autonomy have come from not only federal and state involvement in education, but also, more significantly, the privatization of education. Privatization advocates argue that universities should be more market driven and accountable; some suggest the elimination of tenure, which inhibits the flexible allocation of teaching resources, and the substitution of contract teaching. Tailoring the curriculum and research to that which is profitable and "relevant" to the market will further threaten academic freedom and institutional autonomy. Basic research, which may have no immediate payback, and course work in the humanities and social sciences may be jeopardized. An increased focus on local issues in research may improve public support for academic freedom.

420. Birley, Sir Robert. **The Real Meaning of Academic Freedom.** London: World University Service, 1972. 24 p. ISBN 0-9016-5819-7.

This volume reproduces the text of a 1972 lecture given at the tenth annual Council of World University Service in the United Kingdom. Providing a short history of academic freedom in Germany, Birley goes on to consider the state of academic freedom in South Africa, The United States and the Soviet Union. Citing some of the earliest academic freedom cases in 18th century Germany as well as some post-World War II examples, Birley notes that German universities consistently professed neutrality on all extra-university matters. In contrast, South African universities fought since 1959 the forced racial segregation that their government imposed on them. South African universities also supported the political and anti-governmental activities of students. The issue of the intense influence of business interests on higher education is addressed in discussing United States higher education. The influence of the State, Communist Party, and Marxist dialectic on academic freedom in the Soviet Union are also covered. Birley cites academic freedom issues in the developing world by examining the 1963 founding of the University of East Africa and the comments of its first Chancellor, Julius Nyerere. Nyerere thought that universities should fight racial discrimination and always work to better serve the needs of the society they were in, but should also never waver from the search for truth. Nyerere's comments are quoted at length as an antidote to the problems of university as detached ivory tower (as in Germany), as prejudicial institution (as in South Africa), as controlled by commercial interests (as in the US), or as servant to the goals of the State (as in the Soviet Union).

421. Brown, Cynthia Stokes. "Academic Freedom at Göttingen Before 1815." **School and Society** 100(2340): 173-178, March 1972.

The author details specific freedoms, and specific limitations on those freedoms at the University of Göttingen. The common assertion that academic freedom was invented and fully realized in 19th century Prussian universities must be revisited and revised, particularly in the light of the easy capitulation of universities to the Nazi regime. Four facets of academic freedom at Göttingen are addressed: freedoms of teachers, freedoms of students, and freedom from both internal and external controls. That such freedoms depended in large part on the social and political stabilities of the monarchy is not often recognized.

422. Burke, Maria. "Suffer for Your Thoughts." **Physics World** 8(5): 29-30, May 1995.

Burke profiles the activities of a number of scientific and human rights organizations on behalf of imprisoned academics and scientists worldwide. Frequently, these scholars are imprisoned for their human rights activities, which are considered an outgrowth of their scientific search for truth and devotion to free expression. Organizations such as the American Association for the Advancement of Science (AAAS), Amnesty International, and the Committee of Concerned Scientists (CCS), among others, attempt to mobilize other scientists to write and lobby on behalf of hundreds of scholars, with a disproportionate number being engineers and medics. Some of the cases and countries cited for abuses include Burma, Syria, China, and Cuba. Overall, the AAAS has identified 468 cases, which represents an increase of 119 over the previous year. The American Physical Society (APS) also works with the above organizations and focuses on more traditional academic freedom cases in such countries as Germany, the United States, and China. In addition, it is active in trying to free travel restrictions on scientists worldwide, since such restrictions limit the free exchange of scholarly ideas.

423. Caston, G. "Academic Freedom." In Burton R. Clark and Guy R. Neave, editors. **The Encyclopedia of Higher Education: Volume 2, Analytical Perspectives.** New York: Pergamon Press, 1992. pp. 1295-1305. ISBN 0-0803-7251-1.

Caston's primary focus is on academic freedom in nonfree and Third World or developing countries. He argues that "free" versus "nonfree" is an overly narrow categorization of societies in relation to academic freedom. Such factors as a society's political configuration, wealth, or ethnic and ideological homogeneity also influence the degree to which academic freedom is allowed. Furthermore, threats to academic freedom may also come from dominant groups in university departments, from the administration, or from the trustees. Though wary of generalizations, Caston suggests that universities in developing countries are often asked to contribute in practical ways to development. Consequently, much is expected of these universities and their faculty, and university debates can loom large nationally. A country's former colonial status can further complicate its university faculty's political values and relationship to the international scholarly community. Pre-existing ethnic differences may also impact the staffing of positions and the goal of relying upon meritocratic criteria. In light of the above challenges, universities can preserve academic freedom if they are perceived as promoting the public interest, having international credibility, and fulfilling their educational role. Compromises of academic freedom, autonomy and meritocracy may be necessary in the practical, political context of developing countries.

424. Caston, Geoffrey. "Academic Freedom: The Third World Context." **Oxford Review of Education** 15(3): 305-338, 1989.

The author addresses the variety of definitions and constraints on academic freedom in educational institutions of developing countries, the general societal context that universities operate under in Third World countries, and those elements of academic freedom that can and should be preserved in such contexts. Defining limits imposed on academic freedom in "non-free" societies include such things as specifically anti-university powers of the state and disparities between class and ethnic groups, which sometimes play a part in deciding who attends or teaches at universities. Issues relevant to the societal context in which the Third World university operates are the cost vs. contributions of universities to economic development; the influences from overseas and from ethnic groups within the developing country; and the political fragility and strength of or domestic role of the military. Preserving academic freedom in this context requires that universities serve the public interest, both in hiring and educating; maintain their international standings; and refrain from political activities not directly related to primary teaching and research functions. The author concludes that it is almost always better to preserve the existence of an educational institution than, in the name of higher principles of academic neutrality or special privilege, to refuse to submit to the demands of the state.

425. Daniel, John, et al, editors. **Academic Freedom 3: Education and Human Rights.** Atlantic Highlands, N.J.: Zed Books, 1995. 244p. ISBN 1-8564-9301-6.

See World University Service, entry #469.

426. Daniel, John, et al, editors. **Academic Freedom 2: A Human Rights Report.** Atlantic Highlands, N.J.: Zed Books, 1993. 168p. ISBN 1-8564-9219-2.

See World University Service, entry #469.

427. Erazo, Ximena, Mike Kirkwood and Frederiek de Vlaming, editors. **Academic Freedom 4: Education and Human Rights.** Atlantic Highlands, N.J.: Zed Books, 1996. 246p. ISBN 1-8564-9377-6.

See World University Service, entry #469.

428. Fekete, John. "Against Zero Tolerance." **Journal of Canadian Studies** 29(1): 144-147, Spring 1994.

The second part of two in a section called "Point-Counterpoint: Human Rights and Academic Freedom," this essay argues that a new Ontario "Framework Regarding Prevention of Harassment and Discrimination in Ontario Universities" violates principles of academic freedom and is symptomatic of a new left authoritarianism. The author holds that the universality of rights already accorded under human rights laws is the best means for providing a level playing field for women and minorities in Canadian higher education. Fekete holds that zero tolerance efforts made in conjunction with the framework stifle freedom of expression. See also Sangster (entry #454) and Stark (entry #459).

429. Fernando, Laksiri, et al, editors. **Academic Freedom 1990: A Human Rights Report.** Atlantic Highlands, N.J.: Zed Books, 1990. 192p. ISBN 0-8623-2972-8.

See World University Service, entry #469.

430. Flynn, James T. "Magnitskii's Purge of Kazan University: A Case Study in the Uses of Reaction in Nineteenth-Century Russia." **Journal of Modern History** 43(4): 598-614, December 1971.

One of the most infamously oppressive nineteenth century Russian university curators, Mikhail Leontevich Magnitskii unsuccessfully recommended in 1819 to the minister of education that Kazan University should be closed. Alexander I had established a system of universities based on a liberal Western (primarily German) model but towards the end of his reign rejected principles of liberalism. This essay explores the Kazan University situation at the time, and explores the strain in Russia between rationalism and religious conservatism.

431. Furedy, John J. "Velvet Totalitarianism on Canadian Campuses: Subverting Effects on the Teaching of, and Research in, the Discipline of Psychology." **Canadian Psychology/Psychologie canadienne** 38(4): 205-211, November 1997.

Furedy examines the effects of political correctness on academic freedom in Canadian universities, with specific attention to the field of psychology. He suggests that Canadian campuses are more repressive than the society at large, constituting "islands of repression in a sea of freedom." He terms this repression "velvet totalitarianism" and says that it has five identifying features: ambiguous and uninterpretable laws or rules; adjudicating experts who lack expertise; pervasive fear on campus of running afoul of acceptable political and social positions; the evaluation of behavior by the "identities of the actors"; and the demonization of enemies. In such a climate, the pursuit of truth with logic and facts gives way to a "culture of comfort" in which acceptable ideas must not give offense. This has lead to serious compromises of academic freedom in certain research areas in psychology, such as studies of group differences. Furedy reviews three cases of Canadian academic psychologists whose academic freedom was sacrificed to this "culture of comfort" and its manifestations.

432. Graham, John F. "University Funding and Academic Freedom." **Dalhousie Review** 63(1): 135-146, Spring 1983.

The author considers the threat to academic freedom from Canadian governmental proposals and actions in the area of funding higher education. That a threat exists is supported by an historical overview of funding going back to World War II, focusing on what has happened since funding restrictions were put in place, and on the way government funding has become more oriented towards vocational education.

433. Graycar, Adam. "Autonomy in Higher Education: Some Research Findings." **Journal of Educational Administration** 13(2): 37-45, October 1975.

The author interviewed a sample of 40 engineering academics in two Australian educational institutions, including professors, lecturers, and a Dean regarding their self-perception of "subjective" or "objective" autonomy in their work. The terms here are borrowed from Richard Hofstadter's "Academic Freedom in the Age of the College." Subjective autonomy is defined as existing at the level of coursework, the selection of texts, and teaching strategies. Objective autonomy is at the level of the profession, whether through autonomy of the professional organization (in this case, the Institution of Engineers, Australia), autonomy of professional schools, or autonomy of those educational institutions employing engineers. Most respondents had internalized the values expressed by the professional organization, the industry at large, and the State, and therefore did not see these interests as constraints on their subjective academic freedom. The author noted, however, that while some respondents claimed to have a high degree of objective autonomy, his findings indicated a low degree of objective autonomy.

434. Harrison, M. J. and Keith Weightman. "Academic Freedom and Higher Education in England." **British Journal of Sociology** 25(1): 32-46, March 1974.

The authors hold that the sociological study of academic freedom is a study of the sort of expectations, demands, and disciplinary controls that are imposed on individuals who are in positions of academic freedom. They rely in part for their formulation of academic freedom on the work of Ben-David and Collins (see entry #418). But they take issue with Ben-David's and Collins' analysis of higher education in England, and also with their claim that the U.S. model would provide a viable basis for academic freedom in English universities. These authors contend that the future of academic freedom in England should be of concern.

435. Herriman, Michael. "Academic Freedom in Australia." **Interchange** 14(4)-15(1): 82-93, 1983-1984.

Academic freedom in Australia is more like an incantation or a slogan than a historically rooted tradition, says Herriman. Of the two major aspects of freedom, freedom to pursue truth and freedom from institutional constraints, the latter is most threatened by the structure, finance and governance of Australian higher education. Due to changes in the sources of funding in the early 1970s, Australian universities are more dependent on the Commonwealth and state parliaments, thus increasing the opportunity for de facto outside control. In addition, administrative control is more centralized, with Australian academics having relatively less decision-making input than their American counterparts. Furthermore, Australian universities, being mostly in urban settings, are primarily commuter campuses with little sense of community. Nor are the universities well integrated into their local communities, which are often seen by the academics as anti-intellectual. These factors affect the level of support for universities and, indirectly, institutional autonomy and academic freedom. Fiscal accountability has led to an emphasis on the utility of education and degree programs, thus hurting the job market and freedom of academics in "non-utilitarian" disciplines. Overall, the growth of governmental power over education has led to a decrease of institutional autonomy and academic freedom.

436. Hoch, Paul. **Academic Freedom in Action: An Up-to-date Account of the Counter-Insurgency Activities Pursued by Scholars Around the World Under the Banner of 'Academic Freedom.'** London: Sheed and Ward, 1970. 212p. ISBN 0-7220-0600-4.

Hoch critically examines Harvard, London University, the London School of Economics and the Institute for Defense Analyses (a corporation founded in 1956 by MIT, Cal Tech, Case Institute of Technology, Stanford and Tulane), and the influence of various Pentagon- or CIA-funded private foundations in British and U.S. higher education (including the Carnegie and Ford Foundations). The means by which universities are made to serve the interests of imperialist and militaristic governments and for-profit corporations are laid out. Ways in which pure and social science research is put to military or CIA ends are detailed, as are efforts to write off critics of such university activities as radicals or nihilists. Further efforts to categorize student activism as a threat to academic freedom are outlined, along with an accounting of the "victims of academic freedom" who attempt to oppose militaristic or politically biased institutions of higher education.

437. Horn, Michiel. **Academic Freedom in Canada: A History.** Toronto: University of Toronto Press, 1999. 446p. ISBN 0-8020-0726-0.

Based on research in 26 university and public archives, Horn's history covers academic freedom in English speaking Canada from 1860 to the present. He examines the influence of the German university model on the development of academic freedom in Canada, and also discusses the distinctively Canadian influences that tempered its adoption. Early academic freedom controversies typically revolved around such issues as religion, institutional governance, and the free speech rights of professors. Numerous academic freedom cases are discussed as the book analyzes the extent of and restrictions on academic freedom in various historical periods, such as World War I, the Depression, World War II, the Cold War, and the student movement of the 1960s. Horn also addresses more recent controversies, such as those over political correctness and tenure.

438. Horn, Michiel. "The Mildew of Discretion: Academic Freedom and Self-Censorship." **Dalhousie Review** 72(4): 439-466, Winter 1992/1993.

Horn recounts numerous specific cases from the 1930s through the 1980s of what he sees as an inappropriate discretion in the face of controversy among Canadian academics. Evidence is cited to support his claim that a desire to get along with peers and not endanger one's institutions pushed Canadian professors toward self-censorship.

439. Horn, Michiel. "Professors in the Public Eye: Canadian Universities, Academic Freedom, and the League for Social Reconstruction." **History of Education Quarterly** 20(4): 425-447, Winter 1980.

Horn describes the "near-quiescence" of Canadian academics during the inter-war years, and the unwritten limitations on academic freedom, both self- and institution-imposed. The first organization of left-wing intellectuals in Canadian history, the League for Social Reconstruction (LSR), was founded in 1931/1932. Though the LSR had no formal political affiliation, many of those academics that joined were pressured to resign their affiliations with a recently established Socialist party, the Cooperative Commonwealth Federation. Outside Toronto and Montreal, few academics belonged to the LSR; those members such as Frank Underhill (historian at UT) who gave commentary on public events were much criticized. Dr. Underhill was officially reprimanded in 1931 for criticism of the then-Prime Minister R.B. Burnett. He was almost dismissed in 1941 over his comments about the war. Though dismissals were rare, so was outspokenness. The self-image of academics, it is argued here, precluded social criticism; an anti-intellectualism on the part of public officials also contributed to limiting the participation of academics in public life.

440. Human Rights Watch. **Academic Freedom and Human Rights Abuses in Africa: An Africa Watch Report.** New York: Human Rights Watch, 1991. 153p. ISBN 0-9296-9277-2.

This research report provides country-by-country coverage of threats to and serious abuses of human rights and academic freedom in Africa. A brief essay on the evolution of African universities opens this volume. Recommendations made by Africa Watch (a division of Human Rights Watch) include (among others) calls for African universities to either immediately put on trial or unconditionally release all detainees, to permit student and staff participation in political activity, and to cease deployment of security forces on campuses. Recommendations are made to academics, organizations of academics and those outside of Africa to support and assist exiled or detained scholars and students. A list of academics currently in detention is provided in an appendix.

441. Hutcheon, Pat Duffy. "Academic Freedom: An Evolving Concept?" **Journal of Educational Thought** 7(1): 25-35, April 1973.

Hutcheon makes the claim that the concept of academic freedom should rightly be applicable only within liberal arts universities and removed from influence on professional colleges. This claim is based on the notion that higher education serves two disparate roles in industrialized societies such as Canada's: that of credentialing and that of liberalizing. The author calls for creation of three distinct sets of institutions: professional colleges designed to certify objectively measurable professional competencies, with their own entrance qualifications, diplomas and degrees conferred upon completion; and universities, with no entrance requirements and only a certificate of attendance awarded. The third would encompass all postgraduate research which would be conducted at separately administered research institutions. Arguing that "polarization and confrontation are always obstacles to reasoned inquiry," Hutcheon claims that while students and professors must be free to participate in social and political movements outside the university, academic freedom cannot survive for either students or professors unless it is narrowly restricted to scholarly, intellectual pursuits and unless the student's freedom to learn has precedent over the professor's freedom to teach.

442. Johnson, Alvin. "Intellectual Liberty Imperiled." **American Scholar** 2(3): 312-319, May 1933.

The author discusses academic proscriptions in Germany, Italy, Russia and other European countries. There is an increase in the number of European scholars being expelled for political reasons from faculty positions. The author, Director of the New School for Social Research, compares academic freedom in the U.S. with that in Europe and calls on individual American scholars to pledge one to five percent of their earnings to help their peers who are victims of political oppression in other countries.

443. Ludwikowski, Rett R. "Personal Reflections of Academic Freedom in Poland." **Center Journal** 3(2): 69-88, Spring 1984.

An émigré political scientist, Ludwikowski discusses the extent to which limited academic freedom was possible for him in Poland under Communist Party rule. Ludwikowski refused official demands that he lecture on the benefits of martial law. Experiences of limitations on academic freedom as a student, the pragmatic Communist concept of "partiinost" (or "silent obedience"), and his academic career in Poland are all here addressed.

444. Mason, John Brown. "Academic Freedom under Nazism." **Social Science** 15(4): 388-394, October 1940.

Mason presents the views of the Reich Minister of Education Bernhard Rust as the official governmental response to international concerns about academic and scientific freedoms. In a 1936 speech at the jubilee celebration of the University of Heidelberg, attended by representatives from universities around the world, Minister Rust described the relationship of National Socialism with science. Science must be rooted in the values of "racial and national character," as it cannot possibly be universalized or pursued in value-free objectivity. Mason goes on to recount similar pronouncements by Nazi scientists and an American condemnation of Nazi theory signed by 1,284 American scientists. Mason concludes by noting that the 1937 bicentenary celebrations at the university at Göttingen were largely boycotted by foreign scholars.

445. Mazrui, Ali A. "Academic Freedom in Africa: The Dual Tyranny." **African Affairs: Journal of the Royal African Society** 74(297): 393-400, October 1975.

Mazrui sees academic freedom as under threat in Africa from the political tyranny of newly installed governments in African countries, and from the Eurocentrism that saturates the university tradition, even in Africa. How to make universities into African (not European) institutions is one question addressed here; another is how to ensure academic freedom at those African institutions under white control as well as at those under black control.

446. Mohanon, Edward. "Tenure and Academic Freedom in Canadian Universities." **Interchange on Education** 14(4)/15(1): 94-106. 1983/1984.

Mohanon provides an overview of the history and current limitations (including financial) on the tenure system in Canadian universities. In response to those who would abolish or substantially modify the tenure system, a section on the future of tenure discusses the role of tenure in protecting academic freedom and in attracting and retaining the best academics. The author asserts that alternative means of reaching these important goals are too often unaddressed by those who criticize the tenure system.

447. Munger, William L. "Academic Freedom under Péron." **Antioch Review** 7(2): 275-290, June 1947.

Munger recounts the undermining of academic freedom in the higher education institutions of Argentina since the military coup of June 1943. Long standing freedoms of teaching and learning and the autonomy of universities were swept away after the coup d'état. The first groups in Argentine society to openly protest the seizure of power were students. Government takeover of the schools was slow, but by the beginning of 1947 over 1,200 professors had been forced to resign, with no formal charges ever filed in most cases. Representatives from the Military and from the Catholic Church were appointed to take their places. Mass arrests and torture were used against student leaders (many visited by Munger in prison), and rival nationalist student organizations were put in place by Juan Péron.

448. Neave, Guy. "Accountability and Control." **European Journal of Education** 15(1): 49-60, 1980.

Neave describes a polarization between the concepts of academic freedom and accountability, posing such questions as: Is academic freedom an ideological mask hiding the fact that education serves the ruling elites and status quo?; or, Is academic freedom the guarantee that truth can be pursued without restraint? Are academics accountable to those outside academe? Should they be? These questions are explored with reference to institutions in a variety of European countries, where accountability "from above" (state-imposed limits on academic freedom) and accountability "from below" (locally- or internally-imposed limits) can both be found. In France and the Netherlands, financial constraints begin to make higher education more beholden to government (and therefore more compliant to its demands). In Sweden and Spain, there are an increasing number of participants in the internal running of the university (such as student movements or local involvement in governing boards). Sweden provides an exception to this "binary model." Regional Boards of Education decentralize planning and administration, giving at least some control to locals. Neave predicts that states will only increase their intervention into higher education, thereby reducing university autonomy. One indicator of this trend is the long term development across Europe of power shifting from legislative branch politicians to executive branch civil servants.

449. Neave, Guy. "The Changing Boundary Between the State and Higher Education." **European Journal of Education** 17(3): 231-41, September 1982.

Neave discusses his concept of "boundary relationships" as it plays out in three major models of the relationship between the state and the university. The first of these is that proposed in the late 18th century by Kant, which distinguished between areas of teaching and research where the state might intervene legitimately and areas where it may not. In contrast to this is the Humboldtian organization which, in 19th century Prussia sought to disallow any intervention by the state in research and teaching. This organization worked only to the extent that professional schools with direct governmental oversight existed in a parallel but legally distinct educational sector. The third model is that derived from the Anglo-Saxon university, where formal state intervention is absent, but only because of the certifying role played by professional organizations. Questions posed by Neave to clarify the shifting boundaries between state and higher education include: Who teaches?; Who is taught and for how long?; What national regulations (if any) govern degree-granting or departmental/curricular structure?; Who pays, how much, and how? Neave's conclusions are that while there is growing intervention by the state in higher education, that a more thorough exploration of the Kantian model might help universities maintain some degree of autonomy from outside intervention.

450. Oppenheimer, Martin. "Academic Freedom in the Federal Republic of Germany." **AAUP Bulletin** 63(2): 45-49, April 1977.

Oppenheimer reviews the mid-1970s movement in Germany referred to as "Berufsverbot." It was a systematic government policy of banning from civil service positions, including teaching positions, individuals whose loyalty to the constitution was in question. Any number of political or civil activities, including some free speech and legal political affiliations, were prohibited. The effect of this law was to precipitate the firing or non-hiring of individuals who were deemed not to meet the loyalty standard. According to Oppenheimer, the criteria that would designate one an "enemy of the constitution" were subjective, including the expectation that civil servants demonstrate "measured and reserved" behavior. This latter expectation, though vague, was often invoked in terminations, taking precedence over one's civil liberties. Along with German civil liberties groups, Oppenheimer sees this as having a chilling effect on the exercise of civil liberties and academic freedom.

451. "The Power of the State and the Dignity of the Academic Calling in Imperial Germany: The Writings of Max Weber on University Problems." **Minerva** 11(4): 571-632, October 1973.

In this collection of critical newspaper articles from the turn-of-the-century, Weber, the famous German sociologist and economist, criticizes bureaucratic policies that diminish academic freedom and compromise the proper role of German academics. He is particularly critical of patronage appointments that bypass faculty selection of their colleagues, of the subtle imposition of political and ecclesiastical limits on academic appointments, of the growth of a market or entrpreneurial orientation among German faculty, and of restrictions on the free movement of faculty from one institution to another. Weber also engages in some comparison of academic life in American and German universities. Other topics addressed include ethical neutrality and science as a vocation.

452. Pritchard, Rosalind M. O. "Academic freedom and Autonomy in the United Kingdom and Germany." **Minerva** 36(2): 101-124, Summer 1998.

Pritchard provides a thorough review of the cultural and historical context of and changes in academic freedom in Germany and the United Kingdom. Germany has historically had a close relationship between the state and higher educational institutions. Academic freedom has been supported by law, and the concepts of Lehrfreiheit (freedom to teach) and Lernfreiheit (freedom to learn) are embedded in the culture and ethos of higher education. In the United Kingdom, the support for academic freedom has historically been more implicit, given the freedom and autonomy that was granted higher educational institutions. Pritchard notes the changes in both countries in the context of academic freedom in the current political and economic climate. In Britain, the policies of Prime Minister Margaret Thatcher helped bring about more government influence over higher education, leading to a more market orientation in curriculum, research and accountability. In Germany, the traditional view of how students and faculty should pursue knowledge has conflicted, somewhat, with more practical concerns for meeting marketplace demands for educated labor. Pritchard argues, however, that academic freedom has fared better in Germany than in Britain, and she provides some historical observations explaining why that is the case.

453. Pybus, Cassandra. **Gross Moral Turpitude: The Orr Case Reconsidered.** Port Melbourne, Australia: William Heinemann, 1993. 238p. ISBN 0-8556-1457-9.

The academic freedom case of Sydney Sparkes Orr is easily the most famous in the history of Australian higher education. Orr, a philosopher at the University of Tasmania, was fired from his position in the 1950s for allegedly seducing a female student. He contested the firing and received considerable support from other academics, philosophy associations in Australia and abroad, and Australia's Federal Council of University Staff Associations (FCUSA), among others. Orr had been a strident critic of the university, and his defenders contended that the charge of seducing a student was a pretext for a political firing. In this book, Pybus reexamines the case and its key characters and documentation. She finds ample evidence to suggest that Orr did in fact seduce the student in question, not to mention other students at previous places of employment. Pybus's social history attempts to explain the level of support Orr received, despite his objectionable personality and suspicions that he was in fact guilty. Many of his supporters felt it was important to defend the principle of academic freedom against abridgements by an arbitrary administration. Some philosophers argued that faculty - student relationships were not the university's business. Reflecting the anti-communist hysteria of the period, still other of Orr's supporters contended that a national, political conspiracy was involved in his firing. Pybus demonstrates that there were procedural and political irregularities not only in Orr's firing, but also, more importantly, in his hiring. She also suggests that the male-dominated higher education culture in Australia fostered a contemptuous and sexist attitude toward the female student involved.

454. Sangster, Joan and Paul Zeleza. "Academic Freedom in Context." **Journal of Canadian Studies** 29(1): 139-144, Spring 1994.

One part of two in a section called "Point-Counterpoint: Human Rights and Academic Freedom," this essay makes the argument that a new Ontario "Framework Regarding Prevention of Harassment and Discrimination in Ontario Universities" does not violate principles of academic freedom. A response to this Framework came from Trent University faculty, many of whom signed a manifesto on academic freedom asserting faculty rights to "offend." The anger of academics and the ideological nature of some anti-feminist and anti-humanist opposition to the Framework results in a debate about academic freedom that has a broad political context. The authors question whether reactions against equality, inclusiveness and anti-harassment policies are really a direction that will advance academic freedom. See also Fekete (entry #428) and Stark (entry #459).

455. Savage, Donald C. "Keeping the Professors Out: The Immigration Department and the Idea of Academic Freedom, 1945-90." **Dalhousie Review** 69(4): 499-524, Winter 1989-90.

Savage reviews the history of Canadian immigration policy toward allegedly radical or subversive professors from other countries. For years, the immigration authorities would routinely deny landed immigrant status or visitors' visas to foreign faculty who might be suspected of radical political views or affiliations. However, definitive explanations for the denials were somewhat difficult to verify since immigration generally refused to divulge the reasons for its decisions. Savage discusses some notable cases, their resolution, and the involvement of various interest groups, such as the Canadian Association of University Teachers (CAUT). Recent changes in rules and appeals procedures are discussed.

456. Schrank, Bernice. "Responding to Academic Freedom." **Interchange** 28(4): 351-362, October 1997.

Responding to articles by W. Richard Bond, Fred Wilson, and Michael Kubara in an earlier issue of this journal (Vol. 27, #2), Schrank provides another perspective on academic freedom in Ontario and Canada. Schrank generally agrees with Bond's critique of Ontario's policy against discrimination and harassment in the workplace. The policy's reliance upon the concept of a "negative environment" privileges a person's subjective feelings over demonstrable facts of harassment and discrimination. This creates a threat to free speech and academic freedom. Kubara argues that academic feminists, in their efforts to support a positive learning environment for all, are placing limits on the freedom of academics. In this model, pedagogy becomes too much like therapy. While Schrank agrees with Kubara's critique, she thinks that he underestimates the "systemic discrimination" against women in academia. Wilson's article continues the thread of the other two in arguing that well-crafted speech codes on campus can prevent the "silencing" of legitimate views on campus. Schrank's problem with this argument is that there are no objective criteria to determine when silencing has occurred. Consequently, speech codes will inevitably abridge academic freedom. See also Fekete (entry #428) and Sangster (#454).

457. Shils, Edward. "Stanford and Berlin: The Spheres of Politics and Intellect." **Minerva** 10(3): 351-361, July 1972.

Shils compares the 1972 case of Stanford's revoking of tenure from Associate Professor H. Bruce Franklin with a 1972 West Berlin case involving dismissal of Rudolf Stein from the Free University of Berlin. Both involved Communist scholars found to be engaging in political activity more or less disruptive to the academic community, though Franklin's dismissal came after a committee of his colleagues recommended it, and Stein's dismissal was at the behest of a politician. Shils provides a comparative discussion of student protest and university autonomy in Germany and the U.S. and the implications for academic freedom of faculty dismissal on political grounds.

458. Sigmund, Paul E. "Chilean Universities and the Coup." **Change** 5(10): 18-22, Winter 1973.

Sigmund recounts the events in Chilean universities in the years leading up to and immediately following the September 11, 1973 military coup. The junta replaced all University Chancellors with military officers and put Rear Admiral Hugo Castro in place as Minister of Education in an attempt to "cleanse" the university system of all Marxist of leftist influences. House-to-house searches and seizure of leftist books, newspapers, and magazines were among the methods used under what Castro called "a profound restructuring of Chilean education." The author was a visiting professor in 1967 at the University of Chile and at the Catholic University of Chile.

459. Stark, Cannie. "Academic Freedom, 'Political Correctness', and Ethics." **Canadian Psychology/Psychologie canadienne** 38(4): 232-237, November 1997.

The term "political correctness" has negative connotations and its use as an epithet "results...in trivialization of serious issues and invalidation of injustices experienced by particular populations" (p. 233). An Ontario document, "Framework Regarding Prevention of Harassment and Discrimination in Ontario Universities," has been particularly controversial, suggesting the creation of policies to avoid "negative environments" on campus. However, the policy does raise the legitimate importance of ethics in the professional responsibility of psychologists. Politically incorrect behaviors, such as abusive or discriminatory treatment, can contribute to psychological violence on campus, and psychologists should be ethically obliged to oppose them. Academic freedom should entail an ethical responsibility to nurture "respect and caring in relationships" (p. 236), says Stark. See also Fekete (entry #428) and Sangster (entry #454).

460. Tasker, M. E., and D. E. Packham. "Freedom, Funding and the Future of the Universities." **Studies in Higher Education** 15(2): 181-195, 1990.

According to Tasker and Packham, the 1980s financial crisis in British higher education has compromised the academic freedom and autonomy of faculty and their institutions. Government agencies have used the financial crisis to exert more control over the academic process, which has correspondingly reduced the role and influence of academics. Similarly, industry has provided more financial support for higher education through funded research, university-industry collaborations, and endowed faculty positions. However, these developments have compromised faculty autonomy in selecting research topics and freely sharing knowledge and findings. The authors suggest that industry priorities, such as the creation of a trained workforce and the generation of profitable research, are potentially in conflict with university goals, such as the pursuit of truth and the exploration of knowledge.

461. Tight, Malcolm, ed. **Academic Freedom and Responsibility.** Philadelphia: Open University Press, 1988. 150p. ISBN 0-3350-9531-3.

This edited compilation was commissioned in advance of the 1988 Annual Conference of the Society for Research into Higher Education. The authors are for the most part British, and address such issues as: academic freedom as it relates to professional education; human rights, the limits of academic freedom, and sexual harassment. The editor concludes the volume with an essay synthesizing the contributors' views and spelling out ten basic questions related to academic freedom which he attempts to answer. Includes essays by Anthony O'Hear, Mary Hawkesworth (entry #246), Guy Neave, Sinclair Goodlad, Bhikhu Parekh, Margherita Rendel (entry #28), Ronald Barnett, and John Turner.

462. Veit, Fritz. "Academic Freedom in Germany Before and after 1933: Under the Republic of Weimar and Under Hitler." **Peabody Journal of Education** 15(1): 36-44, July 1937.

Comparing academic freedom under the democratic Weimar republic and the National Socialist Nazi republic, Veit finds that institutions once focused on detached objective study had changed to a focus on studies based on the philosophical outlook promulgated by the state. Freedoms of teaching, study, and research were all written into the Weimar Constitution and broadly interpreted by governmental and legal authorities to allow wide freedoms for academics to pursue studies of their choice and to express findings openly without fear of governmental interference. Under Hitler, however, the concept of a leading philosophical and political viewpoint was extended to cover science, research, and teaching; all of which were conditioned and restricted by National Socialist ideas and under the strict scrutiny of the State.

463. Waters, Malcolm J. "The Institutionalization of Academic Freedom: Implications of Some Findings from the Third World." **Journal of Educational Thought** 13(3): 150-162, December 1979.

Waters provides a country-by-country comparison of academic freedom in Great Britain, Canada, Jamaica, Nigeria, and the West Indies. This author defines academic freedom as "the view that scholarly activity, in the form of research and teaching, is subject to the authority only of academic communities and of no external authority source." Waters finds differing "value consonance" between academic freedom in Third World institutions and the societal systems of which they are a part. This value consonance depends to some degree on the general perspective on the role of a university in society, whether as a place of disinterested scholarship and unfettered criticism, or as the training ground for the country's elites. Specific examples of each perspective are cited in the countries being compared.

464. Weiker, Walter F. "Academic Freedom and Problems of Higher Education in Turkey." **The Middle East Journal** 16(3): 279-294, Summer 1962.

Weiker addresses actions taken in 1960 by the military junta (the National Unity Committee, or NUC) to dismiss 147 faculty members from the six universities in Turkey. A background and brief history of higher education in Turkey is provided, along with details about opposition to the dismissals and what happened after the NUC went out of power in 1962, when many of the faculty were permitted to apply for reinstatement.

465. Weir, Ruth. "Darwin and the Universities in Canada." **Interchange on Education** 14(4)-15(1): 70-79, 1983-1984.

An historical account of academic freedom in 19th century Canada, this essay examines a case study of the conflict between the established (Christian) intellectual traditions and both Darwin's theory of evolution and the ideas of modern biblical exegesis. The essay examines the academic freedom aspects of both religious doctrine and scientific investigation. Acceptance of evolutionary theory occurred through new methods of biblical exegesis and was an important milestone for the exercise of academic freedom of scientists from clerical influence. Methodist influence on scientists at the University of Toronto and scientists' influence on biblical exegesis at Queens University both played important roles in the process described here.

466. Williams, R. J. P. "Science in Universities: Teaching, Research and Autonomy." **Studies in Higher Education** 16(1): 15-22, 1991.

Science teaching and research are necessarily intertwined, says Williams, and depend upon university autonomy to flourish. However, there are threats to this autonomy growing out of the increasing costs of research and government interest in wealth creation. These financial pressures have led government research councils in Britain to increasingly support university research that may help create wealth, but which slights fundamental research. Similarly, corporate involvement in and support of university research can privilege marketplace and profit-oriented concerns over fundamental research. Applied and basic research are and should be different, says Williams. "University research must be more closely based on underlying ideas without any initial view to market-place advantage" (p. 17). Under financial pressures, universities may accept such research support and its accompanying constraints even at the expense of their autonomy.

467. Wilson, Fred. "In Defense of Speech Codes." **Interchange** 27(2): 125-159, 1996.

Wilson argues that principles of academic freedom are compatible with speech codes that aim to limit any linguistic behavior on campus whose intent is to silence marginalized groups. Certain types of speech can limit the freedom to learn, and can silence minority viewpoints from campus discourse. Various written policies of the Canadian Association of University Teachers, including the 1983 Policy Statement on Non-Discrimination, the 1977 CAUT Policy on Academic Freedom, the Canadian Charter of Rights and Freedoms, and Canadian Supreme Court decisions are all cited in support of the argument that professors are obligated to create and maintain a climate both free from discrimination and also supportive of academic freedom. Explicit procedures banning discriminatory or harassing speech or behavior do not violate academic freedom, though blanket prohibitions against incivility may. Wilson argues that academic freedom is not an unconditional right, and that speech codes can help foster an atmosphere of rational debate rather than one in which those with unpopular or non-mainstream views are "silently silenced."

468. Wood, Fiona. "Factors Influencing Research Performance by University Academic Staff." **Higher Education** 19(1): 81-100, 1990.

Based on a survey of faculty at the University of New England (Australia), this study attempted to determine factors that faculty thought were important for research productivity in a changing funding environment. This new and tighter funding environment reflected a national policy to encourage and expect greater productivity from those faculty receiving federal research grants. A number of factors were identified as important in a researcher's productivity, including personal characteristics; styles, processes and techniques of research; and availability of funding. On the last point, many faculty expressed concern that, despite national research funding priorities, they must have autonomy in selecting their research topics.

469. World University Service. **Academic Freedom: A Human Rights Report.**
Atlantic Highlands, N.J.: Zed Books, 1990- .

Published irregularly in association with the World University Service, this
series of publications aims to fill a void in international human rights monitoring by
reporting on governmental abuses of the academic freedom rights of students,
teachers, and institutions of higher education. In 1988, the World University Service
formally adopted a "Lima Declaration on Academic Freedom and Autonomy of
Institutions of Higher Education" which spells out criteria by which countries around
the world will be judged on issues of academic freedom. Each volume includes
signed articles providing case studies of Third World country situations, reprints of
pertinent international agreements (such as the Lima Declaration) as well as overview
articles covering such topics as "Monitoring the Right to Education: Reporting to U.N.
Treaty Bodies" by Andrew Chapman (*Academic Freedom 3*, 1995) and "Core
Contents of the Right to Education" by Fons Coomans (*Academic Freedom 4*, 1996).
See entries #425-427 and #429.

470. Zeleza, Paul Tiyambe. "Academic Freedom in the North and the South: An
African Perspective." **Academe** 83(6): 16-21, November-December 1997.

Zeleza suggests that the industrialized North and the developing South need to
"redefine and defend" academic freedom in light of fiscal constraints, governmental
interference, and public hostility. In the North, critics have challenged the value of
tenure because of the alleged lack of accountability of faculty. Other critics, such as
postmodernists, have suggested that the concept of academic freedom is rooted in a
narrow, modernist belief in a "single notion of truth." There is further debate over
campus speech codes and whether they have a chilling effect on critique and debate.
In the South, other historical factors figure prominently in the development of
academic freedom. In Africa, which is Zeleza's focus, higher education is often
historically rooted in colonialism. Consequently, autonomy is a significant factor for
newly independent countries. In educational institutions, this has sometimes led to a
prescribed nationalism and emphasis on development. Religious fundamentalism and
other cultural forces have also influenced and limited the range of topics that
academics can examine, as well as the ways in which they explore them. Independent-
minded academics have responded by leaving academe, founding independent
research centers, and engaging in strikes and protests. Ultimately, academic freedom
necessitates being free from political and ideological constraints that minimize the rich
cultural diversity of Africa.

Chapter 11

World Wide Web Sites

471. **Academic Freedom Lecture Fund (AFLF).**
    Web Address: http://www.umich.edu/~aflf/index.html
    Accessed: July 15, 1999.

The Academic Freedom Lecture Fund was started by the University of Michigan Senate in 1990. Its purpose is to honor three faculty members who were terminated in 1955 for refusing to testify before a House Un-American Activities Committee hearing. The fund sponsors an annual Davis, Markert, Nickerson Lecture on Academic and Intellectual Freedom. Included on the Web site are the goals of the fund, the enabling University of Michigan Senate resolution, a brief history of the fund's origins, the advisory board members, and a list of past lectures. The most recent lectures are available full-text.

472. **American Association for the Advancement of Science.**
    Web Address: http://www.aaas.org
    Accessed: July 15, 1999

The American Association for the Advancement of Science awards the annual Scientific Freedom and Responsibility Award, and includes on its web site information on such projects as the "Anonymous Communications on the Internet Project" and "Cryptography: Scientific Freedom and Human Rights Issues."

473. **American Association of University Professors (AAUP).**
    Web Address: http://www.igc.apc.org/aaup/
    Accessed: July 15, 1999.

Included on the AAUP homepage are links to association position statements, press releases, policies and guidelines on a variety of matters of interest to faculty and administrators. These cover such topics as university governance, collective bargaining, sexual harassment, faculty workload, part-time faculty, unionization, affirmative action, faculty salaries and academic freedom and tenure, among others. Under academic freedom and tenure one can find texts of the AAUP positions on post-tenure review, tenure, and electronic communications. Also included is the *1940 Statement of Principles on Academic Freedom and Tenure*, as well as the association's list of censured administrations. Additional information describes the association's committee structure, political and legal activities, and membership procedures.

474. American Civil Liberties Union Freedom Network.
Web Address: http://www.aclu.org/
Accessed: July 15, 1999

Included on this web site are descriptions and updates of ACLU activities on a variety of legislative and legal issues. Of particular relevance to the topic of academic freedom are the ACLU positions on hate speech, speech codes on campus, affirmative action, censorship, and students' rights. The students' rights page provides material for students and teachers in secondary and higher education interested in defending civil and academic liberties on their local campuses. An online registration form is provided for college student groups to register with the ACLU. Also available is the full text of a "Student Organizing Manual," an index of relevant court cases, and the full text of ACLU briefing papers on such topics as hate speech, racist speech, and affirmative action. In addition, the students page includes "Ask Sybil Liberty," a forum for questions and answers on students' rights, and a free Macintosh-based interactive software package ("Express Yourself") which explores First Amendment issues related to high school students. The ACLU web site also includes links to related web sites, membership forms, an email alert on important issues, and an electronic form for notifying members of Congress on relevant legislation.

475. American Council of Trustees and Alumni (ACTA).
Web Address: http://www.naf.org/
Accessed: July 15, 1999

Formerly the National Alumni Forum (founded in 1995), ACTA's goal is "to mobilize alumni on behalf of academic freedom and excellence on college campuses" (Web page). The organization considers "political intolerance on campus" to be the "main threat" to academic freedom. Accessible from the web site are copies of newspaper articles dealing with ACTA issues, other interesting web sites (e.g., the National Association of Scholars), a recent issue of the ACTA newsletter (*Inside Academe*), and ACTA special reports (e.g., on the tenure debate).

476. **CAF Computers and Academic Freedom Archive.**
   Web Address: http://www.eff.org/CAF/
   Accessed: July 15, 1999.

The particular focus of this Web site is free speech and censorship on the Internet, though much of the information does focus on such violations in higher education. These include library policies, banned or restricted information on campus networks, banned and challenged academic computer material, and more. The Web site has subsections for and links to hypertext documents, services, papers, CAF archives, and other archives (e.g., American Civil Liberties Union).

477. **Human Rights Watch.**
   Web Address: http://www.hrw.org/
   Accessed: March 23, 1999

While Human Rights Watch researches, reports on, and defends human rights around the world, it also addresses specific incidents and policies abridging academic freedom. The various efforts to defend academic freedom are part of the organization's Academic Freedom Program. Much of this work is carried on by the Human Rights Watch Academic Freedom Committee. At the present time, this Web site includes reports, letters, news updates, and summaries of investigations on academic freedom-related issues in Indonesia, China, Malaysia, Serbia, and Ethiopia, among others. The academic freedom of both faculty and students is defended, including the freedom of academics to travel for the exchange of ideas.

478. **The Lima Declaration on Academic Freedom and Autonomy of Institutions of Higher Education.**
   Web Address:
   http://www.igc.apc.org/hrw/reports98/indonesia2/Borneote-13.htm
   Accessed: July 15, 1999

Passed at the 68th meeting of the World University Service in 1988, this declaration ties academic freedom into broader declarations of social, political, civil and human rights (e.g., Universal Declaration of Human Rights; International Covenant on Economic, Social and Cultural Rights; International Covenant on Civil and Political Rights; the UNESCO convention against Discrimination in Education). The declaration not only talks about academic freedom as "an essential pre-condition" for academic work, but also argues for equitable and open access to the academic community. Academic freedom should include the freedoms to teach, conduct research, and communicate findings, including to international counterparts. Students should be free to study and to choose a course of study. Governments should provide needy students with aide and should strive to have no fees for higher education. The declaration also defends the autonomy and democratic self-government of institutions of higher education that, for their part, should also be obliged to address social problems and defend persecuted members of the academic community.

479. **National Association of Scholars.**
      Web Address: http://www.nas.org/
      Accessed: July 15, 1999

The National Association of Scholars (NAS) is "dedicated to the restoration of intellectual substance, individual merit, and academic freedom in the university" (Web page).   It sponsors conferences, supports local affiliates, publishes a journal (*Academic Questions*), and issues reports on topics of interest, among other things. The NAS critiques speech codes on college campuses, and is also involved in defending traditional curricular content and standards and opposing preferential faculty hiring and student admissions. Numerous NAS and affiliate reports and press releases are available in full-text on the web site.   There are also links to some affiliates and sister organizations.

480. **The Society for Academic Freedom and Scholarship.**
      Web Address: http://www.safs.niagara.com/
      Accessed: July 15, 1999

The goals of this Canadian organization are maintaining 1) "freedom in teaching, research, and scholarship," and 2) "standards of excellence in academic decision about students and faculty" (Web page).   Its activities include promoting its aims, disseminating information, forming local chapters, and more. There are links to its newsletter and press releases, as well as to a description of its annual meeting. The SAFS is a sister organization of the National Association of Scholars (see entry #479), which is an organization of academics in the United States.

481. **World University Service - International.**
      Web Address: http://antenna.nl/wus-i/
      Accessed: July 15, 1999

The World University Service defends and promotes, among other things, academic freedom, university autonomy, the right to education, and "the human rights of members of the educational sector" (Web page). Included here are bulletins and news items updating abridgements of human rights and academic freedom in various countries. There is also an announcement of recently published volumes in the organization's Academic Freedom book series.

Name Index

Numbers refer to entry numbers.

Subject Index

Numbers refer to entry numbers.

American Philosophical Association, 54, 57
American Physical Society, 422
American Political Science Association, 79
American Psychological Association, 54, 57
American Sociological Society, 79
Amnesty in Academia, 307
Amnesty International, 422
Anthropology, 109
anti-Communism, 61, 77, 98, 103, 105, 114, 120, 127, 133, 135, 141, 155, 161, 162, 163, 186, 453; faculty attitudes, 135; history, 51, 153, 163; legislation, 172. *See also* Communism; investigations, legislative; McCarthyism; Neo-conservatism
anti-immigration, 76, 159. *See also* immigration policy
anti-Nazism, 94. *See also* Nazism
anti-Semitism, 261, 308
anti-slavery, 45, 57, 76
apartheid, 34, 415
appeals procedures, 380
appointments, 70, 184, 298, 378, 393
APS. *See* American Physical Society
Area Studies, 109
Argentina, 447
Arkansas, 256
Arms Export Control Act, 280
Art Institute of Chicago, 250, 300, 301
artistic expression, 185, 217, 219, 243, 250, 271, 279, 299; history, 265; legal aspects, 69, 300, 301; threats to funding, 278
Association of American Colleges, 74, 97, 212

Association of American Universities, 74, 103, 161
Association of Governing Boards, 74
Association of Land Grant Colleges, 74
Association of Students of Mexican Origin, 204
Association of Theological Schools, 366
Association of Urban Universities, 74
associations, scholarly, 318
atheism, 105, 120
athletics, 107
Atlanta, Georgia, 97
Atomic Energy Act, 280
Atomic Energy Commission, U.S., 120
Australia, 419, 433, 435, 453, 468
autonomy, 14, 16, 18, 33, 40, 193, 201, 231, 237, 306, 340, 433; accountability in, 268, 406; in Argentina, 447; in Australia, 419, 433; in European institutions, 448, 452, 457; federal government and, 273, 311; history, 4, 20; institutional size and, 175; in newly independent countries, 470; in religious institutions, 356, 361, 363; research and, 322, 460, 466; state government and, 119; in United Kingdom, 452, 460
awards, 472

B
Baptist institutions, 96, 361
Baylor University, 96
benefits, 2, 180
Bennington College, 412

About the Compilers

STEPHEN H. ABY is Education Bibliographer and Associate Professor at Bierce Library, the University of Akron. His previous books include *The IQ Debate: A Selective Guide to the Literature* (Greenwood, 1990).

JAMES C. KUHN IV is Head of Technical Services at the Folger Shakespeare Library. He has chaired the Ohio Library Council's Intellectual Freedom Committee and has an ongoing professional involvement with issues of intellectual and academic freedom.

ISBN 0-313-30386-X

9 780313 303869

EAN

90000>

HARDCOVER BAR CODE